THE HANDBOOK ON MUSIC BUSINESS AND CREATIVE INDUSTRIES IN EDUCATION

Music Industry Studies

Series Editor: Sarah Raine, University College Dublin

Founding Series Editor: Dave Laing†, Honorary Research Fellow at the University of Liverpool and Senior Research Associate at the University of East Anglia.

In recent years, there has been a rapid growth of interest in the music industry, from policy-makers, educationalists, the media and others. This new series aims to satisfy the demand for in-depth knowledge and analysis of all facets of the industry, from recording to live music and the publishing sector. It will include both historical and contemporary approaches and draw on contributions from economics, geography, sociology, legal studies, cultural studies and other disciplines.

Published:

Beyond 2.0: The Future of Music
Steve Collins and Sherman Young

She's at the Controls: Sound Engineering, Production and Gender Ventriloquism in the 21st Century
Helen Reddington

Sounds Irish, Acts Global: Explaining the Success of Ireland's Popular Music Industry
Michael Mary Murphy and Jim Rogers

Venue Stories: Narratives, Memories, and Histories from Britain's Independent Music Spaces
Edited by Fraser Mann, Robert Edgar and Helen Pleasance

Forthcoming:

Elements of Music Management
Sally Gross

Turntable Stories: Narratives, Memories and Histories from In-between the Grooves
Edited by Fraser Mann, Robert Edgar and Helen Pleasance

THE HANDBOOK ON MUSIC BUSINESS AND CREATIVE INDUSTRIES IN EDUCATION

EDITED BY
DANIEL WALZER

SHEFFIELD UK   BRISTOL CT

Published by Equinox Publishing Ltd.

UK: Office 415, The Workstation, 15 Paternoster Row, Sheffield, South Yorkshire, S1 2BX
USA: ISD, 70 Enterprise Drive, Bristol, CT 06010

www.equinoxpub.com

First published 2024

© Daniel Walzer and contributors 2024

All rights reserved. No part of this publication may be reproduced or transmitted in any form or by any means, electronic or mechanical, including photocopying, recording or any information storage or retrieval system, without prior permission in writing from the publishers.

British Library Cataloguing-in-Publication Data
A catalogue record for this book is available from the British Library.

ISBN-13 978 1 80050 592 6 (hardback)
         978 1 80050 522 3 (paperback)
         978 1 80050 523 0 (ePDF)
         978 1 80050 590 2 (ePub)

Library of Congress Cataloging-in-Publication Data
Names: Walzer, Dan, editor.
Title: The handbook on music business and creative industries in education / edited by Daniel Walzer.
Description: Bristol, CT : Equinox Publishing Ltd, 2024. | Series: Music industry studies | Includes bibliographical references and index. | Summary: "The Handbook on Music Business and Creative Industries in Education provides a practical and engaging resource for faculty, staff, administrators, graduate students, and industry members working on the "front lines" in teaching and learning"-- Provided by publisher.
Identifiers: LCCN 2024014008 (print) | LCCN 2024014009 (ebook) | ISBN 9781800505926 (hardback) | ISBN 9781800505223 (paperback) | ISBN 9781800505230 (pdf) | ISBN 9781800505902 (epub)
Subjects: LCSH: Music trade. | Business education. | Music trade--Vocational guidance. | Sound recording industry--Vocational guidance.
Classification: LCC ML3795 .H288 2024 (print) | LCC ML3795 (ebook) | DDC 381/.45780--dc23/eng/20240329
LC record available at https://lccn.loc.gov/2024014008
LC ebook record available at https://lccn.loc.gov/2024014009

Typeset by S.J.I. Services, New Delhi, India

Contents

Introduction: Editor's Welcome   1
DANIEL WALZER

1   Music Business Education: A German Perspective   12
MARTIN LÜCKE

2   Running a Student-Led Music Label: Design, Delivery and Evaluation of Music Business and Professional Practice Training   30
IAN STEVENSON, JEFF CRABTREE AND MONICA ROUVELLAS

3   Embedding Effectual Entrepreneurship across the Music Business Curriculum   51
JEREMY PETERS

4   Thinking Out Loud: The 5Rs of Musicians' Project and Career Decision-Making   67
MATHEW FLYNN

5   How Do I Look? The Importance of Visual Analysis for Musicians in Popular Music Higher Education   91
HELEN ELIZABETH DAVIES

6   Songwriting, Visuality, and Technological Determinism: Exploring Artistic Responses to Perceived Negative Effects of Streaming on Songwriting and Production   109
HUSSEIN BOON

7   Anyone Can be a Musician: Art School Pedagogy and the Rise of the Non-Musician   129
SIMON STRANGE

8   Scaling Up: Teaching Contemporary Music through Repertoire Structures   147
SEAN FORAN, JADE O'REGAN, VINCENT PERRY AND TOM O'HALLORAN

9 'How NOT to land an internship': A Case Study of Experiential
Learning in Sound Recording and Music Production Education   171
KIRK MCNALLY

10 Putting Down Roots: Making Music and Embracing Messiness
in Graduate School   191
TAYLOR ACKLEY WITH JOE SFERRA

11 Reconceptualizing Higher Education Programs in Music for
a Rapidly Changing Global Creative Industries Sector:
An Australian Perspective   210
RYAN DANIEL

Index   227

Introduction: Editor's Welcome

Daniel Walzer

Welcome to the *Handbook on Music Business and Creative Industries in Education*, the first compendium dedicated to exploring educational issues central to teaching, learning, and creativity in the music business, the performing arts, and related sectors. The eleven chapters in this collection represent a broad range of perspectives from researchers and practitioners in Contemporary Performance, Recording Technology, Arts Education, Business and Entrepreneurship, Community Music, Engineering, Popular Music Studies, American Roots Music, and Music Education among others. The volume includes contributors from Canada, Australia, Germany, the UK, and the US – aiming to present a wide-ranging perspective on the growing body of scholarship exploring the relationship between the creative arts professions and education.

A primary aim of this collection is to present a broad overview, or 'state of the field', of the creative industries. While adjacent disciplines, including Popular Music Studies, Arts Entrepreneurship, and Music Technology, are more established, there exists a gap in the literature on what might be best described as the *hybrid creative researcher* – performers, music producers, social scientists, social justice advocates, academics, and industry veterans drawing on rich, interdisciplinary research methods discussing issues central to applied theory and practice in education. Suppose one subscribes to the view that educational institutions provide essential training opportunities for those entering creative fields, including music business, media, and the arts. In that case, a pedagogical resource seems warranted for educational stakeholders.

The last few years have brought unprecedented challenges to the arts and entertainment sector and all types of educational institutions. A once-in-a-generation global pandemic brought on by the novel coronavirus upended global society – including an ever-increasing number of deaths and extended periods of forced isolation. At the same time, scientists raced to develop a vaccine. Seemingly overnight, everything was cancelled as it was too unsafe to be near others. Educational institutions scrambled to figure out how to deliver classes remotely, and virtually everything in the performing arts ground to a halt with no end.

Analysis of 2020 Bureau of Labor Statistics (BLS) employment data released by the US-based National Endowment for the Arts' COVID-19 Recovery Support Function Leadership Group (RSFLG) shows a loss of 2.3 million jobs in the creative arts sector between April and July 2020 (US Bureau of Labor Statistics 2020; Guibert and Hyde 2021). A similar study by the Brookings Institution (Florida and Seman 2020) reported that performing arts professions accounted for over a quarter of total employment losses in the US in 2020 (see also Guibert and Hyde 2021). Statistics in the UK were equally grim. As reported by the BBC in October 2021 (BBC 2021), data from UK Music's *This Is Music* 2021 report show that revenue from live performances declined by 90%, while the music industry reported a loss of nearly 70,000 jobs in 2020 (UK Music 2021). As reported by the World Economic Forum, data from UNESCO showed that 10 million jobs were lost in the creative industries in 2020 (Bateman 2022), resulting in an overall net loss of $750 billion to the global economy (Sherwood 2022; UNESCO 2022).

Another overarching goal for the *Handbook* is to share pedagogical ideas and perspectives in straightforward, accessible language. The *Handbook*'s authors draw on case studies, ethnographies, and narrative-style prose alongside qualitative and quantitative methodologies. At first glance, one might assume that an autoethnography from Early Career Researchers (ECRs) on American roots music shares little in common with the empirical methods used by social scientists presenting visual analysis of music videos and performances. Yet, there is a shared thread among these distinct examples – music and art are deeply personal and describe an ever-changing 'industry' in flux. In essence, aiming to professionalize one's vocation presents numerous challenges for those on the front lines of mentoring young people, namely teachers, researchers, and industry experts.

While most chapters explore perspectives from those working in higher education, the pedagogical and socio-cultural issues identified throughout broadly apply to various learning environments. Here, the concept of 'education' is both flexible and variable, as is our definition of the creative industries. In actuality, the myriad options to study popular music (and all its related fields) extend beyond the classroom to online tutorials, internships, and 'on the job' training. In many instances, music business and the creative industry professionals transition to academia. For higher education institutions, this proves advantageous as educators often bring valuable professional experience to the classroom. Students benefit from instructors with a network of contacts, industry credibility, and an understanding of how the arts professions function in the 'real world'.

Indeed, pursuing a career as a touring artist, actress, or A&R representative has always been fraught with uncertainty. Even before the Great Recession, and the recent pandemic, creative people have always had to hustle to make a living. For performers of all types, years of painstaking dedication to one's craft requires a tremendous amount of focused discipline, often in solitude. Likewise, those working as technicians (such as recording engineers and lighting designers) or in the business side of entertainment (publishing, A&R, promotion, publicity, and legal, for example) have also spent years honing a broad range of skills: technical, interpersonal, critical thinking, problem-solving, collaboration, and networking. And while many of these skills are cultivated in colleges and universities, many are acquired informally and on the job. Prescient is the observation that one's success is equally dependent on a solid network of contacts, timing, and old-fashioned luck. Beyond that, however, barriers to entry and success are often the result of political gatekeeping and inequality (Strong and Raine 2018).

Like misogyny, racial gatekeeping is endemic in the creative industries. In the film sector, workers are often biased towards actors of colour, viewing them as higher-risk and less capable of generating profits. Erigha (2021) describes this behaviour as racial valuation; actors of colour are expected to fail, whereas their white counterparts are seen as lower risk, thus overlooking the unpredictable nature of the entertainment industry and reinforcing white supremacy. Furthermore, gatekeeping is manifested in the power dynamics between booking agents and artists at festivals and by controlling promotional efforts by a select few (Järvekülg and Wikström 2022; Thorkildsen and Rykkja 2022). These trends tell us that while there have been many efforts to address Diversity, Equity, and Inclusion (DEI), social change in the music industry and associated sectors remains precarious and is a trend that educators must remain cognizant of when mentoring young students.

Adding to an already precarious career pathway is the rapid (and sometimes blinding) pace that technology changes. More than twenty years ago, Apple introduced the iPod, changing how people listen to music. Eventually, the iPod was replaced with improved mobile technology. Today, one would be hard-pressed to find the average music fan without their phone listening to tracks and podcasts on Spotify or YouTube. Along with technological innovations come new business models, each competing for a share of an already saturated marketplace. Today, interest in contemporary music is at an all-time low, yet people are consuming legacy recordings more and more (Gioia 2022). While recording and producing media have never been easier, monetizing one's product remains difficult partly due to the glut in artists online and the fact that streaming royalties pay a fraction of more traditional revenue streams, including ticket sales, merchandise, and licensing (Hesmondhalgh 2021).

After acknowledging these global trends, an educator might ask why all this matters. After all, there are no guarantees in show business. And, as the adage says: 'it's not what you know, but who you know'. A career in the arts has always been unpredictable; supply always outpaces demand as there are many more people vying for opportunities than available slots. Yet, educational stakeholders are vested in staying abreast of current trends as colleges and universities have replaced the apprenticeship model made famous by recording studios, record labels, and the media industry. Record labels have consolidated, recording studios have closed, and people aren't buying physical products like they once did. For the budding artist or music producer, how does one learn their craft and build the requisite skills needed for the twenty-first-century arts sector?

The *Handbook* examines the music business and creative industries practically and holistically. As with changing business and technology trends, educational institutions also navigate a precarious path with funding cuts, and casual/adjunct hires replacing full-time teaching staff, rising tuition and student loan debt, and increased scrutiny by government agencies. Education is not immune to global challenges, either. Increasingly, like their students, faculty and staff experience higher rates of burnout and increased workloads (Jääskeläinen, López-Íñiguez, and Phillips 2022; Taylor and Frechette 2022). And as much of the discourse here has addressed the creative industries; there are few degrees designed to help music business professionals learn how to teach compassionately and promote an inclusive learning environment. The music business, for example, is not unlike many academic fields. Pursuing a terminal degree such as a PhD often comes with little guidance on being an effective lecturer.

For argument's sake, one might put forward the notion that industry expertise outweighs an academic credential. Another perspective might consider years of research and theory useful for understanding and explaining business trends. Just as dancers refine their technique, researchers spend years reading, synthesizing, and producing new insights. Academics and industry practitioners need not exist in silos. On the contrary, and in very practical ways, *educational institutions have become incubators for the creative industries*. As such, it makes sense to assemble a coalition of viewpoints addressing prevalent issues in education. Among such topics include peer-to-peer learning, inclusion, racial and gender equality, pedagogical best practices, assessment, the role of theory, decision-making, and creativity. Likewise, providing a forum for such research is essential if the field is to grow.

Suppose there is one takeaway from the complete disruption of the global arts economy and upheaval to learning environments. In that case, it may be that the pandemic's *forced* pause in daily life gave educators a chance to reflect on their teaching praxis. Without gigs, audiences, and associated revenue, artists had to find ways to stay relevant and connect with others. Likewise, educational stakeholders had to meet the moment, devising innovative ways to deliver learning modules. Much like the creative industries during 'normal' times, unrelenting instability forces adaptation and innovation. But, as noted scholar Bettina Love states: 'we want to do more than survive' (Love 2019).

A few points are worth considering. First, the creative industries often mirror what's happening in the world. Composers, playwrights, poets, photographers, and game developers are not immune to global events, nor are educators and learners. As expressed, much of the training for popular music and the entertainment industry happens in colleges and universities. Therefore, the barriers to entry (whether due to socioeconomic status, gender, race, and so on) and success in the creative industries are not dissimilar to those found in educational environments. Music technology professional roles are dominated by white men, and such trends are also reflected in undergraduate enrolments and teaching staff (Born and Devine 2015).

Second, though music business and similar degrees are not particularly new, balancing general education courses with industry-specific training remains challenging (Hatschek 2011). One reason may be that music business, performing arts, and similar fields have primarily focused on vocational training. Employability is a relative term; however, for many young people, a freelance path and entrance into the gig economy seem more likely. Traditionally, higher education has been slower to respond to the rapid changes in business as the creative industries expand, consolidate, and retract every few years. Training schemes can be quickly outdated by the time someone finishes a typical three- or four-year baccalaureate degree.

Earlier in the Introduction, I described a hybrid creative researcher. This might explain a creative practitioner with industry experience who also conducts research. An example might include a music producer who has transitioned into academia and writes on issues relating to creativity in teaching and learning with technology. Another example might be a long-time arts administrator that pursues doctoral studies and writes a thesis drawing on their experience working in a particular arts sector such as orchestral management or publicity. Yet another example might include someone like Daniel Levitin, a famous neuroscientist who started his career as a keyboardist, session musician, and audio engineer (Levitin 2006), or Susan Rogers, an accomplished audio engineer and close collaborator with Prince, who, after receiving her doctorate now researches music cognition and teaches at the Berklee School of Music.

Hybridity is difficult to package, both for the creative practitioner and the academic. Multi-genre music is like interdisciplinary research: both are difficult to classify, and each distinct element is represented proportionally. As with music business research, the few peer-reviewed publications dedicated to pedagogy are somewhat narrow. 'Cross-over' research in the creative industries finds a broader audience as several peer-reviewed journals (including the *Creative Industries Journal*) publish articles on music production, distribution, and media topics. What is missing here is a steady stream of research dedicated to the scholarship of teaching and learning (SOTL) in what has long been considered a vocationally focused and industry-led field. The *Handbook* addresses the gap in this area of scholarship as pedagogy, and the ways it is defined is a strong focus throughout the volume.

Chapter Summaries

Analysing developments in Music Business Education in Germany, Martin Lücke opens the volume by contextualizing the significant differences between more traditional universities and those focusing on applied science, and comparing public and private institutions. After a synopsis of how Music Business Education has evolved in Germany, Lücke generates empirical data by examining curricula, accreditation standards, programme length, and qualitative analysis of teaching and learning across the sector. Lücke concludes with future directions of Music Business Education in Germany and implications for educators working in similar departments in other countries.

In their chapter on instructional design in the music business with tertiary students in a music and sound design course, Ian Stevenson, Jeff Crabtree, and Monica Rouvellas identify three primary areas – design, delivery, and student evaluation – and discuss how these components support self-regulated and authentic learning for educators in the creative industries. Through qualitative analysis of reflective writing and semi-structured interviews, Stevenson and colleagues analysed student participation and project assessment across multiple domains with a university-affiliated record label. Results suggest that mirroring a real-world scenario improved student collaboration, reflective practice, and a sense of autonomy.

Jeremy Peters writes on efforts to integrate entrepreneurship across various undergraduate music business courses to improve job readiness for soon-to-be graduates. Analysing survey data from the Strategic National Arts Alumni Project (SNAAP), Peters discusses effectuation theory and addresses five hybrid skill sets, including financial and business, entrepreneurship, creative thinking, and problem solving, networking, and project management. Peters argues that repetition helps build confidence in these areas and concludes with ways to incorporate experiential learning through internships and relevant coursework.

Drawing on his survey of 500 UK-based musicians, Mathew Flynn uses grounded theory and research in behavioural economics to propose the 5R Model of Decision-Making: Role, Repertoire, Representation, Reputation, and Remuneration. With little extant scholarship on decision-making for musicians and designed with practitioners and educators in mind, Flynn's 5R Model allows musicians to apply a visual toolkit of decision-making concepts in smaller, collaborative environments and when working independently. The result is a more comprehensive and visual understanding of how best to navigate an unpredictable music industry in the future.

Helen Elizabeth Davies writes about visual imagery, a relatively under-researched area of popular music and the creative industries. Central to the music business, visual content in promotional materials, packaging, live events, social media, and technology connect artists with their audience. Davies delves into visual analysis and its relationship to Popular Music Higher Education (PMHE). Using an 'analytical toolkit' that considers musician persona, images, costuming, performance, and music video, Davies describes how students create visual content to accompany their musical practice and how such efforts promote multisensory pedagogy in vocationally focused coursework.

In his critical examination of songwriting, Hussein Boon argues that modern technology and visual media affect how practitioners write music and how popular music educators might address such tensions in their teaching. In Boon's view, technological determinism and songwriting are inextricably linked; crafting songs with and through technology opens possibilities to advance the craft. Moreover, as Boon suggests, creative practice is equally shaped by visuality, namely, how artists communicate beyond music and sound. Through his analysis of music videos and industry case studies, Boon leads us to a better understanding of the interwoven politics of the music industry, artist creativity, and technology. Boon concludes by cautioning educators to guide students to balance creativity with meeting market demand and to view the craft of songwriting across multiple domains: creative, technological, and business.

Undertaking an extensive history of UK art education, Simon Strange's chapter draws on interviews with visual artists and musicians – including Brian Eno, Dexter Dalwood, Gina Birch, Gaye Black, and others – to conceptualize a punk-inspired, DIY model of teaching and creating in popular music. UK art schools in the 1960s and 70s served as a breeding ground for postmodernist experimentation, where artists dismantled or 'unlearned' traditional models of practice, favouring new technologies and aesthetics, and blurring the lines between visual art and popular music. Strange concludes with a vision for how popular music educators might replace more commercially focused concepts for a more expansive, art-inspired model of music-making.

Sean Foran, Jade O'Regan, Vincent Perry, and Tom O'Halloran discuss a study on popular music repertoire and ensembles conducted at three Australian universities. Foran et al. encouraged students to blend historical analysis of popular music to reimagine cover material, compose original works, and consider factors including performance skills, staging, technology, music cognition, and group dynamics. The authors consider the broader aims of ensemble pedagogy, namely guiding students towards autonomy, improved communication, and advocating for a more profound conception of repertoire built on creativity and collaboration.

Using community-engaged learning and participatory action research, Kirk McNally presents a case study on the collaboration between upper-level sound recording students and a local Canadian record label. McNally argues that the standard practice of internships in the music industry is at best limited in its scope and exploitative at its worst. Community Engaged Learning (CEL) presents a useful alternative where students apply their skills in real-world scenarios, thus improving their applied knowledge and learning outcomes. McNally's qualitative analysis of semi-structured interviews suggests that, while CEL promotes a sense of lifelong learning and reflective practice, educators must use care to align the industry component with existing music business curricula so that both support each other equally.

Taylor Ackley with Joe Sferra describe the Deep Roots Ensemble, a student-run mixed chamber group drawing musical inspiration from American folk and roots music, jazz, and classical styles. Written primarily as an autoethnography undertaken by the two authors, the chapter explores aspects of the complicated history of American music, institutional politics in higher education, and how an inclusive pedagogical style inspires deeper and more meaningful connections to ensemble performance, creativity, and professionalism. Along with interviews with former students, Ackley and Sferra challenge the hegemonic and limiting structures commonly found in academic music departments. The chapter concludes with a clarion call for how educators might adopt a similar ethos in their ensemble pedagogy.

Adopting chaos theory as a framework through which to examine the impact of COVID-19 on the creative industries and higher education, Ryan

Daniel describes a future where freelance and portfolio careers become more commonplace in the performing arts. Daniel argues that the traditional model of teaching and learning embraced by conservatory-style education is no longer sufficient to prepare students for sustainable employment. In its place, Daniel advocates for a new conceptual model of self-guided pedagogy, where students acquire knowledge across several domains, including agency, practice, industry engagement, well-being, critical thinking, and peer learning.

The eleven chapters in this volume examine educational issues from myriad perspectives that could be viewed as epistemologically oppositional. Writings on inclusive performance practices accompany chapters examining visual content in music videos and how universities must better prepare students for the inevitable failures they will encounter in the music business and creative industries. Their inclusion in this volume is intentional and aims to provide broad and varied perspectives on teaching and learning in the music business and its related disciplines. The chapters represent perspectives from educators and industry professionals spanning multiple countries, including England, Scotland, Germany, Australia, Canada, and the United States. As the scholarly literature on education and music business advances, future handbooks will likely expand to additional countries and explore policies and perspectives using robust research methods. As the relationship between the creative industries and education simultaneously grows and evolves, relevant global scholarship discussing pedagogy, identity, socio-cultural issues, economics, and inclusion becomes prescient. *The Handbook on Music Business and Creative Industries in Education* aims to contribute to the discussion and advance a multi-faceted perspective on teaching, learning, creativity, and contemporary issues in the creative industries into the future.

Daniel Walzer, PhD
Volume Editor
September 2023
Indiana University-Indianapolis

References

Bateman, K. 2022. 'COVID-19 hit the creative industries particularly hard. How can they be supported in future?' *World Economic Forum*, 22 February. https://www.weforum.org/agenda/2022/02/creatives-job-losses-covid-employment/

BBC. 2021. 'One in three music industry jobs were lost during pandemic'. *Entertainment and Arts*, 19 October. https://www.bbc.com/news/entertainment-arts-58959179

Born, G., and K. Devine. 2015. 'Music technology, gender, and class: Digitization, educational and social change in Britain'. *Twentieth-Century Music* 12, no. 2: 135–72. https://doi.org/10.1017/S1478572215000018

Erigha, M. 2021. 'Racial valuation: Cultural gatekeepers, race, risk, and institutional expectations of success and failure'. *Social Problems* 68, no. 2: 393–408. https://doi.org/10.1093/socpro/spaa006

Florida, and M. Seman. 2020. 'Lost art: Measuring COVID-19's devastating impact on America's creative economy'. *Metropolitan Policy Program at Brookings*. https://www.brookings.edu/wp-content/uploads/2020/08/20200810_Brookingsmetro_Covid19-and-creative-economy_Final.pdf

Gioia, T. 2022. 'Is old music killing new music?'. *The Atlantic*. https://www.theatlantic.com/ideas/archive/2022/01/old-music-killing-new-music/621339/

Guibert, G., and I. Hyde. 2021. 'Week of 4 January 2021: Analysis: COVID-19's impacts on arts and culture'. *National Endowment for the Arts: COVID-19 RSFLG Data and Assessment Working Group*. https://www.arts.gov/sites/default/files/COVID-Outlook-Week-of-1.4.2021-revised.pdf

Hatschek, K. 2011. 'Balancing music industry curricula in undergraduate degree programs: A course distribution survey and analysis'. *Journal of the Music and Entertainment Industry Educators Association* 11, no. 1: 161–211. https://doi.org/10.25101/11.7

Hesmondhalgh, D. 2021. 'Is music streaming bad for musicians? Problems of evidence and argument'. *New Media and Society* 23, no. 12: 3593–3615. https://doi.org/10.1177/1461444820953541

Jääskeläinen, T., G. López-Íñiguez, and M. Phillips. 2022. 'Music students' experienced workload in higher education: A systematic review and recommendations for good practice'. *Musicae Scientiae* 27, no. 3. https://doi.org/10.1177/10298649221093976

Järvekülg, M., and P. Wikström. 2022. 'The emergence of promotional gatekeeping and converged local music professionals on social media'. *Convergence* 28, no. 5: 1358–75. https://doi.org/10.1177/13548565211032376

Levitin, D. J. 2006. *This is Your Brain on Music: The Science of a Human Obsession*. London: Penguin.

Love, B. 2019. *We Want to Do More than Survive: Abolitionist Teaching and the Pursuit of Educational Freedom*. Boston, MA: Beacon Press.

Sherwood, H. 2022. 'UNESCO warns of crisis in creative sector with 10m jobs lost due to pandemic'. *The Guardian*, 7 February. https://www.theguardian.com/culture/2022/feb/08/unesco-warns-of-crisis-in-creative-sector-with-10m-jobs-lost-due-to-pandemic

Strong, C., and S. Raine. 2018. 'Gender politics in the music industry'. *IASPM Journal* 8, no. 1: 2–8. https://doi.org/10.5429/2079-3871(2018)v8i1.2en

Taylor, D. G., and M. Frechette. 2022. 'The impact of workload, productivity, and social support on burnout among marketing faculty during the COVID-19 pandemic'. *Journal of Marketing Education* 44, no. 2. https://doi.org/10.1177/02734753221074284

Thorkildsen, K. L., and A. Rykkja. 2022. 'Showcase festivals: Gatekeepers and bridge builders in the music industries'. *International Journal of Music Business Research* 11, no. 2: 47–58. https://doi.org/10.2478/ijmbr-2022-0006

UK Music. 2021. 'This Is Music 2021'. *This Is Music 2021 Report*. https://www.ukmusic.org/research-reports/report-archive/this-is-music-2021/

UNESCO. 2022. 'Re|shaping policies for creativity: Addressing culture as a global public good'. *UNESCO*. https://www.unesco.org/reports/reshaping-creativity/2022/en

US Bureau of Labor Statistics. 2020. 'Current employment statistics – CES (National)'. https://www.bls.gov/ces/

About the editor

Daniel Walzer is Assistant Professor of Music and Arts Technology at Indiana University-Indianapolis. Originally trained as a percussionist, Walzer maintains an active career as a composer, performer, and audio production specialist. Walzer's research and writings on music technology and the creative industries appear in *Leonardo Music Journal*, *Journal of Music, Technology & Education*, *Creative Industries Journal*, *Music Educators Journal*, and in numerous edited collections. He is the co-editor of *Audio Education: Theory, Culture, and Practice* (with Mariana Lopez), and the author of *Leadership in Music Technology Education: Philosophy, Praxis, and Pedagogy*, both with Focal Press.

1 Music Business Education: A German Perspective

Martin Lücke

Introduction

In 2015, the first comprehensive study on the German music market was presented at the Reeperbahn Festival, initiated by the relevant German music associations.[1] Among many other numbers from the study, one was very surprising: 127,000 people were employed in the German music business, both self-employed and employees covered by social security, a number that had previously been estimated to be much lower (Seufert, Schlegel and Sattelberger 2015). This number does not yet include the employees in the classical concert and opera business. In 2019, the music market study was repeated, and now close to 158,000 employees could be counted (Seufert, Schlegel and Sattelberger 2021). These numbers have demonstrated how important the German music business really is and what economic significance it has within the cultural and creative industries.

In the last two and a half decades, a complex coexistence of public and private training institutions has emerged, each of them proclaiming that they train specifically for the needs of the music business. The question arises whether the music business – with its different, intertwining sub-sectors (recording industry, live industry, etc.) – requires specific training, dual or academic? Isn't the well-known – and often practised – lateral entry, a drop-out from studies, coincidence enough to work successfully in the music business? Can the required (but seldom formulated) 'skills' of this industry be accurately represented in an academic degree programme? In the near future, it will become clear whether existing and future jobs in the sub-sectors are available to a sufficient degree to absorb the number of graduates at all. Also, these very different programmes of training will have to adapt to the constantly changing music industry in terms of structure and content in the coming years, either

---

1. E.g. Bundesverband Musikindustrie (BVMI), Bundesverband der Konzert- und Veranstaltungswirtschaft (bdkv), Deutscher Musikverleger-Verband (DMV).

to provide employers with new and qualified employees or to help start-ups get off to a good business start. First, this chapter looks at the German higher education system and the differences between universities and universities of applied sciences as well as private and public institutions. Next, I discuss why the quantity of academic training opportunities has changed significantly in recent years. Finally, various programmes are analysed qualitatively.

The German Higher Education System

In the winter semester 2021/2022, almost 3 million students were enrolled in colleges and universities (Destatis 2021). The demand on the education market is largely covered by public universities. In Germany, the higher education system is divided into three different types of institutions (universities, universities of applied sciences, and colleges of art and music), and three possible types of ownership. Likewise, an increasing number of higher education institutions are privately funded. According to Werner and Steiner (2010), private universities in Germany have little basis to exist, as the publicly funded system is diversified in the number of study places as well as the range of study programmes. Public programmes are usually free for students, and there is a large number of placement opportunities in universities. However, student needs have changed in recent years. As a result, more and more private institutions are supplementing the public education system, both in terms of the content of the study programmes and the number of places that are available. Private higher education institutions are more market-oriented and create new study programmes more quickly and efficiently. However, the efficiency of private institutions is an economic end in itself, to work cost-effectively with their own organization and staff. The dual system of tuition-fee-financed private universities and tuition-free public universities will continue into the future.

Table 1.1 Number of higher education institutions by type and ownership (Hochschulkompass 2022)

	Public	Private	Religious	Total
Universities	87	20	13	**120**
Universities of Applied Science	102	86	17	**205**
Colleges of Art and Music	46	3	8	**57**
Other Universities	4	3	0	**7**
Total	239	112	38	**389**

Table 1.1 shows that private investors mainly run universities of applied sciences. While only a few private universities were founded in the 1950s (e.g., Frankfurt School of Finance and Management), 1960s (e.g., Wedel University of Applied Sciences), 1970s (e.g., EBS University of Economics and Law) and 1980s (e.g., Witten/Herdecke University), there has been strong growth since the 1990s. In the 2000s alone, forty-seven new institutions were founded. Since then, the trend has not only flattened out, but some universities of applied sciences are no longer present on the market at all, either through insolvency or sold to other private higher education institutions.

In the winter semester 2020/2021, around 307,000 students (more than 10% of total students) were enrolled at private higher education institutions (Wissenschaftsrat 2021). At the same time, almost a quarter of all higher education institutions were privately funded. This shows very clearly that many private universities are relatively small. While public universities have an average of more than 11,000 students, private ones have just over 2,500. Certainly, tuition fees play a significant role in this. Public universities receive a large part of the required funding (approx. 70%) from the government. In addition, there are third-party funds, assets, and tuition fees (4%). Private universities, on the other hand, are entirely financed by tuition fees (Frank et al. 2010: 31). These fees are several thousand euros per semester, depending on the university and the degree. The total costs for a bachelor's or master's degree can add up to €40,000. However, this type of university funding is dependent on constantly growing student numbers in order to survive economically in the long term.

A major difference between public and private universities is the selection of academic programmes. While public universities offer an extensive range of disciplines (humanities, medicine, natural sciences and engineering), private universities focus on business-related degree programmes that are focused on the specific needs of the employment market. Private institutions frequently offer very specific programmes. They have programmes including music management that are not yet offered by public universities along with programmes that have admission restrictions in the public system – such as journalism, psychology, fashion design, acting and popular music. The next few years will show whether the current range of programmes and services offered by the private higher education institutions is sufficient as the competition between public and private universities and the numerous private institutions will surely increase.

Education in the Music Industry

The dual training system, a combination of part-time vocational college or academy and three-year apprenticeship in a specialized company, is typical for German industrial training. The minimum requirement for an apprenticeship is a secondary-school completion certificate, but the so-called 'Abitur' (A-levels) may also be required; 'Abitur' or A-level means the highest school-leaving qualification that can be obtained. Dual-training programmes have existed for a long time in the music business. Examples include the Management Assistant in Audiovisual Media (since 1998), which is geared towards the requirements of the music industry, the Management Assistant in Event Organisation (since 2001) and since 2006, the Management Assistant in Digital and Print Media (formerly: Publishing Assistant), which prepares for activities in the publishing industry (Scholz 2010: 78–109). There is already a specific training path for music dealers, who sell musical instruments and sheet music, since 1954.

On the basis of this basic apprenticeship – comparable to a master craftsman – the Music Business Administrator (Musikfachwirt) was introduced in 2010, the Event Business Administrator (Veranstaltungsfachwirt) and the Publishing Business Administrator (Verlagsfachwirt) in 2008. To date, many music companies have the opportunity to train their junior staff internally for the entry-level and mid-level management positions of the organization's hierarchy. But if there are internal training programmes at labels (Universal, Sony, Warner), publishers (Budde Music, Peer Music Group) or concert promoters (DEAG, Eventim), what are the reasons for setting up a number of academic programmes for the music business in recent years?

The German Music Market

Economic benchmark numbers can provide an important clue in this context. Over the last twenty-five years, the music industry has been in a period of global change, where the conditions of production, distribution, and reception have fundamentally shifted. In 1997, the German music industry generated a record revenue of 2.7 billion euros (BVMI 2021). Due to parallel evolutions (MP3, Napster, CD burner), a digitalization of almost all areas in the music business that continues to this day, the music industry experienced a massive collapse in revenue (Limper and Lücke 2013; Tschmuck 2017). Streaming services have contributed to increased revenue in the music industry. Production, distribution, and reception conditions have changed massively in a way that traditional business models do not work anymore, and new revenue models have been established (Tschmuck 2017).

It is not surprising that as the music industry has lost revenues, it has also lost jobs. The decline between 1997 and 2010 – the year of the last official numbers for the recording sector published by BVMI, the German major labels association – was nearly 40%, comparable to the decline in revenues (BVMI 2011: 12). The live sector is an important segment of the music business as well. But live revenues have not increased at the same rate as recorded music revenues have decreased. Although live business revenues are growing, they are not stable – as the Coronavirus pandemic clearly shows – and are always dependent on economic and conjunctural developments. The last figures before the pandemic show this impressively: while the revenue from live music was around 3.7 billion euros in 2017 (an increase of 1 billion euros compared to 2013), the recording industry turned over 1.45 billion euros (bdv 2018; Initiative Kultur- und Kreativwirtschaft 2020).

Ongoing digitalization and globalization have presented many challenges for music companies. The dual training programmes are not yet prepared for these changes. This provides the opportunity for new and innovative academic programmes that combine more theoretical knowledge with practical elements to respond to the emerging market conditions. The future of the music business is in the effective development and implementation of new business models. The new academic programmes that have been created are trying to find answers to the most urgent questions of a changing and evolving music business.

The German capital Berlin is an excellent location for institutions that offer degree programmes specifically focused on the music business. One reason for this is that, in addition to numerous and well-known music companies (Universal Music, Sony Music, BMG Music, DEAG), the relevant music business associations (BVMI, VUT) and music networks (Berlin Music Commission, Club Commission) are also located in Berlin. To develop relevant music business curricula at the university level, cooperation with music business stakeholders is crucial (Lücke and Paulus 2015: 307). This is because the majority of study programmes include project courses that are to be realized with partners from the business sector. Likewise, these companies or associations are potential internship providers or employers for the students. Higher education institutions must be aware of the changes within the music business and adjust their curriculum accordingly.

Historical Development of Academic Programmes

In Germany, music industry programmes are common. Among these include business studies (business administration, economics) and law. A quick look at large German music companies shows that the majority of executives have a business or law degree (Jóri, Lücke, and Wickström 2015). Franz Willnauer, former artistic director of the Salzburg Festival and professor of cultural management, identified the professional skills of a music manager. In his view, aspiring music managers should have knowledge of economics, art and media law, business administration and organizational theory. Beyond this, implementing various cultural science disciplines is also important. Additionally, a music manager should have good communication skills (Willnauer 1997). After all, the music industry is a so-called 'people's business'. Therefore, cultivating networks is essential. In this context, the network as a construct should also be questioned. Are they open to everyone? Is it possible to join existing networks at all? And is it always necessary to create new networks, which in the end lead to too many of them? These and many other interesting questions would have to be analysed separately, but they would go beyond the limits of this case study.

The existing music management study programmes date back to the establishment of specific arts and cultural management pathways. In 1976, the first university programme in cultural management in the German-speaking world was introduced at the University of Music in Vienna. In 1989, the first full German degree programme started at the College of Music and Theatre in Hamburg, then one year later at the University of Education in Ludwigsburg. Today, the number of programmes continues to rise across Germany. The Cultural Policy Society (Kulturpolitische Gesellschaft, KuPoGe) lists more than 360 programmes (bachelor's, master's, further education) for arts and cultural education, including numerous specializations for arts and cultural management. However, the majority of these courses are oriented towards public-funded high culture (opera, orchestra, theatre, museum, and so on) (KuPoGe 2021). Examples for that are the master's degree programmes Theatre and Orchestra Management at the College of Music and Performing Arts Frankfurt and Music and Cultural Management at the Conservatory in Munich (Jóri, Lücke, and Wickström 2015).

In 2003, the Mannheim-based Popakademie initiated a popular music business programme. Former students are active in leading positions in the German music business (Jóri, Lücke, and Wickström 2015). Examples of successful graduates are Julian Butz, Managing-Director and Co-Founder at NEUBAU Music; Michael Stockum, Head of Four Music; Jonas Weber, Director of Strategic Management at Universal Music.

In the meantime, the number of music business programmes has expanded, especially at the bachelor's level and in private institutions. Most of the public degree programmes focus on opera, theatre, and related fields. In addition, the first master's programmes have been established in recent years. One can assume that there are many types of music business degree programmes in Germany. On the one hand, there are the more practice-oriented programmes at universities of applied sciences which provide training for middle and higher management jobs in the music business. There are also degree programmes at public universities or at music and art colleges which provide a well-rounded theoretical education.

One question must be asked: Are there not too many music management programmes because the number of well-paid jobs is limited? Private institutions are usually financed by high tuition fees and attract students paying out of their own pocket. On the other hand, institutions depend on their reputation, especially the relatively new and expensive private universities. Therefore, they want graduates to take up good positions in the music business or become entrepreneurs by creating new business models.

Quantitative Analysis

The current German study programmes are listed in Table 1.2. The list focuses on those degrees using terms such as music or music management in their description. Cultural management programmes covering a more extensive cultural spectrum have not been included in this table.

Nine accredited and three non-accredited bachelor programmes (see Table 1.2) are compared to nine accredited master programmes (see Table 1.3). But what does accreditation mean in this context? Since 2001, the German Science Council (Wissenschaftsrat) has been responsible for reviewing private universities to ensure that they fulfil the scientific standards in research and teaching. This so-called institutional accreditation is awarded for three to ten years. Degrees from institutionally accredited (private) higher education institutions are equivalent to those from public institutions (Wissenschaftsrat 2021).

The Popakademie Baden-Württemberg in Mannheim, the University of Paderborn, and the Macromedia University of Applied Sciences offer music management courses both as bachelor's and master's degrees. The two master's programmes at the College of Music Munich (Cultural and Music Management) and the College of Music and Performing Arts Frankfurt a.M. (Theatre and Orchestra Management) are geared towards the graduates' later work in the orchestra or opera business.

Table 1.2 Bachelor's degree programmes with a music business focus

Institution	Place	Programme name	Private/public University/ University of Applied Sciences	Number of semesters	Accreditation
BIMM Institute Berlin (validated by the University of West London)	Berlin	BA (Hons) Music Business	private	6	no
Deutsche POP (validated by the University of West London)	13 locations, including Berlin, München	BA (Hons) Music Management	private	6	no
FHAM (University of Applied Management) together with SET-School (School of Entertainment & Technology GmbH)) / FHAM (Hochschule für angewandtes Management) together with SET-School	Berlin, Erding, Treuchtlingen	Bachelor of Arts in Business Administration, Branch Focus: Music & Culture Management	private	6	yes
Fresenius University of Applied Sciences / Hochschule Fresenius	Hamburg, Köln	Bachelor of Arts in Music Management	Private	6	yes
Macromedia University of Applied Sciences / Hochschule Macromedia	8 locations, including Berlin, Köln, München	Bachelor of Arts in Media Management – Field of Study: Music Management	private	6/7	yes
Popakademie Baden-Württemberg	Mannheim	Bachelor of Arts in Music Business	public	6	yes
Robert Schumann Conservatory of Music Düsseldorf / Robert Schumann Hochschule Düsseldorf	Düsseldorf	Bachelor of Music in Music and Media	public	8	yes

SAE Institute (validated by Middlesex University London)	9 locations, including Berlin, München	BA/BSC (Hons) Advanced Music Business	private	4–7	no
SRH University of the Popular Arts (HdpK) / SRH Hochschule der populären Künste (HdpK)	Berlin	Bachelor of Arts in Media Management – Field of Study: Music and Event Management	private	7	yes
University of Erfurt / Universität Erfurt	Erfurt	Bachelor of Arts in Music Education	public	6	yes
College of Music of the Westphalian Wilhelms University Münster / Musikhochschule der Westfälischen Wilhelms-Universität Münster	Münster	Bachelor of Music in Music and Communication	public	8	yes

Table 1.3 Master's degree programmes with a focus on music management

Institution	Place	Programme name	Public/private University/ University of Applied Sciences	Number of semesters
College of Music and Performing Arts Frankfurt a.M. / Hochschule für Musik und Darstellende Kunst Frankfurt a.M.	Frankfurt a.M.	Master of Arts Theatre and Orchestra Management	public	4
College of Music and Theater Hannover / Hochschule für Musik, Theater und Medien Hannover (hMtMh)	Hannover	Master of Arts in Media and Music	public	4
College of Music of the Westphalian Wilhelms University Münster / Musikhochschule der Westfälischen Wilhelms-Universität Münster	Münster	Master of Music in Music and Communication AND Master of Music in Music and Creativity	public	2
Institute for Cultural Management Ludwigsburg / Institut für Kulturmanagement Ludwigsburg	Ludwigsburg	Master of Arts in Cultural Studies and Cultural Management	public	4
Institute for Culture and Media Management / Institut für Kultur- und Medienmanagement	Hamburg	Master of Arts in Culture and Media Management	public	4
Macromedia University of Applied Sciences / Hochschule Macromedia	Berlin, Hamburg, Köln	Master of Arts Music Management	private	3/4
Munich Conservatory / Hochschule für Musik München	München	Master of Arts Culture and Music Management	public	4
Popakademie Baden-Württemberg	Mannheim	Master of Arts in Music and Creative Industries	public	4
University of Paderborn / Universität Paderborn	Paderborn	Master of Arts Popular Music and Media	public	4

Further analysis focuses on the programmes offered in Berlin, where many higher education institutions are competing with each other. These institutions are all privately funded, although a distinction must be made between companies in the form of foundations (e.g., SRH HdpK) or private equity (Macromedia University of Applied Sciences). Nevertheless, many of the analysed programmes are not accredited by the German Council of Science and Humanities, so their degrees are not on an equal status with public degrees. Globally active institutions such as SAE compensate for this disadvantage by cooperating with foreign universities to award a bachelor's degree (Hons).

Qualitative Analysis

The following is a qualitative look at six selected music management study programmes:

- **BIMM Institute Berlin:** BA (Hons) Music Business
- **Deutsche POP:** BA (Hons) Music Management
- **FHAM (University of Applied Management):** Bachelor of Arts in Business Administration, Branch Focus: Music & Culture Management
- **Macromedia University of Applied Sciences:** Bachelor of Arts in Media Management / Field of Study: Music Management
- **SAE Institute:** BA/BSC (Hons) Advanced Music Business
- **SRH University of the Popular Arts (HdpK):** Bachelor of Arts in Media Management / Field of Study: Music and Event Management

For the survey, both the freely accessible documents of the institutions and the various module catalogues were evaluated. In addition to aspects such as the structure of the degree programme, the modules were categorized into different content areas, including business administration, music management, event management, musicology, and foreign languages.

Study Programme vs. Field of Study

The individual names of the study programmes show that it is necessary to distinguish between degree programmes in music management and music management as a field of study. In the second case, more generalized modules must be passed. Thus, some structural and content-related differences between music management as a programme and music management as a field of study can be identified. BIMM, Deutsche Pop, and SAE offer music management as a degree programme. It is remarkable that those institutions are not institutionally accredited. Music management as a field of study is offered by FHAM, SRH HdpK, and Macromedia. The fields of study are part of a specific degree programme: Business Administration at FHAM, and Media Management at both SRH HdpK and Macromedia. Advantages and disadvantages exist for both forms: in the case of music management as a degree programme, the specialized knowledge is more detailed, but it is limited to the music business. In the case of music management as a field of study, students are taught an extensive range of subjects. However, this implies the danger that this leads to a superficial education. This means that it may be difficult to enter the music business due to a lack of depth in the field of music management.

Accreditation and Duration of Studies

When deciding on a degree programme, it is important for students to know whether both the programme and the institution are accredited, because institutional and programme accreditation guarantees quality in teaching (Wissenschaftsrat 2021). The non-accredited institutions (BIMM, Deutsche POP, SAE) cannot award degrees recognized by the government. Their degrees are authenticated by other cooperating universities (e.g., Deutsche POP with the University of West London and the SAE Institute with Middlesex University London), but graduates of these institutions are usually not accepted into accredited master's programmes in Germany.

The study programmes analysed have a different number of semesters, due to the federal state in which the university is accredited. The shortest standard period of study is five semesters at Deutsche POP and 24 months at the SAE Institute. These 'fast track' programmes are aimed at people who are already working in business but do not yet have an academic degree. All other universities offer full-time programmes with six or seven semesters.

Students who study part-time have the same opportunities for a career in music business as students who study full-time. Ultimately, the quality of the study programme depends on various characteristics. But a shorter study programme will usually cover less material than is possible in a six- or seven-semester programme. In a short study programme, the self-learning aspect plays an even more important role.

Teaching and Learning

The teaching staff is *the* key aspect of the quality of higher education institutions. Especially in a practice-oriented study programme like music management, a practical teaching approach is of great importance. Does this specific professional experience count more than academic merits such as a doctorate or the so-called 'habilitation' (a postdoctoral qualification, typical for the

German academic system)? Thus, teaching quality in real terms is a very complex issue that cannot be measured exclusively with the number of doctoral researchers and lecturers as a variable. The right mix of academic and industry-based teaching staff is the key to success here. However, concerning academia, the output of publications and research projects is more common at universities with a stronger research orientation, and thus (more likely) at accredited higher education institutions.

The music business operates globally in all its market segments. Therefore, this aspect plays an important role in a programme like music management. Performers, business partners, sponsors, and so on, have different cultural and industry-specific backgrounds. For this reason, it is important for students to acquire international experience during their studies. A (compulsory) semester abroad, usually with a partner university, can be helpful here. The institutions analysed deal with this aspect in two different ways:

1. At Macromedia, the curriculum includes (at least in the seven-semester variant) a mandatory semester abroad (arranged in the third semester) at one of more than a dozen partner institutions.
2. A semester abroad is possible, but not obligatory, at BIMM, FHAM, SRH HdpK, and SAE. If someone is studying at Deutsche POP to receive a BA Hons Diploma in 'Music Management' from the University of West London, one has to study in London for two semesters.

Learning a second language is an important skill to be competitive internationally, as students should have a good knowledge of the lingua franca English at the end of their studies. The programme at BIMM is the only one that is taught exclusively in English. Macromedia teaches a few courses in English. SRH HdpK offers Business English as a course for three semesters, FHAM for two semesters.

Curriculum

Another benchmark for the comparability of study programmes is the analysis of curricular content. But it is hardly possible to verify in detail what has really been taught. This would require an analysis of the specific course content taught and the selection of teachers, but this cannot be done within the limits of this study. Only the module catalogues of all institutions were evaluated. One problem occurred with the exact module names, because some modules with comparable content were named differently, depending on the university. For this reason, the differences in the module names were modified for further analysis. In addition to twenty different subject fields, the sum of the credit points and the location in the study programme were considered, too.

Table 1.4, arranged alphabetically, lists the different subject fields offered in the individual degree programmes.

Table 1.4 Curriculum analysis

	BIMM	Deutsche Pop	FHAM	Macromedia	SAE	SRH HdpK
Academic Writing	x		x	x	x	x

Most institutions teach the basic rules of academic writing, both in introductory courses in the first semesters and through colloquia, which focus on the final thesis. Academic research methodologies and further in-depth courses are only offered by accredited institutions.

	BIMM	Deutsche Pop	FHAM	Macromedia	SAE	SRH HdpK
Coding						x
Communication Management			x	x	x	x
Design		x				x
Economics	x		x	x	x	x

A total of nine different subjects/courses can be identified within this category. It is remarkable that FHAM and Macromedia offer a relatively extensive economics curriculum (five and four courses respectively). At least four institutions teach a (basic) course in business administration (BWL). In contrast, the Deutsche POP does not have any subjects with an economic focus in its curriculum.

	BIMM	Deutsche Pop	FHAM	Macromedia	SAE	SRH HdpK
Event Management	x	x	x	x	x	x
Foreign languages	x		x	x		x

The internationalization of the music business has been obvious for years; therefore, corresponding knowledge is important for the graduates' later professional activity. In addition to the English-language programme at BIMM, the accredited institutions in particular teach corresponding courses. They strengthen the aspect of internationality through semesters abroad, which are sometimes obligatory.

	BIMM	Deutsche Pop	FHAM	Macromedia	SAE	SRH HdpK
Human Relations			x	x		
Journalism						x
Law	x		x	x	x	x

For many aspects of music management, knowledge of national and international legal rules is important, along with keeping abreast of the issues in the music business over the past two decades.

	BIMM	Deutsche Pop	FHAM	Macromedia	SAE	SRH HdpK
Leadership			x	x		x
Marketing	x	x	x	x	x	x

The topic of marketing in its various forms (physical, digital, general product marketing or specific music marketing) is integrated into the curricula of most programmes. Only Macromedia and the SAE offer current specialized courses in the field of marketing, such as marketing psychology.

Media Management				x		x
Media Science				x		x
Music Management	x	x	x	x	x	x

The topic of music management can be subdivided into Artist Management, Music Market, and (New) Business Models. The SRH HdpK is the only institution that does not offer a course in this field. However, it has to be pointed out that music management-immanent contents can be found in other curricular courses, for which a specific analysis of the individual lessons would be necessary. A general overview of the music market is included in all programmes (except SRH HdpK and FHAM).

Music Production				x		x	x
Musicology	x			x		x

Music management is based on the cultural heritage of music, which has a centuries-old tradition. Macromedia offers a range of courses in the category of musicology. BIMM and SRH HdpK have at least one course in pop music (history).

Project Management	x	x		x	x	x

Project management is the basis of most business activities. BIMM and Macromedia show that a study programme can lead to self-employment with specific start-up courses. These types of courses can be offered extracurricular, too.

Projects and Internship	x	x	x	x		x

According to the module catalogue, the SAE does not offer any courses with partners from music practice. Macromedia, on the other hand, has three teaching projects of 5 weekly semester hours each as well as a 20-week compulsory internship. Macromedia is the only institution that offers a so-called Student Initiative, in which students have to initiate a further practical project.

Sales	x		x	x		

Summary and Outlook

As similar as the analysed programmes appear at first glance, they are different in their structure and realization.

The differentiation of the existing programmes indicates that there is still no blueprint for academic training for the music business that institutions can follow. Instead, all universities are in a trial phase in which they want to establish a new music business programme without referring to best-practice models. Because most of the private higher education institutions are trying to distinguish themselves from each other, they are competing in a relatively small market. The private education players see education as a business model that is to be monetized. But this business model will only exist on the market in the long term if it succeeds in placing graduates in the music business.

It is clear that music business education at the university level is a field that will continue to change, much like the music industry as a whole. It will be interesting to see which new players appear on the market and whether public universities (at least in Berlin) discover this interesting economic sector for themselves. The boom of the last few years, both from domestic and foreign players, is considerable. More research is needed to understand how institutions will specialize, and if they will continue to offer an extensive range of training options or focus on specific areas such as the live sector or the publishing industry.

Empirical research will demonstrate whether future graduates succeed in entering the music business without any problems and what experiences companies from the industry have with these young, academically trained employees. Data will reveal whether educational institutions can adapt to the ongoing changes in the music industry and incorporate new solutions into their curricula. At this time, it is not (yet) possible to say whether training and study are the right way to enter the field of music business, which university offers better training from the point of view of the industry, and so on. The focus is always on the potential student. What does the student expect? An academic education that opens the way to a master's degree? In that case, an accredited institution must be chosen. Or a reliable career entry? Then they have to choose the university with the largest (promised) network.

In analysing German music business curricula, the data suggests that linking theory and practice as early as possible will be the key to professional success. It is not surprising that all analysed players operate as universities of applied sciences. The more theory-oriented universities have not yet discovered this field of science and education for themselves. And it is remarkable that there is only one master's degree (at least in Berlin). In general, one might ask whether the music business in particular needs an even more scientifically oriented master's degree, or whether a bachelor's degree is not sufficient here. Furthermore, one can conclude that the private higher education sector and foreign institutions have discovered the education market for themselves. BIMM was the first provider in the field of music management, but it must be assumed that other international higher education institutions will follow, further complicating an education market that has long been complex.

References

Bundesverband der Veranstaltungswirtschaft (bdv). 2018. 'Live entertainment in Deutschland'. http://gwvr.de/wp-content/uploads/2020/04/GfK-Studie-2018.pdf (accessed 26 October 2021).

Bundesverband Musikindustrie (BVMI). 2011. *Musikindustrie in Zahlen 2010*. Berlin.

Bundesverband Musikindustrie (BVMI). 2021. *Musikindustrie in Zahlen 2020*. Berlin.

Destatis. 2021. 'Zahl der Studierenden im Wintersemester 2021/2022 auf Vorjahresniveau'. https://www.destatis.de/DE/Presse/Pressemitteilungen/2021/11/PD21_538_21.html

Frank, A., S. Hieronimus, N. Killius, and V. Meyer-Guckel. 2010. *Rolle und Zukunft privater Hochschulen in Deutschland*. [pdf] Essen: Edition Stifterverband.

Hochschulkompass. 2022. 'Suche nach Studiengängen'. https://www.hochschulkompass.de/studium/studiengangsuche.html (accessed 26 October 2021).

Initiative Kultur- und Kreativwirtschaft. 2020. 'Monitoringbericht Kultur- und Kreativwirtschaft 2020'. https://www.kultur-kreativ-wirtschaft.de/KUK/Redaktion/DE/Publikationen/2020/monitoring-wirtschaftliche-eckdaten-kuk.html (accessed 26 October 2021).

Jóri, A., M. Lücke, and D.-E. Wickström. 2015. 'The higher education of musicians and music industry workers in Germany'. *International Journal for Music Business Research* 1: 55–88. https://musicbusinessresearch.files.wordpress.com/2012/04/volume-4-no-1-april-2015-not-without-music-business.pdf

KuPoGe. 2021. 'Studium und Arbeitsmarkt Kultur'. http://www.studium-kultur.de/studienangebote.html (accessed 7 June 2021).

Limper, J., and M. Lücke. 2013. *Management in der Musikwirtschaft*. Stuttgart: Kohlhammer.

Lücke, M., and A. Paulus. 2015. *Branchenverbände der Musikkultur / -wirtschaft als Austausch- und Kooperationspartner: Chancen für die Entwicklung und Vermittlung popkultureller Lehrinhalte an (Fach-)Hochschulen*. In *Popmusik-Vermittlung*, edited by Michael Ahlers. 307–20. Münster: Lit-Verlag.

Scholz, L. 2010. *Die Musikbranche. Ausbildungswege und Tätigkeitsfelder*. Mainz: Schott.

Seufert, W., R. Schlegel, and F. Sattelberger. 2015. *Musikwirtschaft in Deutschland. Studie zur volkswirtschaftlichen Bedeutung von Musikunternehmen unter Berücksichtigung aller Teilsektoren und Ausstrahlungseffekte*. Berlin: Die beauftragenden Verbände.

Seufert, W., R. Schlegel, and F. Sattelberger. 2021. *Musikwirtschaft in Deutschland. Studie zur volkswirtschaftlichen Bedeutung von Musikunternehmen unter Berücksichtigung aller Teilsektoren und Ausstrahlungseffekte*. Berlin: Die beauftragenden Verbände.

Tschmuck, P. 2017. *The Economics of Music*. Newcastle: Agenda Publishing.

Werner, C. and E. Steiner. 2010. *Hochschulbildung als Geschäftsfeld?* In *Handbuch Bildungsfinanzierung*, edited by Heiner Barz, 479–90. Wiesbaden: VS Verlag.

Willnauer, F. 1997. 'Musikmanagement'. In *Kulturmanagement. Theorie und Praxis einer professionellen Kunst*, edited by Hermann Rauhe, 223–42. Berlin: de Gruyter.

Wissenschaftsrat. 2021. 'Akkreditierung'. https://www.wissenschaftsrat.de/DE/Aufgabenfelder/Akkreditierungen/akkreditierungen_node.html (accessed 7 June 2021).

Author biography

Martin Lücke is Professor of Music Management at Macromedia University of Applied Sciences, Germany. As Local Head of Faculty, he leads the Faculty of Arts, Media and Psychology at the Berlin Campus. His current research focuses on education research and cultural financing. Previously, he was working on Schlager and progressive rock. Martin Lücke is active in numerous associations and initiatives. He is one of the co-founders of Music Business Research, a new scientific discipline that looks at all kinds of music from economic, legal, and sociological perspectives. His most recent publications include the *Lexikon der Musikberufe* (2021), the anthology *The New Age of Electronic Dance Music and Club Culture* (2021), edited with Anita Jóri, and the anthology *Musikwirtschaftsforschung. Die Grundlagen einer neuen Disziplin* (2017), co-edited with Peter Tschmuck and Beate Flath. Martin Lücke also curates music exhibitions. In 2023, together with Annette Hartmann, he created an exhibition on disco culture for the rock'n'pop museum in Gronau, Germany.

2 Running a Student-Led Music Label: Design, Delivery and Evaluation of Music Business and Professional Practice Training

Ian Stevenson, Jeff Crabtree and Monica Rouvellas

Introduction

This chapter examines practical instructional design responding to the challenge of teaching music business and professional practice skills to tertiary students in the Bachelor Music and Sound design programme at the University of Technology Sydney between 2018–2020. The chapter explores the initial design objectives and iterative refinement over three years of a final-year undergraduate subject, *Music Business and Professional Practice* (MBPP). This analysis is supported by student evaluations of the learning experience captured in interviews and qualitative reflective writing.

The learning design incorporates industry-engaged, real-world, authentic learning incorporating professionally aligned collaborative structures, digital distribution, social media promotion, live events, and cloud-based project management. This design facilitates the motivational, meta-cognitive and strategic action associated with self-regulated learning and provides a stepping stone for students to transition into the diverse workplace contexts typical of today's creative industries. The subject design is contextualized by an examination of elements of authentic learning models that inform it. By focusing on the three components of design, delivery and student evaluation, we aim to offer practical insight that may assist educators seeking guidance on what works and what does not, from the perspective of curriculum designers, instructors, and students themselves.

While research into the future of employment has only recently begun to identify that 'new attitudes and behaviours will be needed by individuals and businesses founded on flexibility, resilience, collaboration, entrepreneurism and creativity' (Störmer et al. 2014: 4), professionals in the music industry have applied these attitudes and behaviours for a long time. These qualities are the everyday reality for those working in popular music's precarious and unpredictable world. As the precariousness typical of the arts sector spreads inexorably into many more workplaces, the skills identified by the UK's *Future of Work* report listed above (Störmer et al. 2014), which have long been prerequisites for a music career, are now needed to survive elsewhere in the economy. The great advantage that some musicians have over those in other sectors is the intrinsic motivation derived from a vocation in music. The university subject described in this chapter aimed to harness this vocation to prepare students not just to survive but to thrive in their music careers.

Learning Design

Overview of the Subject

MBPP is delivered in the third and final year of a Bachelor of Music and Sound Design degree at the University of Technology Sydney. At this stage of their training, students have developed competencies in a range of music and sound production techniques and processes. The initial subject design was premised on the concept that a learn-by-doing model would be most effective in teaching music business and professional practice. Therefore, we conceived the idea to run a student-led music label that would release original music. The label functioned as a commercial enterprise. The complexities of music distribution were simplified by using current commercial online digital distribution platforms and would focus solely on digital and social media marketing campaigns in line with current industry practice. These strategies included a live launch event devised, managed, and run by students, to be presented in an on-campus university venue. The label comprised a series of committees tasked with specific management responsibilities, with each student undertaking a unique role in the label structure. Weekly meetings included guest lectures from current industry professionals drawn from various careers and roles. Teaching staff delivered introductory and scaffolding lectures, provided guidance where required and were intermediaries with the University administration. Students were assessed using a set of professional project documentation tasks, which were authentic versions of documentation they would encounter in industry.

Contextualizing the Learning Design

The subject design drew on a range of key pedagogical approaches that take the traditional learn-by-doing model out of the context of workplace learning (Billett 2010b) and insert it into the university environment (Billett 2010a). The principles of learning-by-doing have been formalized in the educational literature around themes including learner-centred teaching, project-based learning (Stolk and Martello 2018), experiential learning, and 'authentic learning' (Rule 2006). While these theories focus on knowledge and skills acquisition, a further goal was to enhance our graduates' capacity for self-management and self-regulated learning, key capacities for success in the insecure work environment of the creative industries.

Learner-centred Teaching

The learning-by-doing method conforms to the broad concept of learner-centred teaching, which de-emphasizes the role of the instructor in the transmission of knowledge. Weimer's (2002) five key practices for learner-centred instructional design comprise the balance of power between teachers and learners, the function of content, the role of the teacher, the responsibility for learning, and the purpose and process of evaluation. These practices have been implemented in a range of higher education contexts and can include any number of approaches that involve engaged or active learning. Weimer herself draws evidence to support the benefits of learner-centred approaches from a range of group-based approaches such as problem-based, project-based, process oriented, peer-led and other models. Despite the diversity and differences in each approach, these models all in some way address Weimer's key changes associated with learner-centred teaching by empowering learners to define the scope and sequencing of instructional content, transforming the role of the teacher and shifting responsibility for learning, and evaluation, to the learner. The syncretic approach to instructional design suggested by this method gave us licence to mix and match elements from these diverse approaches within the overarching framework of a student-led enterprise.

Project-based Learning

Project-based learning ('PjBL')[1] is a teaching and learning strategy that aims to engage students by asking them to apply their learning and understanding to a project (Bransford and Stein 1993) whilst expanding their understanding through situational learning (Barak and Zadok 2009). Students

---

1. The lowercase j differentiates project-based learning from the distinct approach of problem-based learning.

apply previously acquired knowledge, such as audio production skills, or new knowledge gained from workshops, carried out both individually and in teams (Mills and Treagust 2003). In PjBL, teachers become facilitators and guide students through a project (Mou 2020). According to Deci et al. (1991), students are more likely to become self-regulated learners through intrinsic motivation created by appropriate scaffolding of tasks by teachers within an applied learning environment.

MBPP was also designed to incorporate more traditional approaches to learning-on-the-job, particularly in digital music distribution, social media marketing and event management. Enterprise training has recognized the increasing importance of learning-on-the-job in a time of rapid workplace transformation (Arets et al. 2016; Johnson et al. 2018).

PjBL allows students to engage in a project that is similar to ones they will face in the workplace, and as an authentic form of learning, engages students with a problem that requires them to plan and organize activities that result in a tangible product or artefact that not only showcases their developing expertise (Blumenfeld et al. 1991; Savery 2006) but also meets project requirements. This tangible artefact is thought to be a 'real-life' bridging of the gap between the classroom and industry that develops a wide range of workplace skills (Bender et al. 2008; Lima et al. 2007) that are highly valued by employers in industry.

Authentic Learning

The primary goal of the subject design was to develop an authentic context for learning that would prepare our graduates for music industry careers. The music industry is a heterogeneous environment that is highly fragmented and yet highly networked (Hughes et al. 2013). It is complex to navigate and success is elusive (Wikström 2013). Further, Williamson and Cloonan (2007) have argued that the music industry comprises three distinct but interconnected spheres of economic activity. Regardless of students' career aspirations, the subject design was intended to create a context that was as realistic as practicable. Educational theorists have argued for the benefits of this approach and have attempted to define the characteristics of authentic learning design. Audrey Rule (2006) outlined four key components: real-world problems, open-ended inquiry, social learning, and student choice. To these, Jan Herrington and colleagues (2010), in a model for authentic learning in an online environment, added nine key requirements: authentic context, authentic task, access to experts, multiple perspectives, collaboration, reflection, articulation of new knowledge, coaching and scaffolding, and authentic assessment.

To these two lists, we have added insights from Schön's (1991) approach to training professionals, and Wilson and Stokes's (2002) work on entrepreneur training. These frameworks have been condensed into eight criteria that characterize our approach and are used as themes to describe and evaluate our successes and challenges in developing the teaching model. Table 2.1 touches on implementing these criteria in the design which will be described later in the chapter.

Table 2.1 Authentic learning inventory (adapted from Herrington et al. 2010; Rule 2006; Schön 1991; Wilson and Stokes 2002)

	Criterion	**Implementation**
1	Authentic context / the activity involves real-world problems that mimic the work of professionals in the discipline with presentation of findings to audiences beyond the classroom	Record label
2	Authentic task and assessment of learning (Herrington et al. support varied tasks with common criteria rather than standardized assessment)	Record label activities
		Compromise assessment design including two authentic tasks: assessment 1 proposal, and assessment 3 acquittal/reflection; plus a presentation of a portfolio outlining individual contribution to the label
3	Access to experts and expert performances	Industry guest presenters
		Observation of expert performance implies an apprenticeship model that is absent from the learning design.
4	Multiple roles and perspectives	Students noted that collaboration resulted in negotiating practical problems from the multiple perspectives of their peers and that this enriched their learning.
		Industry guests demonstrate their diverse perspectives and commercial objectives allowing students to understand various points on the value chain of the music business.
5	Collaboration and collaborative construction of knowledge, students engage in discourse and social learning in a community of learners, incentive structure based on the performance of the whole group/enterprise	Students confirmed the following: learning collaboration skills (communication, negotiation, emotional intelligence) was a value in itself; collaboration facilitated their learning (see item 4); they were motivated by the shared goals of the label

6	Reflection and articulation to enable abstractions to be formed; open-ended inquiry, thinking skills, and metacognition are addressed to enable tacit knowledge to be made explicit through public presentation of argument to enable defence of a position; inherent rather than constructed opportunities for articulation	Weekly committee presentations inherently require authentic reflection and articulation, defining goals and reporting on progress; assessment 2 portfolio presentation is a constructed task that demands reflective articulation; assessment 3 combines authentic acquittal documentation and normalizes reflective professional practice (Schön 1991)
7	Coaching and scaffolding through mentoring at critical times	Guidance provided by teaching staff, pre-session coaching of label executive
8	Students are empowered through choice to direct their own learning in relevant project work	Students propose their role in the label and resource their own learning as required to complete tasks

Self-regulated Learning and Motivation

A final consideration that inspired the design of the subject was the desire to facilitate the development of self-regulated learning (SRL) and motivation. We believe that learning to learn is a key attribute for success in the rapidly changing entertainment industry. To develop intrinsic motivation, we aimed to re-kindle students' vocation in music and sound design, reminding them why they originally chose this field. Boekaerts et al. (2005) define SRL as learners using active learning behaviours and constructive processes to achieve their goals. Students gain awareness of their own learning by monitoring their behaviour, setting goals and reflecting on their progress (Zimmerman 2000). Our aim is to enhance students' self-satisfaction and motivation, helping them to optimistically consider future careers (Zimmerman 2002). Students who employ SRL strategies tend to be highly motivated and confident in engaging with their learning (Stefanou et al. 2013), and are more likely to be successful as students and in their careers (Schunk and Zimmerman 2012; Zimmerman 2002).

SRL does not occur autonomously but needs to be fostered through teaching strategies (Paris and Paris 2001; Zimmerman 1998). Table 2.1 shows the intersections between authentic learning and self-regulation in our subject design. Underpinned by emotional and cognitive processes, self-regulation is an important aspect of student engagement (Fredricks et al. 2004) and was central to the design and delivery of MBPP. Given that SRL provides for learning new skills and the refinement of existing ones, it is deemed essential for professionals in creative industries where much work is self-initiated (Zimmerman 2002).

Zimmermann divides SRL into three phases, with each phase consisting of two key processes (see Figure 2.1). This process is cyclical in that the self-reflection phase influences what the student will do when they return to the forethought phase when they set out on their next task, or creative project (Zimmerman and Kitsantas 1999).

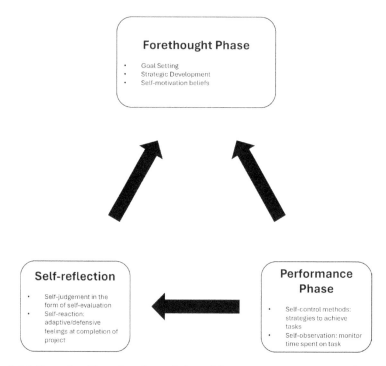

Figure 2.1 Self-regulated learning phases (adapted from Zimmermann 2002 and Bandura 1997)

Essentially, MBPP stimulates the SRL cycle by providing a scaffolding structure in which students are required to plan, perform, and evaluate their own learning (Azevedo et al. 2004; Dabbagh and Kitsantas 2012; Kitsantas 2013). This scaffolded cycle exists at two timescales: at a macro level through the assessment structure and label outcomes, and at a micro level through the weekly workshops in which students plan and monitor the progress of the label project.

Delivery and Adaptation

Initial Design

The MBPP project was to take place over a 12-week semester. Collectively, students would be required to decide the label's identity and artistic direction, undertake artist development and music production culminating in the release of quality recordings of original music composed and performed by the students. To enhance the authenticity of the process, the label was initially conceived as a student club complete with banking facilities under the auspices of the University Student Association. Student association clubs have the structure of an unincorporated association (ATO 2023) typical of early-stage creative cooperatives. A series of committees tasked with roles such as marketing, production, distribution, and event management would report to the executive committee (see Figure 2.2). Conducting committee business would form the principal activity during weekly sessions throughout the semester, with individual students taking on specific roles within each committee and providing professional services to the label.

Figure 2.2 An early illustration of the proposed committee structure

The ongoing weekly committee business was to be scaffolded by lectures to provide an historical overview of industry transformation and an outline of professional practice and portfolio careers (Bartleet et al. 2019). Subsequently, weekly guest lectures would be presented by established industry professionals. These were drawn from artist management, label A&R, radio programming, music streaming, social media and PR, contracts and legal, statutory performance and publishing rights management agencies, music media, and established artists. Ultimately, student feedback surveys in all iterations of the subject recorded high satisfaction levels with the selection of industry guest lecturers, but as we note below, recruiting a continuous roster of industry professionals presents significant challenges.

Assessment

In the original design, the goal of fully authentic learning (Rule 2006) would be enhanced by ensuring that all assessment tasks were real-world activities normally undertaken during professional practice. Due to the diversity of roles, students would not be assessed on their practical contribution to the label but rather on a uniform set of project documentation tasks.

The proposed assessments in the original design are set out in Table 2.2.

Table 2.2 Proposed assessments for MBPP

Assessment 1
• Initial proposal including a description of the work to be undertaken by the individual, • an estimate of the value of the work (representing the fee or in-kind value of their work), • an itemised budget, • a work breakdown schedule and timeline, • an individual SWOT analysis.
Assessment 2
• Students enter into an agreement with the label, • agreements are based on contract templates developed by the University Law School, • contracts cover undertakings such as the provision of professional administrative services, design services, copy writing services, audio production services, music composition, music performance, production and event management services, • contract documents will go through stages: draft schedules of supply and remuneration, contract advice, negotiation of terms, final contract, • artists and label managers negotiate a non-exclusive licence for the release of their creative work. These licences would be revocable in the event of the student artist obtaining a commercial label deal, • peer assessment would be used to monitor the committee performance and contract negotiation.
Assessment 3
• A final acquittal report and a written reflection. • The acquittal would address the undertakings outlined in the project proposal and would list all elements of the student's contribution in summary form, • a budget detailing in-kind and actual costs associated with the student's contribution, • a written reflection to provide the student with experience in developing a formal reflective practice approach to their professional activities. • The reflection was intended to encourage students to identify the strengths and weaknesses of their engagement with the project and to assess future opportunities, risks and strategies associated with their future employment.

Delivery

The subject was delivered in three iterations between 2018–2020. Broadly, students nominated themselves for a specific role within the label either in leadership, management, or in a creative capacity. Leadership roles had responsibilities spanning the whole label, and management roles involved parts of the label such as events manager, marketing manager, or A&R manager. Students were encouraged to nominate for roles that either played to their strengths or had the potential to develop specific soft skills (Blom and Encarnacao 2012), technical or creative skills, or business management skills that they felt might be beneficial to their future careers. The creative roles were related to music production, composition, recording, and performance. In addition to the functions noted earlier, teaching staff established the structure of the label, its objectives, and its time and budget constraints. University funding was sufficient to cover only the cost of hiring technical staff for the live event (a mandatory cost imposed by venue management).

In addition to mentoring and guidance, teaching staff also conducted lectures on a range of topics relevant to the Australian music industry and a portfolio career in music, including the application of industry knowledge to typical music industry roles, project management, business structures, financial management, and developing a press kit.

The intended trajectory of a student through the subject was broadly as follows:

1. Introduction to the subject, the project and the assessments
2. Overview of the project structure and timelines, selection of roles
3. Initial ideation
4. Planning and timeline development and identifying project markers
5. Production and development of creative assets
6. Monitoring of progress and achieving targets
7. Accomplishing the launch event and online release
8. Evaluation

Adaptation

Frith (2013) notes the challenge for academics (and even for professionals) to provide up-to-date information on the current state of industry practices. This was offset in MBPP to some extent by using guest lecturers from industry. Regardless, in undertaking the project, students were able to uncover valuable information about the current and rapidly changing state of local and networked practices as they attempted to promote and distribute the artists they were developing. In addition to the practical details of running the label, annual subject review and modification allowed us to adapt and develop the subject design based on student feedback and evaluation of the design by the teaching staff.

Given that grading students based on their individual contribution to the label was thought too difficult, because the broad range of roles, tasks, and skill requirements were too different, as noted above, the assessment was based on students' engagement with industry concepts and practices as well as on a critical reflection. The second assessment was simplified and adapted to become a portfolio task that required students to document and demonstrate their contribution to the label in a professional format. Further, the disconnect between assessment tasks and the amount of effort that was expected to produce a successful result was addressed in the subject introduction, in the form of a class ethos. This included the open recognition that a student could contribute minimally to the label, complete assessments to a high standard, and achieve an adequate grade with little effort. To counter this, teaching staff pointed to the benefits gained due to their contribution to the project.

Moreover, an appeal was made to their intrinsic motivations for studying music business, as the label was an opportunity to develop various professional skills required for roles within the music industry. Finally, students were actively engaged in the selection and assignment of their roles. Teaching staff based the assignment of roles within the label on a combination of the students' top three preferences[2] and the results of an online personality test.[3] In all iterations, approximately 90% of students were allocated either their first or second preference.

The revised assessment tasks are set out in Table 2.3.

The first delivery iteration featured an organizational structure that divided the label into slightly different committees than subsequent iterations. In practice, the initial committee structure proved to be an effective forum for problem-solving for some parts of the label but not for others, and it became apparent that problem-solving was occurring outside the so-called creative committee. For the second iteration, the label was divided into 'sub-labels' and departments to provide the opportunity for those seeking a leadership role to be engaged in the critical A&R function. This was further modified in the third iteration by dismantling the departmental structure of the label and forming creative teams around an artist, led by an A&R manager, and supported by the service roles of producers, recording engineers, marketing, design and PR, all focused on developing the artist's product and brand (see Figure 2.3). This last change was intended to remove bottlenecks, such as those experienced by the

2. In line with item 8 in the authentic learning inventory.
3. This test was an online version of the NEO Personality Inventory – Revised: a standard measure of the Five Factor Model of personality.

marketing department head, who was overwhelmed by the volume of communication and requests for service. The development of fluid teams around an artist was also thought to more closely resemble a project-based organization or organic network (Morgan 1989; Sedita 2008) typically found throughout newer organizations within both the music and creative industries.

Table 2.3 Assessment tasks for iterations 2 and 3 of MBPP

Assessment 1

• Each student will contribute to the content and/or administration of the digital label project. This document fully describes the student's proposed contribution. It will include the following sections:
   ○ Description of undertaking
   ○ In-kind value of offer
   ○ A work breakdown schedule (WBS) and timeline
   ○ An opportunity analysis

Assessment 2
• Each student will develop and deliver an individual business portfolio that documents the work they have undertaken in the formation, design, and development of the music label. The development of the portfolio will commence immediately on submission of Assessment 1. The portfolio will include evidence of the individual's actual contribution to the business, and can take the form of audio and video files, budget documents, planning and strategy documents, as well as pictorial evidence and screenshots of social media posts. Each portfolio will include a written explanation that links the evidence and demonstrates its significance in explaining the work completed. • Portfolio length will be dependent on format; however, the written explanatory linking document will be 1000 words. • Suitable components of the portfolio may include, but are not limited to, the following: CV, promotional materials, production material, business case, selection of artists, artists' career plan, selecting engineer, production considerations – including metadata logs and coding, strategy (A&R strategy, marketing strategy, promotional strategy, business strategy), financial statements (department budgets, business budget, P&L), media release, promoter planning.
Assessment 3
• On the completion of the project students will produce a final acquittal report and a written reflection (2000 words). • The acquittal will address the undertakings outlined in the project proposal. It will list all elements of the student's contribution in summary form. • The acquittal will detail in-kind and actual costs associated with the student's contribution in the form of a final budget. • A written reflection will provide the student with experience in developing a formal reflective practice approach to their professional activities. • The reflection encourages students to identify the strengths and weaknesses of their engagement with the project and to assess future opportunities, risks, and strategies associated with their future employment.

Figure 2.3 Label structure in the third iteration of the subject

The final adaptation reflected the challenge of financing the label. The first cohort realized that they needed financial resources beyond those provided by the University to facilitate rehearsals for the launch event. They decided to raise these funds by producing and selling merchandise. This initially took the form of T-shirts, but in later iterations students added tote bags, stickers and hats to the merchandise offer. Including event ticket sales revenue, in all three iterations, the project not only covered costs, but left a surplus available for succeeding cohorts.

Table 2.4 450 Records' 2020 financial spreadsheet

Date	Item	Income	Expenditure	Balance
23/9/20	2019 profit carried forward	$431.60		$431.60
28/9/20	Merchandise: Stickers		$107.50	$324.10
6/10/20	Merchandise: Tote bags		$247.50	$76.60
14/10/20	SquareSpace web hosting and EFTPOS		$39.60	$37.00
19/10/20	Venue ticket sales	$350.00		$387.00
19/10/20	Class discount tickets	$190.00		$577.00
19/10/20	Merchandise income (EFTPOS)	$159.37		$736.37
20/10/20	Merchandise income (cash)	$274.00		$1,010.37
20/10/20	Livestream costs		$240.00	$770.37
20/10/20	Rehearsal time venue fees		$100.00	$670.37
20/10/20	Digital distribution (Distrokid)		$59.97 (3x artists)	$610.40
21/10/20	Digital distribution (Ditto Music)		$29.00	$581.40
22/10/20	EFTPOS Terminal		$59.00	$522.40
28/10/20	Stripe (online merchandise income)	$50.50		$572.90
	Balance carried forward to 2021			**$572.90**

Table 2.4 shows the opening balance brought forward from 2019, the 2020 income, expenditure and the surplus balance carried forward to 2021.

Challenges

Internal University and Student Association policies prevented the idea of an independent legal entity for the label, leaving the label without an active bank account. Thus, the label operates on a cash basis. Whilst support from the University was sought, the bureaucratic nature of the university environment does not make this an easy task. Others attempting to emulate our approach are encouraged to seek adequate seed funding and formalize this aspect in a manner appropriate to their local conditions.

Another major challenge is recruiting a continuous roster of industry professionals for guest lecturers. Many working for larger organizations are happy to provide their time gratis, but freelancers often cannot afford to work pro bono. This may pose a threat to presenting a group of guest lecturers who are culturally diverse and gender balanced (McCormack 2016). It is a vital motivational component of learning design to provide students with diverse role models with which they can identify, and Universities must be proactive in resourcing and addressing these issues in the design and delivery of their courses. Fortunately, the teaching staff in MBPP have been able to use their extensive industry contacts to ensure a good level of diversity amongst guest professionals in salaried positions able to donate their time to mentoring the next generation of music industry workers. However, proper resourcing would allow a more diverse representation from those in more precarious, contract, and freelance roles, thereby addressing ethical concerns regarding valuing the time and expertise of music professionals and not perpetuating exploitative practices.

The first two cohorts ran their launch events successfully at on-campus licensed venues; however, in 2020, Covid-19 forced the closure of those venues. Following an appropriate risk assessment, subsequent cohorts negotiated a Covid-safe plan to run their event in off-campus commercial venues. Overcoming this challenge proved beneficial for the students and the project. The heightened risk arguably created greater authenticity, not to mention improved public exposure for the artists. Due to the success of this adaptation, all future iterations of the launch event have run in a commercial, public venue, establishing an ongoing external relationship for the label.

Finally, a project such as this one offers the possibility of collaboration with students in other disciplines. For example, law students could conceivably draft contracts, entrepreneurship students could develop a start-up business, and marketing and design students could contribute expertise. Those seeking to emulate our approach should adapt to local conditions.

Student Evaluation

Student feedback on the learning experience was gathered in a series of group interviews with students and by analysing the students' final written assessment consisting of a critical evaluation and reflection. Students identified four key aspects of the experience that they valued and that they felt contributed to engagement, motivation and learning. These points – realism and professional relevance, collaboration, autonomy, and reflective practice – are largely consistent with elements of the authentic learning model highlighted earlier.

Realism and Industry Relevance

Firstly, students recognized and valued the realism and industry relevance of the learning context that was established through the record label project. One student acknowledged that 'it has been a great learning experience for me as an aspiring artist wanting to set foot into the music industry. I have discovered that there is more to the artist than simply making music, that there is also an entire brand based upon their being which must consequently also be marketed'. Another noted that 'the A&R manager role I undertook ... has been one of the greatest highlights of my degree. I learnt so much about the music industry in such a short amount of time, it has been amazing to see what [the label] could achieve...'. For many this was a distinct contrast to previous learning experiences: 'when I realized we were actually going to get merch and going to pay for a disk jockey and we actually had the money, I realized that it was actually going to be a real thing'.

Collaboration

Three aspects of collaboration had an impact on the students. Firstly, the realization that collaboration occurs throughout the industry and that it is important to develop and practice those skills, and to reflect on their own capabilities. Secondly, the value of collaborative learning in which they could observe and learn from the multiple perspectives their peers brought to the task at hand. The final aspect was that collaboration has its challenges. Some students discovered that they themselves were not strong collaborators and preferred to keep control of many aspects of the projects they were undertaking. Students found that some collaborators were unreliable and less engaged in the week-to-week process leading to frustrations and disappointment. A few highly motivated individuals recognized that unlike typical group assessments in which this would be seen as an unfair or inequitable imposition, uneven work output from colleagues was regarded as a challenge to be managed in order to achieve the goal of making the label happen. One student commented that 'it was clear who had initiative and drive and those who still couldn't see the opportunity as more than just a class to pass for a degree'. For many this was a valuable lesson that would prepare them for developing and contributing to professional networks.

The common goal of the label release and launch event was a great motivator, or 'incentive structure' (Herrington et al. 2010). As one student put it: 'in music business, even though we were all doing different things, it was for the label, and that work was shared with everybody. And we're kind of like working towards the same thing, even though we might have been doing it in different ways'. Smaller unified goals in the collaborative structure of the label in the third iteration were achieved through the fluid project-based teams with a common goal centred around a particular artist. This was reflected in several students' feedback: 'everyone had to collaborate together for working on the label. But it was also interesting to see people own smaller groups, like the one artist I was with had their own dedicated band'.

Autonomy

The third key feature of student feedback expressed how they valued autonomy in directing their own work and managing their own workload. As Rule (2006: 2) notes, 'students are empowered through choice to direct their own learning in relevant project work'. The challenge of this level of autonomy was a learning opportunity: 'as the weeks went by in class it really set in that we were left to our own devices with this label, which was unlike any other class, and made me feel a vague sense of anxiety mixed with excitement for the possibilities'; 'I learnt about my leadership, professional and collaborative values through the management of a budget, partaking in and observing communication between team members, observing accountability in myself and others in the relationship between intention and action'. Students also valued directing their learning in areas of personal interest or in new areas: 'I learnt that I was quite adaptive and quick to learn new aspects of things I never had experience before by trying to do them myself'. This autonomy also directed their learning: 'for instance, we had to create a copyright notice for the stream ... so artists ... can gain royalties from the live stream. Just small experiences like that really contribute to like the feeling of like, hey, I'm actually learning about how this industry works. This subject is a good, like, deep dive into, like, you know, how you'd function job wise in this sort of industry'. Another student noted that 'the subject is unique in that you can set your own goals and achieve what you want to achieve ... [students are] not going to get anything out of it unless they choose to do what they want to do'.

Reflective Practice

Finally, both the learning context and the reflective assessment task stimulated a positive approach to self-awareness, metacognition, and a realization of the value of this to personal and professional growth. Weekly committee processes provided 'inherent ... opportunities for articulation' (Herrington et al. 2010: 32). One student noted that 'it was a great kind of reflective process throughout the entire semester as ... every week, we've kind of talked about where we're at, how we're progressing, what to do next'.

The more 'constructed context' of the assessment also appeared to be embraced as a means to 'enable tacit knowledge to be made explicit' (Herrington et al. 2010: 18). One student reflected that 'it's just making people think more about it like dedicating more focus to it naturally solidifies the lessons that it brings'; and in another reflection: 'I took quite a few missteps during my time in Music Business, however I can use these experiences as positive examples of steps to take going forward'. As a summary observation, one student commented that: 'overall, I was pleased with the achievements of the record label. We achieved our goals of running a successful launch party at an external venue with a live stream and had artists release music on Spotify and Apple Music. However, it took many hours of hard work and perseverance'.

Conclusion

The great advantage that some musicians have over many graduates in other sectors entering the workforce is the intrinsic motivation derived from a vocation in music. Perhaps one of the great successes of this subject design was the reignition of that sense of vocation after three years of navigating the tertiary institution context. The subject described in this chapter aimed to harness this vocation to prepare students to survive and thrive in their music careers.

Overall, the subject design successfully provided students with a rich, authentic experience in delivering all aspects of a music product to an audience, an experience that employers highly value. Students can easily articulate these specific experiences obtained in running a music label in terms relevant to industry professionals. While not without its challenges and compromises, the approach outlined in this chapter allows course designers to provide an avenue for students to gain professional experience that is not generally afforded to students unless they seek external internships or entry-level roles outside the ambit of the institution. We believe that such an approach should be a part of every creative industries programme to equip students with the necessary professional skills and capacities including flexibility, resilience, collaboration, entrepreneurism, and creativity to help them flourish in roles after graduation.

References

Arets, J., V. Heijnen, and C. Jennings. 2016. *70:20:10 towards 100% Performance*. Maastricht: Sutler Media.

ATO. 2023. 'Legal structures for not-for-profits'. Australian Tax Office. https://www.ato.gov.au/businesses-and-organisations/not-for-profit-organisations/getting-started/in-detail/registration/legal-structures-for-not-for-profits (accessed 8 May 2023).

Azevedo, R., J. Cromley, and D. Seibert. 2004. 'Does adaptive scaffolding facilitate students' ability to regulate their learning with hypermedia?' *Contemporary Educational Psychology* 29, no. 3: 344–70. https://doi.org/10.1016/j.cedpsych.2003.09.002

Bandura, A. 1997. *Self-efficacy: The Exercise of Control*. New York: Freeman.

Barak, M., and Y. Zadok. 2009. 'Robotics projects and learning concepts in science, technology and problem solving'. *International Journal of Technology and Design Education* 19, no. 3: 2–16. https://doi.org/10.1007/s10798-007-9043-3

Bartleet, B.-L., C. Ballico, D. Bennett, R. Bridgstock, P. Draper, V. Tomlinson, and S. Harrison. 2019. 'Building sustainable portfolio careers in music: Insights and implications for higher education'. *Music Education Research* 21, no. 3: 282–94. https://doi.org/10.1080/14613808.2019.1598348

Bender, M., M. Fulwider, and M. J. Stemkoski. 2008. 'Linking project-based interdisciplinary learning and recommended professional competencies with business management, digital media, distance learning, engineering technology, and English'. *Journal of College Teaching & Learning* 5, no. 5: 1–8. https://doi.org/10.19030/tlc.v5i5.1255

Billett, S. 2010a. 'Learning through practice'. In *Learning Through Practice: Models, Traditions, Orientations and Approaches*, edited by S. Billett, 1–20. Dordrecht: Springer Netherlands. https://doi.org/10.1007/978-90-481-3939-2_1

Billett, S. 2010b. 'The practices of learning through occupations'. In *Learning Through Practice: Models, Traditions, Orientations and Approaches*, edited by S. Billett, 59–81. Dordrecht: Springer Netherlands. https://doi.org/10.1007/978-90-481-3939-2_4

Blom, D., and J. Encarnacao. 2012. 'Student-chosen criteria for peer assessment of tertiary rock groups in rehearsal and performance: What's important?' *British Journal of Music Education* 29, no. 1: 25–43. https://doi.org/10.1017/S0265051711000362

Blumenfeld, P. C., E. Soloway, R. W. Marx, J. S. Krajcik, M. Guzdial, and A. Palincsar. 1991. 'Motivating project-based learning: Sustaining the doing, supporting the learning'. *Educational Psychologist* 26, no. 3–4: 369–98. https://doi.org/10.1080/00461520.1991.9653139

Boekaerts, M., P. R. Pintrich, and M. Zeidner. 2005. *Handbook of Self-Regulation*. Cambridge, MA: Academic Press.

Bransford, J. D., and B. S. Stein. 1993. *The IDEAL Problem Solver: A Guide to Improving Thinking, Learning, and Creativity*. New York: Freeman.

Dabbagh, N., and A. Kitsantas. 2012. 'Personal learning environments, social media, and self-regulated learning: A natural formula for connecting formal and informal learning'. *Internet and Higher Education* 15, no. 1: 3–8. https://doi.org/10.1016/j.iheduc.2011.06.002

Deci, E. L., R. J. Vallerand, L. G. Pelletier, and R. M. Ryan. 1991. 'Motivation and education: The self-determination perspective'. *Educational Psychologist* 26, no. 3–4: 325–46. https://doi.org/10.1080/00461520.1991.9653137

Fredricks, J. A., P. C. Blumenfeld, and A. H. Paris. 2004. 'School engagement: Potential of the concept, state of the evidence'. *Review of Educational Research* 74, no. 1: 59–109. https://doi.org/10.3102/00346543074001059

Frith, S. 2013. 'Live music exchange'. *Popular Music* 33, no. 2: 297–301. https://doi.org/10.1017/S0261143013000068

Herrington, J., T. C. Reeves, and R. Oliver. 2010. *A Guide to Authentic e-Learning*. New York: Routledge.

Hughes, D., S. Keith, G. Morrow, M. Evans, and D. Crowdy. 2013. 'What constitutes artist success in the Australian music industries?' *International Journal of Music Business Research* 2, no. 2: 61–80.

Johnson, S. J., D. A. Blackman, and F. Buick. 2018. 'The 70:20:10 framework and the transfer of learning'. *Human Resource Development Quarterly* 29, no. 4: 383–402. https://doi.org/10.1002/hrdq.21330

Kitsantas, A. 2013. 'Fostering college students' self-regulated learning with learning technologies'. *Hellenic Journal of Psychology* 10, no. 3: 235–52.

Lima, R., D. Carvalho, M. Assuncao Flores, and N. Van Hattum-Janssen. 2007. 'A case study on project led education in engineering: Students' and teachers' perceptions'. *European Journal of Engineering Education* 32, no. 3: 337–47. https://doi.org/10.1080/03043790701278599

McCormack, A. 2016. *By the Numbers: Women in the Music Industry*. Australian Broadcasting Corporation. https://www.abc.net.au/triplej/programs/hack/girls-to-the-front/7223798 (accessed 29 July 2021).

Mills, J. E., and D. F. Treagust. 2003. 'Engineering education – Is problem-based or project-based learning the answer'. *Australasian Journal of Engineering Education* 3, no. 2: 2–16.

Morgan, G. 1989. *Creative Organisation Theory: A Resourcebook*. Newbury Park, CA: SAGE.

Mou, T. Y. 2020. 'Students' evaluation of their experiences with project-based learning in a 3D design class'. *Asia-Pacific Education Research* 29, no. 2: 159–70. https://doi.org/10.1007/s40299-019-00462-4

Paris, S. G., and A. H. Paris. 2001. 'Classroom applications of research on self-regulated learning'. *Educational Psychologist* 36, no. 2: 89–101. https://doi.org/10.1207/S15326985EP3602_4

Rule, A. 2006. 'The components of authentic learning'. *Journal of Authentic Learning* 3: 1–10.

Savery, J. R. 2006. 'Overview of problem-based learning: Definitions and distinctions'. *The Interdisciplinary Journal of Problem-based Learning* 1, no. 1: 9–20. https://doi.org/10.7771/1541-5015.1002

Schön, D. A. 1991. *The Reflective Practitioner: How Professionals Think in Action* (New ed.). Aldershot: Ashgate.

Schunk, D. H., and B. J. Zimmerman. 2012. *Motivation and Self-regulated Learning: Theory, Research, and Applications*. New York: Routledge.

Sedita, S. R. 2008. 'Interpersonal and Inter-organizational networks in the performing arts: The case of project-based organizations in the live music industry'. *Industry and Innovation* 15, no. 5: 493–511. https://doi.org/10.1080/13662710802373833

Stefanou, C., J. D. Stolk, M. Prince, J. C. Chen, and S. M. Lord. 2013. 'Self-regulation and autonomy in problem- and project-based learning environments'. *Active Learning in Higher Education* 14, no. 2: 109–122. https://doi.org/10.1177/1469787413481132

Stolk, J. D., and R. Martello. 2018. 'Reimagining and empowering the design of projects: A project-based learning goals framework'. 2018 IEEE Frontiers in Education Conference, San Jose, CA, USA.

Störmer, E., C. Patscha, J. Prendergast, C. Daheim, M. Rhisiart, P. Glover, and H. Beck. 2014. *The Future of Work: Jobs and Skills in 2030*. UK Commission for Employment and Skills. https://www.gov.uk/government/publications/jobs-and-skills-in-2030

Weimer, M. 2002. *Learner-centered Teaching: Five Key Changes to Practice*. New Jersey: John Wiley & Sons.

Wikström, P. 2013. 'Commercial successes in the music industry'. In *Music in American Life: An Encyclopedia of the Songs, Styles, Stars, and Stories That Shaped Our Culture*, ed. J. Edmondson, Vol. 1: 256–60. ABC-CLIO.

Williamson, J., and M. Cloonan. 2007. 'Rethinking the music industry'. *Popular Music* 26, no. 2: 305–22. https://doi.org/10.1017/S0261143007001262

Wilson, N., and D. Stokes. 2002. 'Cultural entrepreneurs and creating exchange'. *Journal of Research in Marketing and Entrepreneurship* 4, no. 1: 37–52. https://doi.org/10.1108/14715200280001465

Zimmerman, B. J. 1998. 'Developing self-fulfilling cycles of academic regulation: An analysis of exemplary instructional models'. In *Self-regulated Learning: From Teaching to Self-reflective Practice*, ed. D. H. Shunk and B. J. Zimmerman, 1–19. New York: Guilford.

Zimmerman, B. J. 2000. 'Attainment of self-regulation: A social cognitive perspective'. In *Handbook of Self-regulation*, ed. M. Boekaerts, P. R. Pintrich, and M. Zeidner, 13–39. San Diego: Academic Press.

Zimmerman, B. J. 2002. 'Becoming a self-regulated learner: An overview'. *Theory Into Practice* 41, no. 2: 64–70. https://doi.org/10.1207/s15430421tip4102_2

Zimmerman, B. J., and A. Kitsantas. 1999. 'Acquiring writing revision skill: Shifting from process to outcome self-regulatory goals'. *Journal of Educational Psychology* 91, no. 2: 241–50. https://doi.org/10.1037//0022-0663.91.2.241

Author biographies

Ian Stevenson is a specialist in the field of audible design with over thirty years of experience as an audio engineer, producer, artist, and educator. He is currently senior lecturer in music and sound design at the University of Technology Sydney. His current research is in the areas of sound design, sound studies, soundscape analysis, and music and sound pedagogy.

Jeff Crabtree is a speaker, performer, songwriter, and music producer with 100 composition and production credits. He co-authored *Living with a Creative Mind*, a handbook for nurturing creativity and well-being. He is the founder and director of Zebra Collective, a microlearning platform. Jeff is currently a sessional academic at the University of Technology Sydney and JMC Academy. His doctoral research revealed the extent of workplace and sexual harassment in the music industry.

Monica Rouvellas is a solicitor, composer, music producer, and educator. Monica is currently a sessional academic at the University of Technology Sydney, Macquarie University, and the University of Sydney, teaching in the fields of music, business, and law. She is also the founder of Muzikboxx, a music education app for both music teachers and students. Her current research is in the areas of gamified learning, self-regulated learning, immersive sound, and technology and the law.

3 Embedding Effectual Entrepreneurship across the Music Business Curriculum

Jeremy Peters

We educate students in creative industries programmes in the hopes they will succeed after graduation. Indeed, as Douglas Dempster wrote:

> At the very least, we assume [these educational programmes] are effective at advancing the career ambitions of students who, at high tuition cost and often great debt, aspire to make their way – and a living – in our cultural and creative industries (CCIs). (Dempster 2017: 1590)

Graduates perceive that their post-secondary education is a time to hone skills and prepare themselves for a range of creative careers (Brown 2007). For students who amass significant debt undertaking a creative industries education, there is hope for a return on that investment of both time and money. Students choose to enroll in programmes in music business and the wider creative industries for many reasons. Some are hoping to start careers as performers and want to know how the industry operates. Others wish to work at record labels or in music publishing. Another group enrolls to get a sense of how the creative industries operate, to build skills for a portfolio career comprised of 'different bits and pieces of work for different clients' (Handy 1994: 175). Employment preparedness is especially relevant to students who graduate from traditional conservatoire-style artistic training programmes, which have long lacked focus on aspects other than technical and artistic excellence. Even so, the relevance of preparedness applies to relatively newer programmes designed to train a new generation of workers to build careers in the music business and creative industries.

Although some universities have added practical degree programmes, job readiness is still an ongoing problem. To this end, the 'relative inattention to entrepreneurial and careers skills within post-secondary arts curricula is problematic because it contributes to unequal career outcomes among graduates'

(Frenette 2017: 1458), most especially in comparison to the career training available in traditional business and non-arts fields. To bridge this gap, colleges and universities have scrambled to build support structures such as career offices and entrepreneurship courses. However, these efforts are commonly disjointed. Critics claim that this focus on career training contributes to the neo-liberalization of the university (Kenning 2019; Moore 2016). In reality, students who are hoping for careers in the music business and creative industries (whether as an artist or supporting entity) benefit from a redoubled focus on entrepreneurial and careers skills across the breadth of their training programmes that connect what is currently taught with what recent graduates and industry professionals have reported is necessary to operate in the workforce.

Preparation Gaps

By their own evaluation, arts graduates are unprepared for the workforce. As part of a longitudinal survey of over 200,000 arts alumni, recent graduates reported significant gaps in areas crucial to their success in the creative industries after graduation. In an analysis of responses, 81% stated a need for financial and business management skills in their careers. Yet, only 23% (a gap of 58%) acquired this training during their college and university programme (Skaggs et al. 2017a). These respondents are graduates of United States-based post-secondary universities, colleges, schools, and conservatories with degrees in art, music, design, dance, theatre, and creative writing. They were interviewed as part of the Strategic National Arts Alumni Project (SNAAP).

In the same survey, students stated that they strongly needed entrepreneurial, networking and relationship building, and project management skills after graduation. These needs aligned with similar gaps in attainment, evidenced by 43%, 32%, and 26% deficits, respectively (Skaggs et al. 2017a). While this is troubling, the deficits reported by all artists were worse for musicians. Music alums specifically reported a lack of emphasis on career-oriented skills versus other arts fields (generating new ideas or brainstorming, risk-taking, looking at multiple approaches, and inventing new and unconventional solutions). Musicians face an average 12% deficit in acquiring these skills, compared to the average of all the artistic fields surveyed (Skaggs et al. 2017a).

This information proves beneficial, as specific longitudinal survey data for music business and professional cultural industries graduates in the United States do not exist. Existing research is mainly at the programme-level, is housed in one domain-specific journal, and focuses primarily on internships (e.g., Bruenger 2015; Kopplin 2016; McCain 2002; Sobel 2007). Perhaps the closest comparison to SNAAP is a longitudinal look at music business graduates that investigates the importance of university-sponsored internship programmes. These findings suggest cooperative experiences deliver an in-depth understanding of what work in the music industry is like in the real world (Rolston and Herrera 2000). At a minimum, the data align with the findings from SNAAP, especially regarding long-held beliefs that internship and cooperative experiences can jump-start a student's employment networking.

Scholars emphasize the need for exploratory career experiences during a student's education (Bennett and Bridgstock 2015; Pitts 2013; Rolston and Herrera 2000). Landing an internship leads to career stability. As evidence, internships positively affected SNAAP participants' ability to hold a creative industries job over the long term (Frenette and Dowd 2020) as they have learned the ropes of creative industries careers before graduation. Problematically, internships are simultaneously challenging for students to find and demanding on hosts to support. Worse yet, arts students find it difficult to support themselves during these experiences if they are lucky enough to obtain one (Frenette 2015).

Other research on American music business graduates found employers reporting students need 'music business courses with practical projects built in' (Surmani and Anderson 2018: 9), to exercise skills before they get to an internship, let alone begin their employment in the music industry. The same study noted that students lack the 'basic business skills such as accounting, marketing, and finance' that 'make for competitive employees' (Surmani and Anderson 2018: 4). Once again, these findings match those found in Skaggs et al.'s (2017a) and Frenette's (2017) analysis of the survey data. These projects must be part of a 'practical curriculum' that is relevant to a modern time frame alongside an 'adaptive curriculum' which allows students to analyze problems and adapt to unknown situations (Bruenger 2015: 99–103). These findings are not limited to the United States. European students and non-US artists reported similar skills gaps to those evidenced in the SNAAP surveys in the United States (Bennett 2016; Canham 2016; Dyce and Smernicki 2018; Peters 2018), and found that life after graduation is similarly tough (Campbell 2020). Curricular change is juxtaposed against traditional beliefs that 'an education in the field of music business is not required' and that 'all that is needed is "gut instinct"' (O'Hara 2014: 28).

Critics agree that that a shift in focus is needed. By and large, arts programmes have not embraced the idea of developing employability skills (Bennett 2016; Minors et al. 2017). Curricular approaches to post-secondary training in both music education and the music industry must emphasize skills and topics outside of the traditional academy where they have long been 'isolated' and 'resistant to change' (Campbell et al. 2014: 4). Campbell et al.

state that 'while surface change has occurred to some extent through additive means', there have not been 'fundamental changes in priorities, values, perspectives, and implementation' (2014: 4).

Steering Students toward Success

Educators can help students develop their identity (Pike 2015). Students may, with guidance and opportunity, envision themselves as performers, marketers, venue operators, studio owners, or music publishers. Educators can use coursework in a particular topic area to help them build on those identities across classes. Furthermore, there is a strong need for practicing skills, or as Linda Essig (2012: 71) notes, 'habits of mind', to embed them in the daily actions of music business and creative industries graduates. In these instances, students can draw on habitual frameworks when faced with difficult decisions. But, investing in experiences where students can build upon the habits of mind (where SNAAP research has shown gaps) is crucial. The building process suggested here focuses on the skills these students need to attain a satisfying career through relevant and applicable assignments across the music business and creative industries curriculum and the traditional music curriculum.

Across all forms of the creative industries, successful graduates cultivate an amalgam of 'hybrid roles and skillsets to secure legitimacy and resources', while simultaneously (and one might argue advantageously) 'inventing wholly new titles, products, and markets' (Lingo and Tepper 2013: 348). Music business and arts graduates must function in a world that prizes the 'mobility' of work and requires practice to understand the role of 'digitisation, gender parity, and health and wellbeing', which are ultimately necessary to do the job of 'preparing graduates for a portfolio career reality' (Bartleet et al. 2019: 282). Successfully working in the music industry (as well as other creative industries) in these hybridized roles 'increasingly involve[s] working across multiple sectors (commercial, nonprofit, community), [and] disciplines' (Frenette 2017: 1457).

Unfortunately, examples of how creative industries intersect, profit, schedule, format, and cross traditional industrial boundaries are not well represented in creative arts coursework. To this end, much coursework seems to focus on individual topic areas such as marketing, copyright, and touring, with little to no interaction between course content. Programs often silo these topics, given the lack of solid agreement across the field and in research about what areas music business programmes should focus on and how they should be taught.

Jobs in the music industry will require graduates to work across these topic areas and synthesize information and skills from multiple fields. For example, working at a blockchain-focused music startup such as Imogen Heap's MyCelia requires an understanding of technology, intellectual property, performance, music licensing, marketing, and entrepreneurship. As the internet continues to mediate performance, work, and music consumption, students must learn to embrace a set of skills that allow them to adapt to an undefined future.

Repetition

Programmes need to allow students to repetitively use and reuse the skills they learn in the classroom while they are learning them (Raffo et al. 2000). Yet, arts and creative industries programmes are not necessarily aware of how to embed this self-aware form of training (Myers 2016) where students practice being in the industry rather than learning about it as an external observer. To be successful as graduates and for their training to work, students must look at themselves as active self-agents in building their success (Toscher 2020). As these project management, entrepreneurial, and network-building skills are repetitively used in projects, case studies, assignments, and courses that mimic real-world organizations, students can essentially strengthen the industry-oriented muscles they will need to operate after graduation.

Consistent praxis is key to this transformation. This requires embedded skill practice across multiple courses and touchpoints across a multi-year educational programme. Adding long-frame experience across numerous classes allows students to practice skill sets over time. Longitudinal practice works best in varied situations that approximate the real-world (Bureau and Koufaris 2012), rather than in siloed and disjointed curricular or co-curricular snippets. This in-weaving shines when multiple courses across previously disconnected topic areas 'include contextually rich experiences and conceptualizations, critical reflections, and pragmatic active experimentations' (Baggen, Lans, and Gulikers 2021: 355).

As students grasp the habits of mind and rehearse skills that help them operate in the real world, they build a well of resources from which to draw in the long run. This builds toward the 'broad-based education' called for by arts education researchers, which must connect 'to the workplace' and which 'should focus on more than just technical proficiency (Skaggs et al. 2017b: 7). By embedding these opportunities across multiple experiences, educators in creative industries programmes can deliver the foundational and theoretical content they hope to cover in a course and build resilient graduates. In a music business programme, this could be technical content such as audio engineering, theoretical concepts such as copyright, or practical skills such as marketing and promotion. When students engage in projects in these courses that apply outside the classroom, they practice skills in preparation for the workforce.

Toward Implementing Effectual Creative Works in the Classroom

Many of the same skill sets which graduates are identified as needing align with those traditionally taught in entrepreneurship education. However, most entrepreneurship experiences in creative industries programmes are constrained to a single course (Beckman 2011). Teaching resources exist, and the broader field of entrepreneurship's flagship pedagogy journal has published a consistent line of research and resources on arts-based entrepreneurship pedagogy (Cavalcanti Junqueira and Discua Cruz 2019; Hanson 2021; Hart and Beckman 2021; Hart 2016; Peters 2021; Peters 2022). However, from the curriculum designer's standpoint, what is missing is a framework to place these resources across multiple courses that cover a wide range of topics.

Effectual entrepreneurship practice can be that framework. Effectuation theory is based on five core skills that successful entrepreneurs have practiced, which help them effectuate (or design to bring about) the practice of entrepreneurship (Sarasvathy 2001). These five core skills align quite closely with the skills gaps found by Skaggs et al. (2017b). The connections between these skills gaps and effectuation's core skills are shown in Table 3.1.

These benefits are amplified in consideration of how this focus simultaneously closes gaps in required skills noted by SNAAP, as many align with effectuation practices, as Table 3.1 shows.

Table 3.1 Connecting the principles of effectual entrepreneurship with skills gaps reported by SNAAP participants

Effectuation practices	Descriptions (Sarasvathy 2001; 2008a; 2008b; 2011)	SNAAP skills and abilities (Skaggs et al. 2017b)	Deficit	Severity rank (of 16)
Affordable Loss (Focus on the Downside Risk)	• '… limit risk by understanding what they can afford to lose at each step…' (2011: 2) • '… leveraging limited means in creative ways to generate new ends as well as new means' (2008: 81) • '… choose goals and actions where there is upside even if the downside ends up happening' (2011: 2)	Financial and business management skills	−58%	1st

Start With Your Means	• '... they know who they are, what they know, and whom they know – their own traits, tastes, and abilities...' (2001: 250) • 'begin to imagine and implement possible effects that can be created with them' (2008b: 3) • '... start very small with the means that are closest at hand, and move almost directly into action without elaborate planning' (2008b: 3)	Entrepreneurial skills	–43%	2nd
Lemonade (Leverage Contingencies)	• '... invite the surprise factor... interpret "bad" news and surprises as potential clues to create new markets' (2011: 2) • 'the ability to turn the unexpected into the profitable... how the entrepreneurs *leveraged* the contingencies' (2008b: 6)	Creative thinking and problem solving	–5%	14th
Crazy Quilt (Strategic Partnerships)	• 'Focused on forming alliances and partnerships...' (2001: 261) • obtaining pre-commitments from... key partners early on...' (2011: 2) • '... helps reduce uncertainty' (2008b: 6)	Networking and relationship building	–32%	3rd
		Interpersonal relationships and working collaboratively	–18%	9th
Pilot-in-Plane (Control vs. Predict)	• 'To the extent we can control the future, we do not need to predict it...' (2008a: 91) • '... future is neither found nor predicted, but rather made' (2011: 2) • '... working with human agency as the prime driver of opportunity' (2008a: 16)	Project management skills	–26%	6th
		Critical thinking and analysis of arguments and information	–6%	14th

If we paraphrase Sarasvathy's (2011) descriptions and apply them to creative industries students, programmes built to practice effectual entrepreneurship skills over time will allow these students to do the following:

1. Understand that artists do not need to predict the future but can learn to design and control it.
2. Build fluency in operating in situations where the resources they access seem inconsistent with those they believe are necessary.

3. Imagine the impact their skills, networks, and talents can have on a desired business or artistic outcome.
4. Operate in partnership with others to build stability and value for the recipients of their work, most especially in transforming problems into possibility, progress, and profits.

Effectuation Practice, in Practice

These activities need to be contextualized by enterprising programmes and teachers. For starters, instructors can design courses that build toward the final product of a venture the music business student can pitch externally to community stakeholders (accelerators), pitch competitions both on and off-campus, and arts organizations. The author implemented an example of this type of course during a re-design of the Bachelor of Music in Music Business programme at Wayne State University. The course asks students to tie together in-class exercises and assignments to create a brand-new music industry venture. Student-run ventures from versions of this course taught by the author led to the founding of firms focused on public relations, royalty portfolio investments, musicians' health, and music playing systems.

To get from an idea (or lack thereof) to venture, students are tasked with creatively re-imagining resource dependency. Effectuation scholars have termed this 'starting with your means' (Sarasvathy 2011). Practically, instructors can ask students to participate in Bradley George's *Marshmallow Tower* exercise (Neck, Greene, and Brush 2014: 125), or choose three items on their person and develop a product to pitch – a modification of many popular improvisation exercises. As they practice effectual skills, they are simultaneously asked to put these skills to use to create their venture. They practice being comfortable with ideation and their ability to control the future (Sarasvathy's 'pilot in the plane') while building value with customers using affinity diagrams and customer-oriented mindfulness practices that arrange seemingly disparate ideas into solutions for potential customers. This exercise, developed by the author, is included in the fifth volume of the *Annals of Entrepreneurship Education and Pedagogy* (Peters 2022). The activities described here are in addition to the use of texts such as *Create, Produce, Consume* (Bruenger 2019), and *Creating the Revolutionary Artist* (Rabideau 2018) to develop effectual logics in these young entrepreneurs.

This course is not the only entrepreneurship-oriented experience the student receives in the programme. Activities that emphasize the ability of music business and creative arts students to practice effectual thinking have been included in classes outside of a particular entrepreneurship course. For example, in an introductory survey class, where students look at the music industry in economic terms and consider career pathways, they are introduced to the 'Business Model Canvas' (Pigneur and Osterwalder 2010). Students engage with their career planning through the lenses of resources, skill, and partnerships using the 'Personal Business Model Canvas' (Clark, Osterwalder, and Pigneur 2012). This canvas, in effect, forces students to look at downside risk (otherwise termed 'affordable loss') as a product of the available resources, skills, and networks the student either has on hand ('starting with your means') or must create in partnership with others (creating value via 'strategic partnerships'). As another example, in a course focused on intellectual property and music industry stakeholder relationships, students practice empathy and the importance of interpersonal relationships and collaboration through the use of a negotiation exercise based on Lakshmi Balachandra's *Negotiation for Resource Allocation* (Neck, Greene and Brush 2014: 146; Jacker 1982).

Simulation and investing classroom time in long-form case study discussions every other week allows students to grapple with real-world situations appropriate to the core content in each class while building the core skills which SNAAP researchers (e.g., Skaggs et al. 2017a) and Sarasvathy (2011) found important. Among these case studies are those like *John Branca: Negotiating the Beatles' Northern Songs Catalog*, which focuses on stakeholder relationships between lawyers and music rights owners (Sebenius and Green 2020). Other cases focus on downside risk in the context of tour planning and turning negative contingencies into positive ones, based on effectual logic's 'lemonade principle'. Herein, the *Lady Gaga* case asks students in a module on touring to evaluate the financial implications of a difficult decision (Elberse and Christensen 2011). Elsewhere, the critical thinking necessary for strategic decision-making is highlighted by cases such as *Downtown Music Publishing and Songtrust* (Peters 2021). Each case is meant to reinforce a particular topic in a course and serve the overarching goal of embedding non-causal, effectual entrepreneurship thinking in as many courses as possible. Elsewhere, gameplay is used to simulate real-world transactions that require a deft understanding of how networks are formed based on the means that partners have to offer each other (whether based on skills, finances, or other intangibles). One example of this is the *Fame and Fortune* game which asks students in an introductory course to play a card game and take on the role of a label, venue, or musician (Herzig 2019).

To cement these skills, Wayne State students participate in internships they are tasked with sourcing, including partnerships, and fellowships with real-world companies and organizations such as Live Nation and Detroit Symphony

Orchestra. They also operate a student-run record label that functions as a class. A course focused on strategy asks students to look at the forces of competition (Porter 1979) while evaluating political, economic, sociological, technological, environmental, and legal concerns (Aguilar 1967) as they design solutions as proto-consultants for a real-world music business. Most recently, students in these courses have evaluated the impact of a global pandemic on the operations and competitiveness of local music firms. These student-run, instructor-mentored experiences allow students to generate the higher-order connections necessary to use the skills they have learned once they have graduated, having practiced them over and over against new problems.

The programme's student-run record label, Old Main Records, allows students to work in partnership with artists, faculty, and the department's recording facilities to release records onto platforms using the same tools (e.g., a digital distributor, mechanical rights payments, accounting software, and project management) that record labels would use. Successful examples of these methods and example case studies across the arts are highlighted in *Entrepreneurship in Action: The Power of Student-Run Ventures* (Liguori and Tonelli 2021). In both instances, the instructor serves as a mentor. At the same time, students actively practice the core effectual principles (focusing on downside risk, starting with available means, leveraging contingencies, creating value via strategic partnerships, and controlling the future rather than predicting) in real-time (Sarasvathy 2011). Additionally, they practice the synthesis necessary to reuse the technical skills and individual strengths they have gained in several courses across diverse situations (Bloom et al. 1956).

Expanding Past the Core Practical Curriculum

Coursework outside of the music business and creative industries core provides an opportunity to embed skills practice. Many creative industries students take coursework in the humanities, which serve as a theoretical foundation for their practical coursework. For music business students in a programme accredited by the National Association of Schools of Music, these courses include musicology or music theory but can feel distant for professionally oriented students. However, these courses can incorporate the practice of effectual entrepreneurship skills just as easily as those more explicitly focused on the music industry. In Gary Beckman's *Disciplining the Arts*, musicologist Mark Clague argues that these studies, which can feel 'detached from the real world' for many students, can be reattached through the integration of entrepreneurship (Clague 2011: 167). In his courses, Clague asks students to perform the practice of investigating music history by interviewing practicing musicians and participating in events tied to the course content. For example, he states: 'In my American music courses, a group might produce a Billie Holiday tribute concert or put on a showcase of classical composers from the United States, which highlights the difficult definition of "American"' (Clague 2011: 173). These students learn music history while practicing the skills needed to operate in the real world once they graduate: starting a venture, marketing, managing, and running it. Their ability to do so during their education and not afterward affords students the ability to practice these skills many times in the softer sandbox of college. Comparatively, their struggles and failures after graduation meet the concrete-like hard reality, which is less easy to bounce back from if they have not had ample chance to practice those skills.

Activities similar to those suggested by Clague and others in Beckman's *Disciplining the Arts* (Beckman 2011) can place the study of other core skills such as music theory and music performance in contexts that allow students to engage with them in an entrepreneurial fashion. For example, themed academic years can merge teams of students in disparate courses to grapple with large-scale problems from a wide array of topic areas. The home unit of a programme might choose to look at how musicians and music business practitioners operate as agents for social change and incorporate this theme across classes in music theory, music history, composition, writing, and music business. Of course, practitioners hoping to embed such change must work within the administrative structure of their institutions to make such necessary change take place. These modifications are made not to revise the core-content expertise of those instructors teaching courses outside of the music business core but to incorporate the real-world skill-building students themselves have deemed they need as many times as is possible during their education. Rather than these being included by happenstance, I argue here for a consistent approach.

Ultimately, this sort of curricular transition is by no means easy, especially for programmes that emphasize more of the conservatoire aesthetic rather than a liberal arts or pre-professional training ethos. Nevertheless, given evidence of curricular gaps and further proof that students would benefit from the inclusion of purpose-driven, effectually oriented experiences across the entirety of their time in a programme, it is now incumbent upon postsecondary educators and their institutions to invest time and resources to support such change. Ultimately, if our programmes hope to remain relevant to incoming students, we must show proof of evolution in method and implementation.

References

Aguilar, Francis J. 1967. *Scanning the Business Environment*. New York: Macmillan.

Baggen, Yvette, Thomas Lans, and Judith Gulikers. 2021. 'Making entrepreneurship education available to all: Design principles for educational programmes stimulating an entrepreneurial mindset'. *Entrepreneurship Education and Pedagogy* 5, no. 3: 347–74. https://doi.org/10/gmx3c2

Bartleet, Brydie-Leigh, Christina Ballico, Dawn Bennett, Ruth Bridgstock, Paul Draper, Vanessa Tomlinson, and Scott Harrison. 2019. 'Building sustainable portfolio careers in music: Insights and implications for higher education'. *Music Education Research* 21, no. 3: 282–94. https://doi.org/10/ghth9x

Beckman, Gary D., ed. 2011. *Disciplining the Arts: Teaching Entrepreneurship in Context*. Lanham, MD: Rowman & Littlefield Education.

Bennett, Dawn. 2016. 'Developing employability in higher education music'. *Arts and Humanities in Higher Education* 15, no. 3–4: 386–95. https://doi.org/10/gfx79k

Bennett, Dawn, and Ruth Bridgstock. 2015. 'The urgent need for career preview: Student expectations and graduate realities in music and dance'. *International Journal of Music Education* 33, no. 3: 263–77. https://doi.org/10.1177/0255761414558653

Bloom, Benjamin S., M. D. Englehart, Edward J. Furst, Walker H. Hill, and David R. Krathwohl. 1956. *Taxonomy of Educational Objectives – Book 1: Cognitive Domain*. New York: David McKay.

Brown, Ralph. 2007. 'Enhancing student employability? Current practice and student experiences in HE performing arts'. *Arts and Humanities in Higher Education* 6, no. 1: 28–49. https://doi.org/10/dwcqzz

Bruenger, David. 2015. 'Complexity, adaptive expertise, and conceptual models in the music business curriculum'. *Journal of the Music and Entertainment Industry Educators Association* 15, no. 1: 99–119. https://doi.org/10/gmx28m

Bruenger, David. 2019. *Create, Produce, Consume: New Models for Understanding Music Business*. Berkeley: University of California Press.

Bureau, Sylvain Pierre, and Marios Koufaris. 2012. 'How to teach effectuation: The situationist dérive as a solution?' *Academy of Management Proceedings* 2012 (1): 15819. https://doi.org/10/gmx3cz

Campbell, Miranda. 2020. '"Shit is hard, yo": Young people making a living in the creative industries'. *International Journal of Cultural Policy* 26, no. 4: 524–43. https://doi.org/10/ghgvbw

Campbell, Patricia, David Myers, Ed Sarath, Juan Chattah, Lee Higgins, Victoria Lindsay Levine, David Rudge, and Timothy Rice. 2014. 'Transforming music study from its foundations: A manifesto for progressive change in the undergraduate preparation of music majors: Report of the Task Force on the undergraduate music major'. Missoula, MT: College Music Society.

Canham, Nicole L. 2016. 'Making mavericks: Preparing musicians for independent artistic culture'. *Arts and Humanities in Higher Education* 15, no. 3–4: 407–13. https://doi.org/10/gmx26q

Cavalcanti Junqueira, Miriam Isabella, and Allan Discua Cruz. 2019. 'Crowdfunding and museums: A field trip exemplar in the United Kingdom'. *Entrepreneurship Education and Pedagogy* 2, no. 2: 151–70. https://doi.org/10.1177/2515127418801728

Clague, Mark. 2011. 'Real-world musicology: Integrating entrepreneurship throughout the music curriculum and beyond'. In *Disciplining the Arts: Teaching Entrepreneurship in Context*, edited by Gary D. Beckman, 167–76. Lanham, MD: Rowman & Littlefield Education.

Clark, Timothy, Alexander Osterwalder, and Yves Pigneur. 2012. *Business Model You: A One-Page Method for Reinventing Your Career*. Hoboken, NJ: John Wiley & Sons.

Dempster, Douglas J. 2017. 'Concluding remarks: Policy implications for postsecondary arts education'. *American Behavioral Scientist* 61, no. 12: 1589–94. https://doi.org/10.1177/0002764217742221

Dyce, Andrew, and Richard Smernicki. 2018. 'Bridging the gap: Music business education and the music industries'. In *Proceedings of the 2018 International Summit of the Music & Entertainment Industry Educators Association*, 56–60. Nashville, TN: Music and Entertainment Industry Educators Association. https://doi.org/10/gmx3c7

Elberse, Anita, and Michael Christensen. 2011. 'Lady Gaga (A)'. Cambridge, MA: Harvard Business Publishing. https://hbsp.harvard.edu/product/512016-PDF-ENG

Essig, Linda. 2012. 'Frameworks for educating the artist of the future: Teaching habits of mind for arts entrepreneurship'. *Artivate: A Journal of Entrepreneurship in the Arts* 1, no. 2: 65–77. https://doi.org/10.1353/artv.2012.0006

Frenette, Alexandre. 2015. 'The internship divide: The promise and challenges of internships in the arts'. Special Report. Strategic National Arts Alumni Project. Bloomington, IN: Indiana University Center for Postsecondary Research.

Frenette, Alexandre. 2017. 'Arts graduates in a changing economy'. *American Behavioral Scientist* 61, no. 12: 1455–62. https://doi.org/10/gf542w

Frenette, Alexandre, and Timothy J. Dowd. 2020. 'Careers in the arts: Who stays and who leaves?' Special Report. Strategic National Arts Alumni Project. Bloomington, IN: Indiana University Center for Postsecondary Research. https://eric.ed.gov/?id=ED605409

Handy, Charles B. 1994. *The Empty Raincoat: New Thinking for a New World*. London: Hutchinson.

Hanson, Josef. 2021. 'Best practices for mentoring in arts entrepreneurship education: Findings from a Delphi study'. *Entrepreneurship Education and Pedagogy* 4, no. 2: 119–42. https://doi.org/10.1177/2515127420964120

Hart, James D. 2016. 'Games for the entrepreneurship classroom'. In *Annals of Entrepreneurship Education and Pedagogy – 2016*, edited by Michael H. Morris and Eric W. Liguori, 381–84. Cheltenham, UK: Edward Elgar. https://www.elgaronline.com/view/edcoll/9781784719159/9781784719159.00032.xml

Hart, James D., and Gary D. Beckman. 2021. 'Aesthetics, medium, and method: An introduction to the differences and similarities between arts and non-arts entrepreneurs'. *Entrepreneurship Education and Pedagogy* 6, no. 1. https://doi.org/10.1177/25151274211045696

Herzig, Monika. 2019. 'Fame and fortune: Developing a simulation game for the music industry classroom'. *Journal of the Scholarship of Teaching and Learning* 19, no. 5: 105–22. https://doi.org/10.14434/josotl.v19i5.24276

Jacker, Norbert. 1982. 'Sally Soprano'. PON425-PDF-ENG. Cambridge, MA: Harvard Business Publishing. https://hbsp.harvard.edu/product/PON425-PDF-ENG?Ntt=sally%20soprano

Kenning, Dean. 2019. 'Art world strategies: Neoliberalism and the politics of professional practice in fine art education'. *Journal of Visual Art Practice* 18, no. 2: 115–31. https://doi.org/10/gmx29k

Kopplin, David. 2016. 'Best practices in music industry education'. *Journal of the Music and Entertainment Industry Educators Association* 16, no. 1. https://doi.org/10/gmx28n

Liguori, Eric W., and Mark Tonelli, eds. 2021. *Entrepreneurship in Action: The Power of Student-Run Ventures*. Cheltenham, UK; Northampton, MA: Edward Elgar Publishing.

Lingo, Elizabeth L., and Steven J. Tepper. 2013. 'Looking back, looking forward: Arts-based careers and creative work'. *Work and Occupations* 40, no. 4: 337–63. https://doi.org/10/gf29hp

McCain, Claudia. 2002. 'A model music business curriculum'. *MEIEA Journal* 2, no. 1: 14–28.

Minors, Helen Julia, Pamela Burnard, Charles Wiffen, Zaina Shihabi, and J. Simon van der Walt. 2017. 'Mapping trends and framing issues in higher music education: Changing minds/changing practices'. *London Review of Education* 15, no. 3: 457–73. https://doi.org/10/gmx274

Moore, Andrea. 2016. 'Neoliberalism and the musical entrepreneur'. *Journal of the Society for American Music* 10, no. 1: 33–53. https://doi.org/10/ggmpw5

Myers, David E. 2016. 'Creativity, diversity, and integration: Radical change in the Bachelor of Music curriculum'. *Arts and Humanities in Higher Education* 15, no. 3–4: 293–307. https://doi.org/10/gmm364

Neck, Heidi M., Patricia G. Greene, and Candida G. Brush. 2014. *Teaching Entrepreneurship: A Practice-Based Approach*. Cheltenham, UK: Edward Elgar.

O'Hara, Ben. 2014. 'Creativity, innovation and entrepreneurship in music business education'. *International Journal of Music Business Research* 3, no. 2: 28–60.

Peters, Jeremy J. 2018. 'Strategizing core competencies for arts-entrepreneurs'. Conference presentation at the "Creativity, Knowledge, Cities" conference, University of the West of England, Bristol, 4 July. https://ckc-conf.co.uk/2018/sessions/skills-for-surviving-the-creative-sector/

Peters, Jeremy J. 2021. 'Downtown Music Publishing and Songtrust'. *Entrepreneurship Education and Pedagogy* 6, no. 1. https://doi.org/10.1177/25151274211040418

Peters, Jeremy J. 2022. 'Quickly generating startup ideas with an affinity diagramming and mindfulness exercise'. In *Annals of Entrepreneurship Education and Pedagogy*, Vol. 5, edited by Charles H. Matthews and Susana C. Santos, 303–307. Cheltenham, UK: Edward Elgar.

Pigneur, Yves, and Alexander Osterwalder. 2010. *Business Model Generation: A Handbook for Visionaries, Game Changers, and Challengers*. Hoboken, NJ: Wiley.

Pike, Pamela D. 2015. 'The ninth semester: Preparing undergraduates to function as professional musicians in the 21st century'. *College Music Symposium* 55. http://www.jstor.org/stable/26574399

Pitts, Stephanie E. 2013. 'Would you credit it? Navigating the transitions between curricular and extra-curricular learning in university music departments'. *Arts and Humanities in Higher Education* 12, no. 2–3: 194–203. https://doi.org/10/gmx27r

Porter, Michael E. 1979. 'How competitive forces shape strategy'. *Harvard Business Review* 21, no. 38: 137–45.

Rabideau, Mark. 2018. *Creating the Revolutionary Artist: Entrepreneurship for the 21st-Century Musician*. Lanham, MD: Rowman & Littlefield.

Raffo, Carlo, Justin O'Connor, Andy Lovatt, and Mark Banks. 2000. 'Attitudes to formal business training and learning amongst entrepreneurs in the cultural industries: situated business learning through "doing with others"'. *Journal of Education and Work* 13, no. 2: 215–30. https://doi.org/10/cwkk3h

Rolston, Clyde Philip, and David Herrera. 2000. 'The critical role of university-sponsored internships for entry into the professional music business: A report of a national survey'. *Journal of Arts Management, Law, and Society* 30, no. 2: 102–12. https://doi.org/10/bthsd9

Sarasvathy, Saras D. 2001. 'Causation and effectuation: Toward a theoretical shift from economic inevitability to entrepreneurial contingency'. *Academy of Management Review* 26, no. 2: 243–63. https://doi.org/10/cm47fn

Sarasvathy, Saras D. 2008a. *Effectuation: Elements of Entrepreneurial Expertise*. Cheltenham, UK: Edward Elgar.

Sarasvathy, Saras D. 2008b. 'What makes entrepreneurs entrepreneurial?' SSRN Scholarly Paper ID 909038. Rochester, NY: Social Science Research Network. https://papers.ssrn.com/abstract=909038

Sarasvathy, Saras D. 2011. 'What is effectuation? Effectuation 101'. Society for Effectual Action. Available at: https://effectuation.org/effectuation-101

Sebenius, James K., and Alex Green. 2020. 'John Branca: Negotiating the Beatles' Northern Songs Catalog (A)'. 921009-PDF-ENG. Cambridge, MA: Harvard Business Publishing. https://hbsp.harvard.edu/product/921009-PDF-ENG

Skaggs, Rachel, Alexandre Frenette, Sally Gaskill, and Angie L. Miller. 2017a. 'Career skills and entrepreneurship training for artists: Results of the 2015 SNAAP survey module'. Special Report. Strategic National Arts Alumni Project. Bloomington, IN: Indiana University Center for Postsecondary Research.

Skaggs, Rachel, Alexandre Frenette, Sally Gaskill, and Angie L. Miller. 2017b. 'Arts alumni in their communities'. Annual Report. Strategic National Arts Alumni Project. Bloomington, IN: Indiana University Center for Postsecondary Research.

Sobel, Ron. 2007. 'Music schools: Are we incubating excellence?' *MEIEA Journal* 7, no. 1: 177–87.

Surmani, Andrew, and Carl Anderson. 2018. 'The music products industry as part of a collegiate music industry program's curriculum'. *College Music Symposium* 58, no. 1: 1–10. http://www.jstor.org/stable/26564932

Toscher, Ben. 2020. 'Blank canvas: Explorative behavior and personal agency in arts entrepreneurship education'. *Artivate: A Journal of Entrepreneurship in the Arts* 9, no. 2. https://doi.org/10/gmx3bj

Author biography

Jeremy Peters is an Assistant Professor of Music at Wayne State University, a faculty affiliate of Labor@Wayne, and is the 2023 recipient of the American Musicological Society Career Development Grant in American Music. He maintains an active teaching, performing, and researching practice centred around popular music, vocal performance, the creative and cultural industries, ethnographic studies, archives, organization theory, and entrepreneurship in the home of Motown. He is an active music industry professional who co-owns indie label Quite Scientific Records, and before academia he worked at Ghostly International for many years.

4 Thinking Out Loud: The 5Rs of Musicians' Project and Career Decision-Making

Mathew Flynn

Introduction

Research on decision-making in the music industries is a largely unexplored field. The few studies conducted to date have modelled the decision activities of music industry practitioners. Pioneering work by Seifert and Hadida (2006, 2009) and Tschmuck (2012), and recent work by Schreiber (2014, 2016; Saintilan and Schreiber 2023; Schreiber and Rieple 2018) takes account of the organizational structures within music companies, and focuses mainly on how experienced practitioners make decisions about musicians and music products, through processes such as A&R, PR, and creative management. Research by Lefford and Thompson (2018) has analysed musician decision-making but is focused specifically on studio-based record production. As yet, research has not focused directly on the wider decision-making of musicians. This chapter contributes to the growing body of music business scholarship on decision-making by reflecting on data collected through a survey with 500 UK-based musicians (from all genres and income levels) about the types of decisions they make and how they make them. The results are condensed into a decision-making model, developed using a grounded theory approach, which is designed to be useful to, and used by, all types of practising musicians and music industry educators.

After summarizing research on decision-making, the chapter presents the methodologies employed to research, code, categorize, and explain the five core types of musicians' everyday choices: namely Role, Repertoire, Representation, Reputation, and Remuneration decisions. The process for how the findings were developed into formulating a musician decision model is then explained, and the resulting visual 5R decision model is presented. The chapter concludes by explaining how the 5R model is designed to guide musicians towards better understanding of the types of decision they are making in a sequenced process, and proposes circumstances and methods of use for the model by musicians and educators.

A Short Overview of Flawed Decision-Making

Generally, 'people treat decision making as an event – a discrete choice that takes place at a single point in time' (Garvin and Roberto 2001: 1). Equally, most assumptions are that most decisions taken are founded upon rational judgement (March and Heath 1994: 1). However, since the pioneering work of Edwards (1954) and Simon (1955, 1956), research across various disciplines has established that decision-making is a process rather than an event, and is as influenced by the decision-maker's environment, emotional state, prior experiences, and current attentional focus, as it is by rational judgement (see Bazerman and Moore 2013; Damasio 2004, 2006; Eisenhardt 1999; Kahneman 2011; Klein 1997a, 1997b; March and Heath 1994; Thaler and Sunstein 2009; Weick 1995).

As Boulton, Allen, and Bowman observe,

> We readily accept that the 'real world' is complex and varied, and that to make any sense of it we have to narrow down our focus of interest, ignore some of the information, and make simplifications. The problem of simplification is that we may inadvertently throw out or hide the very issues and information that are critical both to understanding the present and to shaping the future. (Boulton, Allen, and Bowman 2015: 71–72)

A famous experiment that demonstrated that when people focus on something in particular, they can be blinded to other events or information was the invisible gorilla test. First conducted in 1999 by Chabris and Simons (2010a), the experiment asked participants to watch a one-minute video and count the number of passes between one of two basketball teams. While most participants counted the correct number of passes, only half of the observers spotted the person dressed in a gorilla costume walk into the middle of the court and beat their chest. Then in follow-up experiments, where observers knew about the gorilla, only 17% spotted the curtains change colour or one player exit the court (Chabris and Simons 2010b; Choi 2010).

These experiments indicate how everyday situations frame our individual perceptions, and what we pay attention to and ignore are prone to what Kahneman, Slovic, and Tversky (1982) termed cognitive biases. As Saintilan and Schreiber (2023: 214–18) explain, cognitive biases increase our mental efficiency and are often necessary shortcuts to quick and effective decision-making. However, they also cause unconscious errors in our thinking, which leads to false judgements and poor decision-making. As with the invisible gorilla experiment, the numerous different types of cognitive biases (see Drummond 2012) cause us to ignore information that is present, but they can also mean we disregard new evidence in favour of long-held beliefs, and see facts that are not there. As Snowden (2010) observes, given the mental effort required to make rational decisions, it is perhaps unsurprising that most of the time when making decisions people generally default to interpreting situations based on their personal preferences for action.

Decision-Making in the Music Industries

Historically, across the music industries, decision-making has tended to rely upon the informal transfer of knowledge (Williamson, Cloonan and Frith 2011), narrative approaches to management (Wheeldon 2014), and 'the value of going with your gut-feelings over the statistical analysis' (Schreiber 2016: 129). Due to the systemic variability in decisions about the same problems (see Kahneman, Sibony, and Sunstein 2021), and because outcomes are so difficult to predict (Krueger 2019: loc. 1851), as Tschmuck (2012: 230) has observed, historically, heuristics have formed the dominant mode of decision-making across the music industries. Often referred to as rules of thumb, Kahneman defines heuristics as: 'a simple procedure that helps find adequate, though often imperfect answers to difficult questions' (Kahneman 2011: 97).

As technology companies such as Apple, Google, Spotify, Amazon, and TikTok exert increasing influence over how music is released and listened to, heuristic decision-making is supplemented, and to an extent superseded, by major music companies' increasing use of algorithms and probabilistic decision models (Eriksson et al. 2019; Page 2021). Individual and small groups of musicians do not have this option, as they do not have access to this wealth of data, or the interpretation expertise necessary to render statistical models effective (see Maasø and Hagen 2019). However, as Jones asserts, 'whether they recognise it or not, self-management is a central issue for musicians' (Jones 2012: 67). To address the limitations of cognition, access, and expertise, Courtney, Lovallo, and Clarke advocate 'developing your decision-making tool kit' (2013: 70).

A Brief Theoretical Context for Developing a Musician Decision Tool Kit

The theoretical underpinning in developing the decision model recognizes that musicians, of all types, work within and across projects to produce their musical and economic outputs, and musicians pursuing careers invariably work across a portfolio of projects (see Bakker 2011; Bennett 2008; Feist 2013; Hesmondhalgh 2013; Lorenzen and Frederiksen 2005; Ryan 1992). With genre used as an overarching organizing principle (see Hesmondhalgh 2013: 32; Lena 2012; Negus 1999), through their projects, all musicians operate within and across sets of markets that constitute and configure the music industries (Eriksson et al. 2019: 159). From an orchestral performance or band studio recording, to a film score, or non-fungible token (NFT) sale, effectively, all musicians engage in two primary types of market. The first is what White (1981) labelled production markets, where musicians join or form music projects in optimal locations by assuming distinctive roles to engage each other's services to produce musical outputs. From teaching, to rehearsing and working in studios, success in production markets rests on the judgement of the musician's project collaborators (other artists, performers, producers, etc.) of their ability to fulfil their role(s) within the project(s). The second of the two primary markets are the markets for music use. Music-use markets are fundamentally constructed of the core audience-facing music industries of live, publishing, and records (Williamson and Cloonan 2007), but extend to include markets for mainstream and social media, brand association and merchandising, business-to-business clients, and public and private investment (see Meier 2017; Taylor 2016). While operationally distinct but often interrelated, all these music-use markets exist 'to turn objects, services and experiences into products and, ultimately, brands, by differentiating them so that they can then be positioned within the minds of the target customer in order to facilitate exchange' (O'Reilly, Larsen and Kubacki 2013: 56). In music-use markets, musicians are judged by users' perceptions of the projects' ability 'to stand out from the competition – to win the battle for attention' (Elberse 2013: loc. 383). The premise for the development of the decision model recognizes that musicians operate on two definitions of success. One is to be personally recommended by peers in production markets, and the other is to have the project(s) in which they are involved generate sufficient attention in music-use markets. Coles's (2019) research on perceptions of success arrived at similar conclusions. It found that musicians measured success objectively by their annual earnings, but subjectively by the relative prestige of their current projects/performances.

In the pursuit of success, decisions across all music markets carry varying degrees of risk (Krueger 2019; Mauboussin 2012). Billionaire investor Howard Marks (2015) argues that, for all its complexity, risk reduces down to two key concerns: the fear of the cost of a bad outcome contrasted against the potential benefits of a missed opportunity. Most musicians have a limited sense of risk, if any, when making market-based decisions (Portman-Smith and Harwood 2015). Given this, Marx's straightforward premise is a productive way to frame risk in the formulation of a decision model.

Methodology and Overview of the Data

To capture and analyse the everyday decisions of various types of musicians, I developed a self-selecting online survey (see Czaja and Blair 2005; Wolf et al. 2016). The survey was distributed through the e-newsletters, websites, and social media channels of a range of national UK music organizations, universities, and various industry, media, and professional and amateur networks between 15 November–7 December 2018. The questionnaire essentially asked one fundamental question:

> As a musician you need to make decisions about many different aspects of what you do. What is the most recent decision you have made you do not yet know the outcome of?

The primary question was followed by thirty quantitative questions, most of which were multiple choice and related to how, where, when, and with whom the decision was taken, and participants' expectation for the outcomes of such decisions.

The survey generated 500 useable responses that represented a convenient sample of UK musicians. Across the cohort there was a 63% male/35%[1] female split in terms of respondents that is broadly consistent with other recent research (Cloonan and Williamson 2016: 245; PRS for Music 2019). With around ninety musicians in each age bracket there was generally an even age distribution from 18 to 65, with a median age range of 35–44. Broadly consistent with UK population data (ONS 2011), 87% of respondents identified as white, with 10% from global majority backgrounds, and 3% undeclared (n=500). Most musician roles were represented, but the majority of participants identified as songwriters, solo artists, band members, session/function musicians, and producers when making the decision. Equally, most genres were represented but rock, classical, folk, pop, jazz, indie, and alternative were dominant in the sample.

Financial themes from the data showed live music contributing considerably to musicians' incomes, recorded music accounting for only a small proportion, and many musicians engaged in other types of non-music work.

---

1. A total of 2% preferred not to say and non-binary was an option.

These findings are broadly consistent with subsequent research on UK musicians' earnings by Help Musicians (2023) and Hesmondhalgh et al. (2021). However, whereas both reports showed 64% of UK musicians earned less than £30,000 per year, 89% of my survey cohort earned below that figure. This suggests a potential underrepresentation of musicians earning above £30,000 per annum in the decision survey data.

General Decision Themes Emerging from the Data

An analysis of the data produced some general themes. More than half the participants (n=265) took their decision alone. However, demonstrating that decisions are dynamic and sequential (Clemen 1991), as Table 4.1 shows, many other people were involved in the decision-making or wider process. Which types of contributors were involved in a decision was one of the defining characteristics of each decision type, and will be discussed in the following section.

Table 4.1 Who musicians make decisions with

Different roles that contributed to the decision	% Total
Alone (36% made the decision completely alone)	53%
Other band members	12%
Creative partner (co-writer, producer etc.)	13%
Spouse/Partner	7%
Friends/Family/Colleague	5%
Professional collaborator (manager, promoter, A&R etc.)	6%
Education advisor (tutor, lecturer)	2%
Business advisor (accountant, lawyer, bank manager)	1%
Other	1%

Regardless of the decision type, as Table 4.2 illustrates, the majority of decisions were taken in musicians' homes,[2] with all the places in which musicians are usually active accounting for only a small proportion of decision-making sites.

---

2. To clarify, the survey was completed 15 months prior to the UK's national lockdown in response to the COVID-19 pandemic, and therefore results reflect pre-pandemic decision practices.

Table 4.2 Where musicians make decisions

Distribution of places where decisions are taken	Percentage
At home	65%
Rehearsal room	7%
While travelling	5%
At work	5%
At a social occasion	5%
Studio	4%
Other	9%

Table 4.3 shows almost all communication surrounding decisions (88%) was largely discursive and discussion based, reflecting the informality and narrative nature of the music industries' organization (Williamson, Cloonan and Frith 2011).

Table 4.3 Different methods used for discussing and communicating decisions

Decision discussion/Communication method	Percentage of participants using the method
General conversation	28%
Email	22%
Messenger apps	12%
Phone	9%
Scheduled meetings	6%
Plans and lists	4%
No consultation or communication	12%
Other	7%

As Table 4.4 shows, along with 'money', the other key concerns expressed by musicians when making a decision are 'perception',[3] 'ability',[4] and 'opportunity'.[5] Accounting for a combined 75% of underlying concerns when deciding, the self-doubt inherent in these findings reflects the complexity, uncertainty, and precarity musicians experience through their circumstances (Canham 2022) and mental states (Gross and Musgrave 2020).

3. Relating to concerns about others' judgement about the quality of the practical outcome of the given decision.
4. The participants' own concerns about their ability to meet the demands of the decision.
5. Namely, concerns about transitions between circumstances.

Table 4.4 Musicians' underlying concerns when making a decision

Underlying concerns when deciding	Percentage of participants
Perception	24%
Money	18%
Ability	18%
Opportunity	15%
Time	9%
Logistics	6%
None	4%
Well-being	3%
Effort	1%
Protection	1%
Connections	1%

This data reveals that although they generally adopt informal decision-making processes, self-managing musicians assume high levels of personal responsibility for their decisions.

The 5R Decisions Defined and Explained

To establish the distinct types of decisions musicians make, participant responses to question 1 were coded using grounded theory (see Charmaz 2014). The interpreting and coding of decisions proved a difficult and nuanced task, where even short narrative decision expressions presented considerable ambiguity as to the type of decision taken. However, the coding and recoding of the decision data (Charmaz 2014: 1) eventually identified and defined five key decisions all types of musicians make. Table 4.5 shows examples of decisions from participants' responses to question 1, and how they were allocated to one of the five different 'R' decision categories.

The following descriptions outline the distinctive characteristics of each decision type in detail.

Role Decisions

Based upon their established working practices, the musicians' Role decisions concern choices about which roles to assume and where and how to fulfil those roles. Role decisions address a complex combination of factors:

- instrument choice and its contextual function, e.g. violin teacher (Bennett 2008)

- Genre conventions, e.g. classical, rock, grime (Fabbri 1981; Becker 2008; Lena 2012)
- levels of expertise, e.g. novice to virtuoso (Lehmann, Sloboda, and Woody 2007)
- professional status, e.g. amateur to superstar (Shuker 2013: 40–58).

Table 4.5 Example of responses to the first open-ended question of decisions that were coded as each 'R'

Coded decision type	Example 1	Example 2
Role	'Decided to go full time with my music mainly as a weddings and events pianist'	'Moved to Hastings from London as there is much more accessible live music'
Repertoire	'Recorded some guitars for a song a producer is working on'	'The formation of a trio: sax, cello and tabla'
Representation	'To run our own PR campaign for our next release and tour we're putting together ourselves due to a serious lack of money and not really knowing who to approach in the first place'	'To go for a meeting with a potential manager'
Reputation	'Whether a 6-month contract abroad is a good idea'	'Signing album contract deal with UK based Indie Label'
Remuneration	'I declined to waive the mechanical rights to a vinyl release on an independent label'	'Whether to pay additional money to film, record and produce and mix an additional song when recording a live band video recording session'

As Thomson (2013) observes, strategic decisions about building and sustaining careers are highly dependent on a musician's role choices. Role is the primary decision musicians make and continually re-affirm, because the decision to be a particular type of musician in everyday situations places musicians in existing market economies (Towse 2010), which, in turn, continuously define and determine levels of expertise in production markets and professional status in music-use markets.

Although musicians collaborate in delivering projects in production markets, depending on their role within the project, from a copyright and fees perspective, they can operate in different use markets. A simple example of a producer and two songwriters collaborating on a track places their practice in the distinct markets for recording and publishing, respectively. The situation could be further complicated by the producer switching roles into songwriter or vice versa. Moreover, an individual musician can occupy multiple roles, at times almost instantaneously, thereby adding to the depth of market knowledge required to make informed decisions. Analysis of the research data shows that Role decisions are constrained by access to education, geographic location, and the need to balance personal and professional commitments. Various music industry equality initiatives such as Keychange, Black Lives in Music, and Attitude is Everything, alongside a broader focus on mental health by the likes of Help Musicians UK, attempt to level the playing field in terms of role choice constraints, by advocating for a greater diversity of musicians to have the opportunities to pursue and succeed in the music role(s) of their choice.

Consistent with Umney's (2016) observations on a jazz musician's individual sanctity of the decision to work, Role decisions are primarily taken individually or with a spouse or partner, and full-time professional musicians make a higher percentage of Role decisions than less established musicians. Because they are usually important career-based decisions, Role decisions carry a higher than average perceived risk of a bad outcome, with results generally not known for between six months and a year. These characteristics contrast heavily with Repertoire decisions.

Repertoire Decisions

Unsurprisingly Repertoire decisions are the most common everyday decision all musicians make, and they tend to make them with each other. The *Oxford English Dictionary* (OED 2009) has two main definitions of 'repertoire':

1. A stock of dramatic or musical pieces which a company or performer has prepared or is accustomed to play; a person's stock of parts, tunes, songs, etc.
2. In extended use: a stock or range of regularly performed or easily exhibited skills, techniques, abilities, etc.; a collection of typical features.

In both senses, musicians make Repertoire decisions because the binary decision between being a musician and non-musician is to develop a repertoire of skills sufficient to fulfil a role in a project, and then practice and perform a repertoire of music (Attali [1977] 1985). As Bennett observes, 'the ability to accept an engagement depends on the existence of a repertoire' (Bennett [1980] 2017: 133). From highly professional (see Seabrook 2015) to amateur music-making (see Finnegan [1989] 2007), and underpinned by shared values (Frith [1996] 2002: 53), Repertoire decisions relate to the opportunity to be creative and collaborate with other musicians in production markets, and to develop sounds into music products in rehearsal and record production spaces. Becker ([1982] 2008: 201) also remarks that even those musicians who predominantly practice and perform solo cannot completely disconnect from a sense of community values.

Repertoire decisions are constrained and often restricted by the musicians' own genre-determined musical abilities, and their access to instrumentation, performance and recording technologies. As the area where musicians exert most control, Repertoire decisions are perceived as the least risky of all five decision types. This is due to the fact that outcomes are predominantly known within a few days, or at the most within two months, and are usually easily reversible (to re-record, re-arrange etc.). Having made Role decisions to play with other musicians and repeated Repertoire decisions about what music to play and how to play it, to have their work used by a wide range of music users, musicians also need to think about Representation.

Representation

Attali has argued:

> In the economy of representation, profit is linked to the ability of an innovation to accrue value: the remuneration of the author of the innovation can then be a function of the number of valorizations of his innovation, in other words, of the number of representations of his work. (Attali 1985: 80)

The transition from a Repertoire to a Representation decision is evident by the switch in focus from production markets to music-use markets. The objects, services, and experiences musicians have developed have to be presented as products (O'Reilly, Larsen, and Kubacki 2013). This means each live performance, use of a recording, and related tweet, email, or casual professional conversation represents the project and its associated musician(s).

Consistent with recent literature on the demands on twenty-first-century musicians having to operate as various types of self-managed entrepreneur (Beeching 2010; Haynes and Marshall 2018; Hughes et al. 2016; Morris 2014; Scott 2012; Thomson 2013), Representation decisions are the second most common decision taken by musicians. They are opportunity seeking, often commercially driven, and ultimately aim to enhance the project's perception in regard to the judgement of audiences, mainly through online platforms, the media, and live performance. To deliver Representation outcomes, musicians must either assume a host of additional non-music-making roles (see Hracs 2013; Tessler and Flynn 2015), or appoint professional collaborators (agents, managers, labels, etc.) to 'do promotional work, but also take calculated risks ... [about] how to place their artists in the market' (Lizé 2016: 35). This is why musicians will often seek to identify and work with the appropriate representatives to inform Representation decisions, and why, along with creative collaborators, professional collaborators feature prominently in the Representation decision-making process. Although online activities increasingly provide 'real-time' feedback, decision outcomes are usually expected within three to six months. Still, the risks associated with the multitude of different types of Representation decisions are dependent on the combination of two key factors: the level of ambiguity in how the decision is expressed, and the level of involvement of professional collaborators external to the music project. Table 4.6 outlines the four different types of Representation decisions when the two key factors are combined, and the graduating level of risk musicians perceive these types of decision to carry.

Regardless of the ambiguity in the decision's description, musicians' perception of the risk of a bad outcome only becomes serious when (potential) collaborators, external to the project, are involved. And when a decision that affects collaborators is ambiguously framed, outcomes are very difficult, if not impossible, to predict (Courtney et al. 2013), making this type of Representation decision the riskiest of all.

Table 4.6 Four different types of Representation decision which increase in perceived risk

Type of representation decision	Example of the type of decision from the survey	Perceived risk of a bad outcome
No Ambiguity/ No Collaborators	'To change the name of my project'.	Below Average
Ambiguity/ No Collaborators	'To perform at an opera class on Tuesday. I do not know the audience, the stage or the outcome of what the performance will be'.	Below Average
No Ambiguity/ With Collaborators	'Britain's Got Talent have been asking me to audition for 4 years – I usually turn them down – this week I agreed to meet them next week in Belfast'	Above average
Ambiguity/ With Collaborators	'Which records to include in a playlist for the label, then which order... or if to even bother sending them at all!!!'	Very high

In search of attention, musicians can appoint professional collaborators to improve their chances of market success, but in doing so increase their perceived risk of a bad outcome. This is because the cumulative results of Representation decisions accrue to develop or diminish a musician's reputation.

Reputation

Everts, Berkers and Hitters (2022) observe how achieving certain career milestones, such as receiving radio airplay or touring internationally, is indicative of the strength of a musician's reputation. As Becker argues, 'your reputation as an artist depends on your work' (Becker 2008: 173). In production markets musicians compare themselves against each other (see Faulkner 1971; Faulkner and Anderson 1987), and are aware of 'a wide range of stakeholders who either contributed to or otherwise critiqued their reputation' (Portman-Smith and Harwood 2015: 501). In music-use markets, Hearn's (2010) analysis of social media established how fluid and precarious contemporary reputations are, and how beholden they are to the judgements of others. Suggesting professional musicians are more aware that their 'external market value [is] based on reputation' (Menger 1999: 551), Reputation decisions were three times more common amongst high-income musicians than the survey average.

If they are a consequence of the musician's decision at all, Reputation outcomes are often not necessarily a direct result of Reputation decisions, but are a second-order consequence of the indirect and cumulative effect of the outcomes of preceding Role, Repertoire, and Representation decisions. However, as Bataille and de Brabandère (2019) demonstrate, reputation is more robustly reflected in the type, quality, and value of contracts musicians are offered, negotiate, and sign. The conversion of market value into actual economic value through the legally enforceable agreements in contracts is the most tangible – but usually not very visible – measure of a musician's reputation. As Menger remarks, 'an artist's reputation provides him with a temporary monopolistic position on the market, as long as his or her skills and talents are in demand' (Menger 2001: 248).

Influenced by professional collaborators, and underpinned by concerns relating to planning, time constraints, and opportunity, Reputation decisions are concerned with responding appropriately to favourable assessments of the project(s) which lead to formalized contracts. Because Reputation decisions invariably involve professional third parties and variable timelines, like collaborator-based Representation decisions, they carry a very high level of risk. Reputation decisions are deemed important for the project's progress but are crucial for the maintenance of long-term careers, as contracts are the conduit for agreeing the type and share of remuneration.

Remuneration

As Table 4.4 demonstrates, money is a key underlying concern when musicians make decisions. However, in terms of specific characteristics, Remuneration decisions concern the individual musician's assertion of intellectual property rights (see Bosher 2021; Frith and Marshall 2004; Laing 2012), and methods of income generation – via fees, royalties, investors and public funders (see Cameron 2016; DiCola 2013; Tschmuck 2017) – to cover costs, generate profits, and to (re)invest in physical property acquisition (e.g., instruments) and services (e.g., advertising, PR, etc.).

Consistent with other research that earning an income is not the key driver of most musicians' activities (Purnomo and Kristiansen 2018), Remuneration decisions accounted for the lowest number of decisions in the data. However, indicative of levels of professionalism, high-income musicians made twice as many Remuneration decisions as their lower-earning counterparts. In line with standard one- to three-month invoice payment terms, when Remuneration decisions relate to a payment for services (e.g., fees for performances, merchandising, brand association, sponsorship, etc.) they demonstrate a tight association between decisions and outcomes. However, underlining how finance underpins every aspect of the decision-making process, when 'in the moment' creative Repertoire decisions are taken during the project, every decision has a potential commercial, copyright, and contractual consequence, which affects not only the project but the incomes of each musician involved. In situations where Remuneration decisions concern copyrights or shares of project equity, the timing of the decision, in terms of when commercial discussions need to intersect with creative flow, is key. As Osborne observes, 'the most important decision that co-composers will come to financially, creatively and socially [is] how to split the songwriting credits' (Osborne 2016: 1). Musicians appropriating their rights now extends to sound recordings and trademarks, as well as shares of partnerships and limited companies, and this is why the data shows Remuneration decisions are often resolved with the help of experts (business advisors, lawyers, and accountants). Remuneration decisions are often a culmination of preceding negotiations, with the parameters of probable outcomes often well-defined and understood, meaning, somewhat counterintuitively, Remuneration decisions are generally perceived to carry only an average risk of a bad outcome by the time the decision is made.

Designing and Applying the 5R Decision Model

Krogerus and Tschäppeler's (2011) *The Decision Book* collates fifty decision-making tools, and summarizes the core criteria they all share:

- Simple – including only relevant aspects of reality;
- Pragmatic – by focusing on what is useful;
- Sum-up – by reducing complexity;
- Visual – using images and diagrams to convey concepts;
- Organise – by providing a structure;
- Methods – they do not provide answers but ways of asking questions to get them. (2011: loc. 90)

Designed for use by educators when teaching professional development modules, and musicians of all types when making music project and career related decisions, the integrative and sequentially organized 5R decision model, presented in Figure 4.1, attempts to address the complexities all individual musicians encounter when negotiating the ongoing challenges of working in and across projects.

To illustrate how the 5R model aids in dealing with the sequential but fluid nature of the decision process, as an example consider how the participant decision below maps on to the model.

'Paying for an album to be mixed professionally without knowing its commercial worth'.

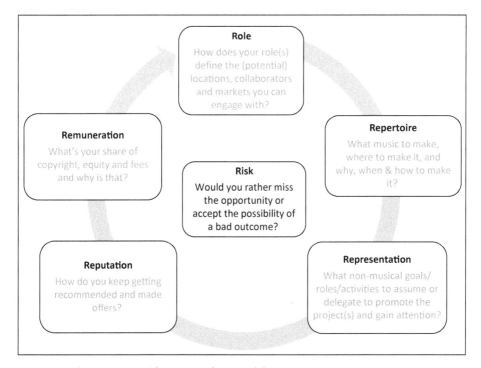

Figure 4.1 The 5R musician decision-making model

Follow the 'album mix' decision-making process example by relating the below decision sequence to the respective sections of the 5R model in Figure 4.1.

1. As the emphasis of this decision is on mixing an album, this is primarily a production market-based Repertoire decision.
2. However, by implication in the act of recording an album, the musician has already made a preceding Role decision to be an artist, and possibly also to be a writer/performer/producer/etc. in this project, or has collaborated with other musicians to fulfil those roles. Therefore, demonstrating the consequential link between Role, Repertoire, and Remuneration decisions, to maximize the album's commercial worth, the musician must be aware of, and able to engage in, the various rights and income streams related to each role, and/or agree splits/fees with all involved in the project, most notably at this stage with the mix engineer.
3. The uncertainty expressed about the album's 'commercial worth' underlines the ongoing dilemma of balancing the risk of missing an opportunity versus a potential bad outcome.
4. Implicit in the 'commercial' element of the decision is advanced consideration of how the repertoire could be represented, and by the time the album is complete more detailed Representation decisions would be required. For example, to self-release or try to engage a label? Or to self-promote or use professional PR? Demonstrating the fluidity within the model, additionally, pre-consideration of the album's remuneration potential could inform the decision as to how much to spend on the professional mix.
5. The eventual music-use market response to the album's representation will deliver reputational outcomes. This prompts the musician to make more detailed Reputation and Remuneration decisions. If outcomes are positive, there may be resulting remuneration in the form of royalties. Or the opportunity to leverage the project's enhanced prestige by signing contracts with more (established) professional and/or business collaborators.
6. If the outcome is negative, then the musician's reputation is not as enhanced and potentially diminished. A negative outcome also risks depleting resources for other projects, and the musician's potential for future work and payment. However, it also provides the opportunity to reflect and improve for the next project.

7. While most music project practices contain some aspect of Role, Repertoire, Representation, and Reputation elements, in either a single decision or sequence of decisions, Remuneration is not always the outcome. Reaching the Remuneration decision point in many instances will have been a long-term iterative process cycling back and forth between the first four stages of the model. However, if making money is the musician's aim, enabling musicians to realize they have not made any money (yet) is an important reminder for them to reconsider the project's potential before risking more time and resources.
8. Remuneration is the fulfilment of the decision cycle. And in terms of investing in future projects and career development, it is the beginning of the next cycle. The outcomes of Reputation and Remuneration decisions impact and influence subsequent Role decisions, by either bolstering or depressing the musician's sense of fulfilment and market achievement in their assumed role(s), which will influence and frame all future decisions.
9. Risk, the hidden R, sits within the model and although there is risk in every decision, the significance of the risk usually depends on the type of decision, the time, effort, and resource committed up to that decision point, and the potential impact of the outcome on the reputations of not only the musician(s) making the decisions, but equally importantly, on other industry professionals associated with representing the project in question.

This example illustrates how the 5R model can be employed in two ways:

First, as with the above example, the visual model can be used by musicians and educators holistically to act as a guide for the broad strategic planning behind the delivery of a music project, illuminating the key considerations from intention through to delivery. In line with Krogerus and Tschäppeler's (2011) principles, the 5R model provides a visual structure that focuses on useful concepts and methodologically prompts the user to question their decision process.

The model's second application is as a mental image, which can be used in a typically discursive live situation (see Table 4.3) where the musician is faced with a decision, and so cycles through the steps mentally in order to identify what type of decision they are faced with, and its possible consequences. More than a broader strategic application, this is about improving the musician's awareness and clarity of thinking, so they know what type of decision is being made. Returning to our album example, using the model in this way would enable the musician to consider if they are primarily taking a Repertoire, Representation, or Remuneration decision. This is important, because the challenges musicians encounter in making informed decisions are compounded by Snowden's (2010) aforementioned observation of the tendency of most people to default to interpreting all situations based on their own frames of reference, i.e. as musicians. Table 4.7 shows examples of the 49% of decisions coded as Representation, that in their survey responses the musicians categorized as musical (Repertoire) decisions.[6]

Table 4.7 Examples of decisions coded as Representation that the participants considered a Repertoire decision

Participants perceiving Representation decisions as Repertoire decisions
'Deletion of my website. Will it decrease the amount of work I get?'
'Reworking the artwork that goes with my podcasts – Branding and Artwork, times, dates etc. I will be creating the artwork to see if it helps the plays'.
'Pitched a project to a publisher'.
'Took on the hosting of a night of music in a local pub. Pay is low, optimism is high. It could be the making of a great venue for live music'.
'Having to choose a single from 15 album tracks, 4 months before it's put out'.

Table 4.7 offers just one example of how cognitive biases influence the predominantly heuristic decision-making of musicians, and the potential pitfalls in perceiving all aspects of the management of a music project from a musician's frame of reference. Musicians who view Representation as Repertoire decisions arguably underappreciate the considerable difference in risk, and their ability to exert control over the respective outcomes. Similarly, the commonplace notion of building a portfolio career masks the fact that careers are not simply built through engaging in straightforward Repertoire decisions across a portfolio of projects, but predominantly rest on the successful outcomes of less frequent but higher risk Role, and collaborative Representation and Reputation decisions. Previous industry-based models encourage decision-makers to engage their professional networks in the judgement process to avoid the narrow framing of decisions (Seifert and

6. Question 2 in the survey was a single option multiple-choice question that asked: 'Would you say this decision was primarily: a) Musical (creating, performing or producing)?; b) Related to project planning?; c) Related to career planning?; d) Related to a specific marketing aim/objective?; e) Related to ongoing/active promotional activity?; f) A response to a marketing/promo outcome?; g) A response to an offer or opportunity?; h) A response to a project outcome?; i) Related to contract / business negotiation?; j) Related to copyright?; k) Financial (earning / spending money)?; l) Other (please describe)'.

Hadida 2009; Schreiber and Rieple 2018). However, for musicians who often make decisions in isolation, and particularly those who operate on the periphery of music communities (such as women and gender minorities within male-dominated music scenes), repeatedly asking the questions posed in the 5R model can not only identify the type of decision being taken, but also guard against the subconscious influence of cognitive bias, the informality of the process, and the inertia of routine.

As a decision-making approach that specifically identifies the types of everyday creative and commercial decisions that musicians make, and formulates them into a sequenced process that better enables musicians to think strategically, the 5R model is designed to expand the musician's decision tool kit, and complement the existing approaches to the teaching and practice of professional development. Use your own most recent decision as a starting point on the model, and test how it could help you think through that specific decision and its relationship to preceding and succeeding decisions.

Conclusion

Research in behavioural economics and other fields demonstrates that decision-making is far more complex than it is assumed to be in day-to-day practice, and that applying decision-making models can improve outcomes. Decision modelling has only recently begun to be applied to the music industries and has generally focused on the practice of music industry professionals, as opposed to the decisions taken by musicians. As individuals and small project teams, musicians have limited access to the tools and techniques that might enable them to fully appreciate their decision circumstances and minimize the risks implied by their choices. This research analysed the everyday decision-making of 500 UK musicians and translated the findings into a simple visual decision tool, designed to help musicians of all types identify five core decisions they make – Role, Repertoire, Representation, Reputation, and Remuneration – and how they differ and relate to each other. In the same way as instrumental practice improves them as musicians, through adoption and repeated use, a decision model – like the 5Rs – could go some way to improving the decision situation for musicians, because, in the uncertain and unpredictable twenty-first-century music industries, being an adept decision maker may be just as important as being an excellent music maker.

References

Attali, J. [1977] 1985. *Noise: The Political Economy of Music*. Minneapolis: University of Minnesota Press.

Bakker, G. 2011. 'Adopting the rights-based model: Music multinationals and local music industries since 1945'. *Popular Music History* 6, no. 3: 307–43.

Bataille, P., and L. de Brabandère. 2019. 'Musical work and its tempi: Some thoughts from the Belgian case'. *Working In Music*. https://wim.hypotheses.org/1008 (accessed 18 April 2022).

Bazerman, M. H., and D. A. Moore. 2013. *Judgment in Managerial Decision Making*. New York: Wiley.

Becker, H. S. [1982] 2008. *Art Worlds*. London: University of California Press.

Beeching, A. M. 2010. *Beyond Talent: Creating a Successful Career in Music*. Oxford: Oxford University Press.

Bennett, D. 2008. *Understanding the Classical Music Profession: The Past, the Present and Strategies for the Future*. Aldershot: Ashgate.

Bennett, H. S. [1980] 2017. *On Becoming a Rock Musician*. New York: Columbia University Press.

Bosher, H. 2021. *Copyright in the Music Industry: A Practical Guide to Exploiting and Enforcing Rights*. London: Edward Elgar Publishing.

Boulton, J. G., P. M. Allen, and C. Bowman. 2015. *Embracing Complexity: Strategic Perspectives for an Age of Turbulence*. Oxford: Oxford University Press.

Cameron, S. 2016. 'Past, present and future: Music economics at the crossroads'. *Journal of Cultural Economics* 40, no. 1: 1–12.

Canham, N. 2022. *Preparing Musicians for Precarious Work: Transformational Approaches to Music Careers Education*. New York: Routledge.

Chabris, C., and D. Simons. 2010a. *The Invisible Gorilla, and Other Ways Our Intuitions Deceive Us*. New York: Crown Publishers/Random House.

Chabris, C., and D. Simons. 2010b. *The Invisible Gorilla*. http://www.theinvisiblegorilla.com/gorilla_experiment.html (accessed 17 December 2021).

Charmaz, K. 2014. *Constructing Grounded Theory*. 2nd edn. London: Sage Publications.

Choi, C. Q. 2010. '"Invisible gorilla" test shows how little we notice'. *Live Science*. https://www.livescience.com/6727-invisible-gorilla-test-shows-notice.html

Clemen, R. T. 1991. *Making Hard Decisions: An Introduction to Decision Analysis*. Boston: PWS Kent.

Cloonan, M., and J. Williamson. 2016. *Players' Work Time: A History of the British Musicians' Union, 1893–2013*. Manchester: Manchester University Press.

Coles, D. X. 2019. 'Perceptions of Success among Music Professionals'. Doctoral dissertation, Teachers College, Columbia University. Available at: https://www.tc.columbia.edu/faculty/dxc2102/

Courtney, H., D. Lovallo, and C. Clarke. 2013. 'Deciding how to decide: A tool kit for executives making high-risk strategic bets'. *Harvard Business Review* 91, no. 11: 62–71.

Czaja, R., and J. Blair. 2005. *Designing Surveys*. California: Pine Forge Press.

Damasio, A. R. 2004. *Looking for Spinoza: Joy, Sorrow, and the Feeling Brain*. New York: Vintage.

Damasio, A. R. 2006. *Descartes' Error: Emotion, Reason and the Human Brain*. New York: Vintage.

DiCola, P. 2013. 'Money from music: Survey evidence on musicians' revenue and lessons about copyright incentives'. *Arizona Law Review* 55, no. 2: 301–70.

Drummond, H. 2012. *The Economist Guide to Decision Making: Getting it More Right than Wrong.* London: Profile.
Edwards, W. 1954. 'The theory of decision making'. *Psychological Bulletin* 51, no. 4: 380–417.
Eisenhardt, K. M. 1999. 'Strategy as strategic decision making'. *Sloan Management Review* 40, no. 3: 65–72.
Elberse, A. 2013. *Blockbusters: Why Big Hits – and Big Risks – are the Future of the Entertainment Business.* New York: Faber & Faber.
Eriksson, M., R. Fleischer, A. Johansson, P. Snickars, and P. Vonderau. 2019. *Spotify Teardown: Inside the Black Box of Streaming Music.* London: The MIT Press.
Everts, R., P. Berkers, and E. Hitters. 2022. 'Milestones in music: Reputations in the career building of musicians in the changing Dutch music industry'. *Poetics* 92: 101647. https://doi.org/10.1016/j.poetic.2022.101647
Fabbri, F. 1981. 'A theory of two musical genres: Two applications'. In *Popular Music Perspectives*, edited by D. Horn and P. Tagg, 52–81. Göteborg and Exeter: International Association for the Study of Popular Music.
Faulkner, R. R. 1971. *Hollywood Studio Musicians: Their Work and Careers in the Recording Industry.* Chicago: Aldine.
Faulkner, R. R., and A. B. Anderson. 1987. 'Short-term projects and emergent careers: Evidence from Hollywood'. *American Journal of Sociology* 92, no. 4: 879–909.
Feist, J. 2013. *Project Management for Musicians: Recordings, Concerts, Tours, Studios, and More.* Boston, MA: Berklee Press.
Finnegan, R. H. [1989] 2007. *The Hidden Musicians: Music-Making in an English Town.* Middletown, CT: Wesleyan University Press.
Frith, S. [1996] 2002. *Performing Rites: Evaluating Popular Music.* Oxford: Oxford University Press.
Frith, S., and L. Marshall, eds. 2004. *Music and Copyright.* New York: Routledge.
Garvin, D. A., and M. A. Roberto. 2001. 'What you don't know about making decisions'. *Harvard Business Review* (September). Available at: https://hbr.org/2001/09/what-you-dont-know-about-making-decisions (accessed 9 May 2024).
Gross, S. A., and G. Musgrave. 2020. *Can Music Make You Sick? Measuring the Price of Musical Ambition.* London: University of Westminster Press.
Haynes, J., and L. Marshall. 2018. 'Reluctant entrepreneurs: Musicians and entrepreneurship in the "new" music industry'. *British Journal of Sociology* 69, no. 2: 459–82.
Hearn, A. 2010. 'Structuring feeling: Web 2.0, online ranking and rating, and the digital "reputation" economy'. *Ephemera: Theory & Politics in Organization* 10, no. 3–4: 421–38.
Help Musicians and Musicians' Union. 2023. *Musicians' Census Financial Insight Report 2023.* https://www.helpmusicians.org.uk/about-us/news/the-first-ever-musicians-census-report-launched
Hesmondhalgh, D. 2013. *The Cultural Industries.* London: SAGE.
Hesmondhalgh, D., R. Osborne, H. Sun, and K. Barr. 2021. *Music Creators' Earnings in the Digital Era: Ground-Breaking Research into How Creators Earn Money through Streaming.* London: Intellectual Property Office.
Hracs, B. J. 2013. 'Cultural intermediaries in the digital age: The case of independent musicians and managers in Toronto'. *Regional Studies* 49, no. 3: 461–75.

Hughes, D., M. Evans, G. Morrow, and S. Keith. 2016. *The New Music Industries: Disruption and Discovery*. Cham: Palgrave Macmillan.

Jones, M. L. 2012. *The Music Industries: From Conception to Consumption*. Basingstoke: Palgrave Macmillan.

Kahneman, D. 2011. *Thinking, Fast and Slow*. London: Penguin.

Kahneman, D., O. Sibony, and C. R. Sunstein. 2021. *Noise: A Flaw in Human Judgement*. London: William Collins.

Kahneman, D., P. Slovic, and A. Tversky. 1982. *Judgment under Uncertainty: Heuristics and Biases*. Cambridge: Cambridge University Press.

Klein, G. 1997a. 'Developing expertise in decision making'. *Thinking & Reasoning* 3, no. 4: 337–52.

Klein, G. 1997b. 'The Recognition-Primed Decision (RPD) model: Looking back, looking forward'. In *Naturalistic Decision Making*, edited by C. E. Zsambok and G. Klein, 285–92. Hillsdale, NJ: Lawrence Erlbaum Associates.

Krogerus, M., and R. Tschäppeler. 2011. *The Decision Book: Fifty Models for Strategic Thinking*. London: Profile.

Krueger, A. B. 2019. *Rockonomics: What the Music Industry Can Teach Us About Economic and Our Future*. London: John Murray.

Laing, D. 2012. 'Copyright in the balance: Notes on some 21st-century developments'. *Popular Music & Society* 35, no. 5: 617–27.

Lefford, M. N., and P. Thompson. 2018. 'Naturalistic artistic decision-making and meta-cognition in the music studio'. *Cognition, Technology & Work* 20, no. 4: 543–54.

Lehmann, A. C., J. A. Sloboda, and R. H. Woody. 2007. *Psychology for Musicians: Understanding and Acquiring the Skills*. Oxford: Oxford University Press.

Lena, J. C. 2012. *Banding Together: How Communities Create Genres in Popular Music*. Princeton: Princeton University Press.

Lizé, W. 2016. 'Artistic work intermediaries as value producers: Agents, managers, tourneurs and the acquisition of symbolic capital in popular music'. *Poetics* 59 (December): 35–49.

Lorenzen, M., and L. Frederiksen. 2005. 'The management of projects and product experimentation: Examples from the music industry'. *European Management Review* 2, no. 3: 198–211.

Maasø, A., and A. N. Hagen. 2019. 'Metrics and decision-making in music streaming'. *Popular Communication* 18, no. 1: 18–31. https://doi.org/10.1080/15405702.2019.1701675

March, J. G., and C. Heath. 1994. *A Primer on Decision Making: How Decisions Happen*. New York: Free Press.

Marks, H. 2015. 'Risk revisited again'. *Oaktree Capital*. https://www.oaktreecapital.com/docs/default-source/memos/2015-06-08-risk-revisited-again.pdf?sfvrsn=2 (accessed 28 March 2022).

Mauboussin, M. J. 2012. *The Success Equation: Untangling Skill and Luck in Business, Sports, and Investing*. Boston, MA: Harvard Business Review Press.

Meier, L. M. 2017. *Popular Music as Promotion: Music and Branding in the Digital Age*. Cambridge: Polity.

Menger, P. M. 1999. 'Artistic labor markets and careers'. *Annual Review of Sociology* 25: 541–74.

Menger, P. M. 2001. 'Artists as workers: Theoretical and methodological challenges'. *Poetics* 28, no. 4: 241–54.

Morris, J. W. 2014. 'Artists as entrepreneurs, fans as workers'. *Popular Music and Society* 37, no. 3: 273–90.

Negus, K. 1999. *Music Genres and Corporate Cultures*. London: Routledge.

OED. 2009. 'Repertoire'. *The Oxford English Dictionary*. Oxford: Oxford University Press.

ONS. 2011. *Ethnicity Facts and Figures*. https://www.ethnicity-facts-figures.service.gov.uk/ (accessed 28 March 2022).

O'Reilly, D., G. Larsen, and K. Kubacki. 2013. *Music, Markets and Consumption*. Oxford: Goodfellow.

Osborne, R. 2016. 'Doing the splits: The creative accounting of songwriting shares'. Proceedings for IASPM UK & Ireland 2016: *Creativity, Practice and Praxis*. Brighton: Academia.edu.

Page, W. 2021. *Tarzan Economics: Eight Principles for Pivoting Through Disruption*. London: Simon & Schuster.

Portman-Smith, C., and I. A. Harwood. 2015. '"Only as good as your last gig?": An exploratory case study of reputational risk management amongst self-employed musicians'. *Journal of Risk Research* 18, no. 4: 483–504.

PRS for Music. 2019. 'New figures from PRS for Music reveal extent of gender disparity in songwriting'. https://www.prsformusic.com/press/2019/new-figures-gender-disparity-songwriting (accessed 21 April 2022).

Purnomo, B. R., and S. Kristiansen. 2018. 'Economic reasoning and creative industries progress'. *Creative Industries Journal* 11, no. 1: 3–21.

Ryan, B. 1992. *Making Capital from Culture: The Corporate Form of Capitalist Cultural Production*. New York: Walter de Gruyter.

Saintilan, P., and D. Schreiber. 2023. *Managing Organizations in the Creative Economy: Organizational Behaviour for the Cultural Sector*. 2nd edn. Oxford: Routledge.

Schreiber, D. 2014. 'An Investigation of Influences on Strategic Decision-Making in Popular Recorded Music Industry Micro-Enterprises'. PhD thesis, University of Westminster.

Schreiber, D. 2016. 'The influence of disruptive technologies on radio promotion strategies in the music industry: A case study of one firm's decision-making practice'. In *Business Innovation and Disruption in the Music Industry*, edited by P. Wikström and B. Defillippi, 114–32. Cheltenham, UK: Edward Elgar Publishing.

Schreiber, D., and A. Rieple. 2018. 'Uncovering the influences on decision making in the popular music industry: Intuition, networks and the desire for symbolic capital'. *Creative Industries Journal* 11, no. 3: 245–62.

Scott, M. 2012. 'Cultural entrepreneurs, cultural entrepreneurship: Music producers mobilising and converting Bourdieu's alternative capitals'. *Poetics* 40, no. 3: 237–55.

Seabrook, J. 2015. *The Song Machine: Inside the Hit Factory*. New York: W.W. Norton.

Seifert, M., and A. L. Hadida. 2006. 'Facilitating talent selection decisions in the music industry'. *Management Decision* 44, no. 6: 790–808.

Seifert, M., and A. L. Hadida. 2009. 'Decision making, expertise and task ambiguity: Predicting success in the music industry'. *Academy of Management Annual Meeting Proceedings* 2009, no. 1: 1–6. https://doi.org/10.5465/AMBPP.2009.44257974

Shuker, R. 2013. *Understanding Popular Music*. London: Routledge.

Simon, H. A. 1955. 'A behavioral model of rational choice'. *Quarterly Journal of Economics* 69, no. 1: 99–118.

Simon, H. A. 1956. 'Rational choice and the structure of the environment'. *Psychological Review* 63, no. 2: 129–38.

Snowden, D. 2010. *The Cynefin Framework*. YouTube, CognitiveEdge. https://www.youtube.com/watch?v=N7oz366X0-8 (accessed 21 April 2022).

Taylor, T. D. 2016. *Music and Capitalism: A History of the Present*. Chicago: University of Chicago Press.

Tessler, H., and M. Flynn. 2015. 'From DIY to D2F: Contextualizing entrepreneurship for the artist/musician'. In *Music Entrepreneurship*, edited by A. Dumbreck and G. Mcpherson, 47–74. London: Bloomsbury.

Thaler, R. H., and C. R. Sunstein. 2009. *Nudge: Improving Decisions about Health, Wealth and Happiness*. London: Penguin Books.

Thomson, K. 2013. 'Roles, revenue, and responsibilities: The changing nature of being a working musician'. *Work and Occupations* 40, no. 4: 514–25.

Towse, R. 2010. *A Textbook of Cultural Economics*. Cambridge: Cambridge University Press.

Tschmuck, P. 2012. *Creativity and Innovation in the Music Industry*. Berlin: Springer.

Tschmuck, P. 2017. *The Economics of Music*. Newcastle upon Tyne: Agenda Publishing.

Umney, C. 2016. 'The labour market for jazz musicians in Paris and London: Formal regulation and informal norms'. *Human Relations* 69, no. 3: 711–29.

Weick, K. E. 1995. *Sensemaking in Organizations*. London: SAGE Publications.

Wheeldon, J. 2014. *Patrons, Curators, Inventors and Thieves: The Storytelling Contest of the Cultural Industries in the Digital Age*. London: Palgrave Macmillan.

White, H. C. 1981. 'Production markets as induced role structures'. *Sociological Methodology* 12: 1–57.

Williamson, J., and M. Cloonan. 2007. 'Rethinking the music industry'. *Popular Music* 26, no. 2: 305–22.

Williamson, J., M. Cloonan, and S. Frith. 2011. 'Having an impact? Academics, the music industries and the problem of knowledge'. *International Journal of Cultural Policy* 17, no. 5: 459–74.

Wolf, C., D. Joye, T. W. Smith, and Y.-C. Fu. 2016. *The SAGE Handbook of Survey Methodology*. London: Sage Publications.

Author biography

Mathew Flynn is a Senior Lecturer in Music Industries at University of Liverpool, Assistant Director of the Institute of Popular Music (IPM), and member of the Liverpool City Region Music Board. His current research interests include decision-making in the music industries, mapping music sectors, the experiences of Black music makers and practitioners, and how to better educate musicians about copyright, data use and self-management.

5 How Do I Look? The Importance of Visual Analysis for Musicians in Popular Music Higher Education

Helen Elizabeth Davies

Introduction

In February 2021, a member of the International Association for the Study of Popular Music (IASPM) mailing list requested information about the global availability of a 'Facts About AIDS' insert with copies of Madonna's 1989 album *Like a Prayer*. The request elicited several responses discussing the packaging of the album, followed by one that called for a shift of focus in list discussions more towards the music itself. This point, in turn, generated a flurry of counter responses asserting the importance of music packaging, as music and its packaging are inextricably connected. Following Auslander (2009; 2021) and Morrow (2020), this chapter explores a related and arguably broader topic: the visual aspects of popular music and the importance of their inclusion in music study, arguing that for students on vocational, practice-focused popular music higher education courses, the value and relevance of contextual study are greatly enhanced by analysing their own creative outputs. Referencing scholars such as Kearney (2017), Korsgaard (2013, 2017), and Machin (2010), the chapter outlines some approaches to and effects of analysing and contextualizing visual elements of students' own musical performances and promotional materials, exemplified through a module taught as part of the BA Music degree course[1] at the Liverpool Institute for Performing Arts (LIPA), UK.

---

1. Throughout this chapter, the term 'course' refers to a programme of study leading to a degree award, in this case at undergraduate level, typically lasting three years. The term 'module' refers to a unit of study focused on a specific subject within the course, such as performance, production, creation, etc.

The chapter begins by considering arguments that visual aspects of popular music are relatively neglected as a primary focus in popular music study and music industry research, yet integral to popular music culture and the music industry. This is followed by a discussion of visual analysis in popular music higher education (PMHE), specifically the importance of contextual study that links together visual aspects of music and students' own practice. Finally, the chapter discusses some analytical approaches and the effects of analysing visual elements of promotional material and performance on students' own visual creativities and musical practice.

Visual Aspects of Music

Several writers who focus on visual aspects of music claim this area of music study is often neglected. For example, for Auslander (2009: 303), 'visual aspects of musical performance … have not received the attention due to them'; while Morrow (2020: 3) notes 'the omission of visual creativities and content' in music business research. A reason for this is the separation of music performance as an audio-visual experience in the late nineteenth century through the introduction of technologies such as radio and gramophone, resulting in conceptions of music becoming audio-focused 'such that visual contributions to music activities are often ignored' (Forde Thompson et al. 2005: 203). This is not to say that visual aspects of music are completely disregarded. As well as publications that celebrate the artwork associated with specific genres and subcultures (e.g., Lavine and Moore 2009; Krivine 2021; Bestley et al. 2022), visual aspects are sometimes considered in critical studies of specific performers (e.g., Tate 2005; Iddon and Marshall 2013; Bailey 2014; Duffett 2020) and scholarly works with an identity focus (e.g., Leonard 2007; Jennings and Gardner 2012; Hawkins 2017; Gregory 2019). Furthermore, audiovisual studies is a well-established field (e.g., Richardson 2015; Chion 2019). However, it can be argued that works that consider all visual aspects of music as their primary focus are relatively few.

There are compelling arguments for taking account of visual aspects of music. For example, Jones and Sorger's (1999: 68) point that artwork 'functions as a visual mnemonic to the music' is supported by Libeks and Turnbull's (2011) analysis of music-related images for indications of music genre, in which they conclude 'both album cover artwork and promotional photographs encode valuable information that helps place an artist into a musical context' (2011: 30). Focusing on music performance, Auslander (2009: 303) asserts physical and visual aspects of musical performance are not separate from or contextual to it, but rather 'convey musical information and shape the audience's perception of the musical event'. He broadens the argument to include other extra-musical aspects:

> Popular musicians do not perform their personae exclusively in live and recorded performances; they also perform them through the visual images used in the packaging of recordings, publicity materials, interviews and press coverage, toys and collectibles, other venues and media, including music video. (Auslander 2009: 308)

Similarly, Morrow (2020: 8–9) argues that design is integral to music, as 'the production of meaning and value' is not limited to music but 'occurs across a number of textual sites' including 'album covers, gig and tour posters, music videos, stage and lighting designs, live concert experiences, websites, XR [extended reality] experiences, merchandise and other forms of non-musical content'. Hansen (2019: 524) also states that extra-musical elements are integral, not supplementary, to music:

> [S]ocial media posts, artwork, music videos, interviews, and so on are not just secondary texts that serve to infuse sound recordings with additional meaning (at the same time as they do). A vast network of meaningful texts and events operate in relation to each other in a complex interplay, and the continuous interweaving of multiple different texts, discourses, and narratives ultimately shape pop personae.

Advice for aspiring popular musicians from industry practitioners mirrors the scholarly arguments. Music lawyer Harrison (2017: 201) highlights the importance of 'getting the artwork right for the record', and the ways in which it can be rolled out consistently across all mediations and platforms that require a visual element: 'It could be used as a backdrop to a stage show and on a poster campaign. It could appear on T-shirts and other merchandise' (ibid.). Similarly, in their guidance on shaping an artist persona, musician mentors Chertkow and Feehan (2019) note the prevalence of fan interactions with the 'website, social media profiles, logo, photos, bio, images, videos, merch, and other public representations' of the artist, all of which are visual or have a visual dimension. In a guidebook written for a musician audience, Cannon and Thomas (2015: 345), advising DIY musicians on growing a fanbase, point out the risk of neglecting visual aspects: 'if your graphics don't fit your music, it usually results in a lack of potential fans giving you a chance'. As Littleton (2023) puts it in a blog for *Music Gateway*: 'Having your own unique "image" is often overlooked by many smaller artists in the industry ... but it's something record labels will notice if they're thinking about signing you as an artist. As an artist you need to have the "whole package", right down to your style choices and social media artwork, it needs to be uniform and consistent'.

Furthermore, the importance of visual creativity is growing, as music consumption and mediation are becoming increasingly tied to visuals. As Sexton (2009: 99) points out, 'as the formats music is stored on become less material ... such loss is compensated by music's increased connection to other visual formats'. Holt (2011: 52) argues that music 'remains distinct as an art form defined primarily by audio, but ... the media distribution, presentation and sharing of music are becoming more visual'. This is not least due to 'audiovisual convergence, with the penetration of video in music industry practices of production, communication and distribution' (Holt 2011: 51). Since these observations, consumption of audiovisual forms has continued to increase. Among the 44,000 internet users surveyed by IFPI in 2022, video streaming was the most popular way of engaging with music (82%), with short form video at 68% (IFPI 2022). In November 2022, it was announced that YouTube had over 80 million paid YouTube Music and Premium subscribers worldwide (Stassen 2022) and, according to Statista, short form video-sharing social media app TikTok had three billion downloads worldwide in July 2021, and over 150 million monthly active users in January 2022 (Ceci 2022). As Ceci observes: 'Whether it is professionally produced or user-generated – online video content is proving vastly popular with social media consumers, and it is, therefore, expanding across established platforms like Instagram and serving as a springboard medium for newcomer applications like TikTok' (ibid.).

Although consumption of physical recordings with artwork has been largely replaced by digital consumption, accompanying online artwork and images are still essential; and the so-called vinyl revival (Paine 2023) indicates that the physical presence of artwork to accompany recordings remains relevant. In relation to music performance, according to Statista, the UK live music industry was worth £1.1 billion in 2018 (Gotting 2023) and in 2022 was still in recovery following the COVID-19 pandemic (UK Music 2022). Visual aspects of music performance are arguably more important than ever, as live streaming has gained a stronger foothold in the live music industry since the pandemic, making live music performance more widely accessible and presenting new challenges for musicians in relation to performance practice and visual presentation, in order to engage audiences (Haferkorn et al. 2021).

It is clear that visual elements of musical performance and promotional material are changing and increasing in importance; and their relative neglect as a main focus in popular music studies and music business studies is unjustified. This chapter now considers how this relates to the context of popular music higher education.

Visual Analysis in PMHE

Warner (2017) explores the state of popular music studies (PMS), noting its flourishing in UK universities since the late 1980s, and the more recent signs of its decline demonstrated by the closure of PMS courses at University of Leeds in 2014 and Liverpool John Moores University in 2015. The increasing vocational emphasis of degree programmes in the post-millennial period, shifting from a free-to-user service to a 'market-driven commodity, coming with an ever-higher price tag for the "consumer"' (Warner 2017: 134), has increased the vocational, industry-facing focus of PMS courses, which has become the mission of many private sector institutions offering employment-focused training and music industry connectivity. The Universities and Colleges Admissions Service (UCAS) operates the application process for post-18, higher education courses in the UK. A search of the UCAS website for undergraduate courses starting in 2023 using the search term 'popular music' finds 364 courses from 64 providers (UCAS 2023), all of which have a practical, commercial, professional element or focus, public and private sector providers alike.

As Warner (2017: 130) notes, popular music degree courses increasingly offer 'practice and theory as complementary models', and students enrolled on practice-based PMHE courses include performers, songwriters, composers, and producers, whose musical practice both motivates and underpins their study. The practical aspects of the course are, therefore, the main priority of students and, from my own experience as a lecturer in popular music studies at LIPA, it can sometimes be necessary to justify (to some students) the inclusion of PMS with an academic focus. However, contextual study (i.e., the study of the cultural and social contexts of music) is integral to even a practice-based music degree (Quality Assurance Agency for Higher Education 2019: 5).

Hooper (2017) makes a convincing argument for the importance of contextual study in PMHE, to foster understanding among musicians of the potential meanings and effects of what they do: 'Students need to be aware not just of what chord they are playing and how to play it, but also how its reception will be altered dependent on innumerable "meta-musical" choices, sociologically contextualized, championed or critiqued' (Hooper 2017: 159). She links a high level of competency in analytical and critical thinking to a greater potential for graduate/professional success for music students; not only an ability to analyse in an abstract way, but an ability to apply the understanding directly to their own practice:

> It is ... keenly important that if student performers are to be expected to succeed, that they are taught fluency in the language of sociology

> and semantics, not as abstract tools for theory and criticism, but as active components of their own performance and a way to understand their potential professional life. (Hooper 2017: 159–60)

Moreover, the current music industry demands visibility from musicians, in part due to the increasing pressures to regularly post and appear on a range of social media platforms; as Baym (2018: 1) puts it: 'today musicians relentlessly seek relationships with audiences, following listeners from platform to platform, trying to establish a presence for themselves and build connections'. Although some musicians 'would like to disappear from sight (and site[s]) and exist only in sound, this is simply not a viable position for current performers. More and more, to be heard is to be seen' (Hooper 2017: 159). In addition, as Hooper argues, educating and enabling music students to analyse and contextualize their own creative practices and products is increasingly important due to technological change, which necessitates musicians undertake more of their own promotion and marketing (Hooper 2017: 161).

So, there are strong arguments for the importance of contextual and critical aspects of popular music study in popular music higher education; and for practice-focused music students, the value and relevance of contextual study can be greatly enhanced by focusing these aspects of study on their own creative outputs. Combined with the evidence for the integral relationship between music and visuals, the importance of visual aspects of music in the music industry, their relative neglect in music study, and the fact that graduate employability is a key criterion in course status, a strong case can be made for enabling students to analyse visual aspects of their own musical creativities within the broader contexts of popular music and music industry culture.

Analytical Approaches and Effects

Students on the BA Music degree course at LIPA are musicians whose practice encompasses various configurations of performance, songwriting, composition, and music production. The second-year contextual module enables them to analyse and explain relationships between musician personae and visual elements of promotional material and performance. Their first task is to construct and deliver a presentation analysing the visual elements of examples of the promotional material and performance of a well-known musician or band. They then turn their analytical attention towards themselves, to write a 4000-word essay focusing on the visual elements of their own promotional material and performance, taking into consideration the relationships between these, their music, and their musician persona. The essay is written in sections, drafts of which students present in seminars for tutor and peer formative feedback, before submitting the final essay for assessment. Students who have not yet developed promotional material or have little experience of performing are encouraged to use the module as an opportunity to begin thinking about potential future directions and analyse examples of other musicians' material and performance to bring their own intentions into focus.

This section outlines approaches to analysing and contextualizing visual elements of students' own promotional materials and musical performances as taught in the module at LIPA and includes some examples of when students' analysis has been effective in helping them to understand and shape their visual choices. The module also includes analysis through a range of lenses including genre, identity, and authenticity, which further informs students' understanding of their visuals. While the length of this chapter precludes an in-depth discussion of these here, some of the implications of the role of gender are considered. The outline focuses on four main areas: images, dress and costuming, performance, and music video. First, however, it is relevant to briefly discuss the concept of the musician persona.

Musician Persona

The term 'persona' is defined as 'the particular type of character that a person seems to have and that is often different from their real or private character' (Cambridge Dictionary 2023). Auslander's (2009; 2021) exploration of 'musical persona' uses Goffman's (1959) concept of 'front' to provide a theoretical framework for analysing 'the means performers use to define and project personae' (Auslander 2009: 309). Similarly, Hansen (2019) and Chertkow and Feehan (2019) argue that a musician's persona is composed of aspects of their image and identity, constructed and performed through their music and a range of mediations such as promotional materials and performances. An understanding of the concept of persona as it relates to musicians, therefore, is an essential starting point in the analysis of visual aspects of promotional material and performance. Furthermore, keeping a consideration of both persona and promotional materials/performance in balance is crucial because, as Hansen (2019: 524–25) contends, there is a dialectical tension between musician personae and promotional materials and performance, with each informing understanding and perceptions of the other. Therefore, as students create promotional materials as part of their development as musicians, and indeed as part of their curriculum-based work, they need to be mindful of their image; and the ability to perceive and analyse their own personae is important to the creative process. In addition, as the persona is constructed through promotional materials and performances, analysis of visual aspects of these contributes to understanding and developing their personae. Table 5.1 illustrates this relationship, with a summary of the visual aspects of promotional material and performance for analysis.

Table 5.1 Musician persona and visual aspects of promotional material and performance

Musician persona ⟷		Visual aspects of promotional material and performance to analyse	
Images	**Dress and costuming**	**Performance**	**Music video**
posture pose gaze distance objects (including clothing) settings salience modality colour typography	everyday dress vs. performance costume gender aspects	venue, props, set – including lighting, artwork, visual media, special effects salience, colour, typography costuming posture, position, gaze, facial expression, gesture, movement	can include analysable features of images, costuming, and performance broad relationship between sound and visuals: illustration, amplification, disjuncture specific relationships between sound and visuals, e.g. texture, intensity, loudness, tempo, rhythm, structure

Images

Methods for analysing visuals are prevalent and diverse, and include content analysis, semiology, psychoanalysis, discourse analysis, and ethnography (Rose 2016). For analysis of the kinds of images that include advertising, fine art and films, which are arguably most similar to music-related images, Rose recommends semiology (Rose 2016: 50–51). While it is not possible to give an in-depth explanation of semiology here, it is worth summarizing a few key points about the approach. Semiology, also known as semiotics, is 'the study of signs' (Rose 2016: 107) and, as Rose states, offers 'a very full box of analytical tools for taking an image apart and tracing how it works in relation to broader systems of meaning' (Rose 2016: 106).

Rose does not include analysis of music-related visuals in her work. However, Machin (2010) is seemingly unique in offering a detailed toolkit for semiotic analysis of music-related images, which includes approaches to identifying and interpreting the posture, pose, gaze and distance/proximity of people in the image, objects in the image, including clothing, and settings

(Machin 2010: 37–48). The toolkit also includes a consideration of salience: how 'certain features in compositions are made to stand out' (Machin 2010: 48), and modality: how 'real a representation should be taken to be or how closely it represents naturalistic truth' (ibid.). Additionally, he explores semiotics of colour (Machin 2010: 61–68), as well as providing an analysis of potential meanings of various typographical features (Machin 2010: 69–76). Although his examples are all album cover artworks, the approach is applicable to other types of image such as promotional images, gig posters and flyers, logos, and images depicted on merchandise and as part of performance sets, all of which are relevant to the promotional outputs of music students.

Students use this toolkit to analyse in detail their own promotional images, as well as other reference images that illustrate their ideas and intentions. Many students conclude that their images are consistent with their persona and music; however, sometimes the process of analysis results in constructive criticism and change. For example, a promotional photograph of a four-piece band in an urban park shows the members standing at various levels on stone steps. Three members are standing close together in a line leaning against a low wall, while the fourth member stands higher up, separately and to the side. After analysing this image, the student realized that the salience given to the fourth member due to his position was misleading, as he was the drummer rather than the front person of the band. Similarly, a band whose intention was to depict all members equally had a photograph taken in which the only female member was standing at the front with the four males standing behind her. Again, position and salience contributed to a misleading representation of the band persona. Another image used by a solo artist showed him sitting on a low outside step, looking away from the camera, with the colour palette of the image dominated by neutral tones such as grey and beige. After analysing the image with a focus on gaze, salience, setting and colour, the student decided it was incongruous with his intended musician persona, which he conceptualized as more engaging and flamboyant.

Dress and Costuming

Physical appearance and personal style are central to visual aspects of musicians' promotional material and performance, and the construction of musician persona. In the module at LIPA, we expand on Machin's (2010: 43) inclusion of clothing with objects, to analyse dress and costuming in more depth. Eicher and Evenson (2015: 4) consider how individual components of dress can be interpreted within a specific time, place and culture, as well as how the various components work together in a single ensemble to create meaning. This approach helps to illuminate how these specific visual aspects of musicians' promotional material and performance contribute to the way the musician is perceived.

For performing musicians, the relationship between everyday dress and performance costume is significant, as 'costume speaks to an assumed identity in opposition to everyday roles' (Eicher and Evenson 2015: 100). Auslander (2023: 25) states the dynamic of performance 'is predicated on the distinction between performers and spectators'. He points out that the identical suits of 1950s doo-wop groups effectively set them apart from their audience, positioning them as 'entertainers', whereas 1960s psychedelic rockers wore 'the same fashions as their audiences' to reduce the performer/audience distinction (Auslander 2009: 312). The costuming conventions of popular music are clearly often genre-dependent and relate to differing relationships between artists, audience, and the concept of authenticity. The distinction between everyday dress and performance costume can also be considered in relation to the various performing roles of musicians, such as featured artist, band member, and session player, as well as to musician roles such as producer, songwriter, composer, and musical director, as in these roles people construct a professional persona through clothing choices that relate to professional and genre expectations.

For students working in a session player role, for example, performing on stage as an accompanist or backing band member for a featured artist, everyday dress is often replaced with all black, plain clothing. As one student working in this way concluded, this gives a more neutral impression, not drawing attention from the featured artist. On the other hand, some session players performing in a backing band are asked by the featured artist to dress in a particular style to create a cohesive image for the whole band. Examples of this at LIPA include session band members wearing all white, all black with different coloured neckties, and blue jeans and Hawaiian-style shirts.

Alongside a musician's specific role, costuming choices are also shaped by gender. As Reilly and Barry (2020: 6) point out, 'dress is one of the most salient ways in which we express, embody and enact our own gender, as well as make assumptions about the genders of others'. While musicians of all gender identities need to consider the impression they are creating through their clothing, it is arguable that female musicians must pay particular attention to this aspect of visual presentation. Kearney (2017: 174) observes the need for female performers to navigate challenges in relation to costuming, due to expectations of females to wear 'tight, revealing clothing to accentuate their physical features'. Furthermore, as Warwick (2015: 339) points out, whether aiming 'to shock or to please', female musicians 'must think carefully about what to wear and how to look, in ways that men can more easily disregard'.

So, while many student musicians tend to dress in their everyday clothing for promotional images and performances, to appear less distant from both their audience and their everyday selves, female musicians are more likely to feel the need to dress in a revealing way and wear make-up due to perceived audience expectations. While negotiating self-presentation as sexual or sexualized, primarily though dress and costume, is undoubtedly a more pressing concern for female than male musicians, some female students have a positive attitude to costuming that accentuates their femininity and sexuality, embracing the notion prevalent in wider popular music culture that sexualized self-presentation and performance can both signify and contribute to self-empowerment.

As Reilly and Barry (2020: 1) argue, by the start of the twenty-first century, concepts of gender were being 'redefined … beyond the western binary of male and female to include agender, non-gender, gender fluid, genderqueer, [and] transgender'. Despite an increasing acceptance of a wider range of gender identities, there is 'an ongoing issue with dress and gender: violations of traditional, binary gender norms are often met with violence' (ibid.). However, popular music culture, and indeed PMHE, can provide an accepting space for the expression and performance of non-traditional identities through costuming; as Hawkins (2016: 1) argues, 'pop music … reconstructs, reaffirms, and challenges fixed notions of gender'. While student musicians at LIPA currently adhere more or less to the traditional gender binary in relation to their dress, it is becoming more usual to see traditionally feminine 'body supplements' (Eicher and Evenson 2015) such as coloured nail polish, extravagant jewellery, and hair ornaments worn by students of all genders in their promotional materials, performances, and everyday life.

Performance

An advantage of the approach used on the music course at LIPA to analyse promotional materials and performance is that it is cumulative: teaching starts with analysis of images, then progresses through a consideration of dress and costuming, to then focus on performance. Consequently, analysis of the visual aspects of music performance can incorporate many of the features already discussed, such as posture, gaze, setting, objects, salience, and colour, as well as costuming. Crucially, however, analysis of performance also involves taking account of the moving body within the context of the performance. According to Dodds (2015: 411), 'popular music artists engage their bodies to visualize the generic categories, aesthetic features and philosophical dimensions of their musical affiliations'. More specifically, Fast (2001: 144–45) directs attention to 'how the performers look and gesture, how they are costumed, how they interact with their instruments and with one another, how they regard the audience'. Alongside the practical tuition and performance opportunities offered at LIPA, this theoretical and analytical approach helps students to understand the significance of various elements of performance, which can inform their practice. To analyse musical performance, it helps to follow Auslander (2009: 309), who, as mentioned earlier, applies Goffman's (1959) theory of front, the means a performer uses to create an impression, which consists of two aspects: setting, which is the physical context of the performance, and personal front, the performer's appearance and manner.

In a similar way to analysis of images, taking account of the setting of a performance, comprising venue and set, is a useful starting point. In relation to set, which includes lighting, artwork, visual media, props and special effects, the degree of complexity depends on the type of musician and music performed (Kearney 2017: 168). As performers at a relatively early career stage, musicians at LIPA can be somewhat limited in relation to the kinds of venues in which they can perform, which typically include LIPA's internal performance venues and local live music venues, all of which are relatively small and stripped back in terms of complexity. Nonetheless, student performers often create imaginative settings for their performance in collaboration with students studying on other courses at LIPA, through lighting, stage sets, and props.

As well as setting, analysis of performance needs to consider costuming, position, posture, gesture, facial expression, and movement. Dress and costuming are crucial elements of the visual presentation of musicians of all kinds. In relation to performance, costuming is 'key to the successful communication of both public persona and song character' (Kearney 2017: 170) and, according to Eicher and Evenson (2015: 332), 'must create a visual impression that will support or supplement performance'. Obviously, performance costume must also be able to accommodate the level of movement involved in performing music, to avoid potentially embarrassing wardrobe malfunctions. This is a consideration for female performers in particular who, as discussed earlier, can be influenced by social expectations to dress scantily and so, during a physically vigorous performance, can sometimes reveal more than they intend.

Students are also encouraged to think about position: where performers are in relation to each other, the set and the audience, and the ways in which this can follow or subvert conventions of performance and genre. Student bands often conform to the conventional stage set-up of vocalist at the front and centre of the stage, drummer back centre, with guitarists and/or keyboardists mid-stage to either side. A five-piece band with two vocalists, one female and one male who was also the keyboardist, changed their positioning after realizing the reason the male vocalist was lacking audience attention was because he was not at the front alongside the other vocalist. By bringing the keyboardist/vocalist to the front, the audience's focus was directed more effectively.

Posture often follows convention as singers, guitarists, and bassists usually stand upright, whereas keyboardists and drummers often sit. As Kearney (2017: 176) points out, standing 'draws attention to ... bodies and music while also allowing for greater flexibility with technology and movement'. In addition, the ways in which performing musicians hold and interact with technology and instruments are significant, as they can develop 'very distinctive personae ... expressed ... in the way they play' (Auslander 2009: 309). Analysis has led several students to reconsider their relationship with their instrument, with some keyboardists choosing a standing rather than a sitting posture to move more freely and create a more energetic visual impression on stage.

Gestures, movements, and facial expressions are all aspects of performance that students are continually encouraged to improve in their practical work, as lack of confidence and performance anxiety can lead to somewhat static performances. Analysis of such elements from a theoretical perspective can draw upon Kearney's work (2017: 176–77), to distinguish between illustrative gestures such as head movements and arm raising, and emblematic gestures, which are more genre specific, for example the sign of the horns; and to recognize the difference between choreographed movements, more common in pop genres, and ritualized movements, which are specific to an individual performer or genre, such as the rock guitarist knee slide. Forde Thompson et al. (2005: 178) offer an analytical approach to facial expression, identifying its key functions as signalling specific musical events, communicating emotion, and strengthening the relationship between performer and audience.

For students, having the tools to analyse the visual details of performance affords them a greater awareness of the significance of individual elements, how these elements contribute to an overall meaning of a performance and, most crucially, how they can work on shaping their own performances using this awareness.

Music Video

Although analysable features of images, costuming, and performance outlined above are also relevant to music video, the task of developing a toolkit for analysing music video is less straightforward. As well as being complex, the form is also highly mutable. As Korsgaard (2013: 504) notes, 'new videolike phenomena take shape all the time through a bewildering proliferation of practices, which are too numerous to follow'. Morrow (2020: 90) observes that social media platforms such Facebook, Instagram, and YouTube have 'led to a fragmentation of the traditional music video into packages of content that can be drip fed into the rivers of content these services facilitate' (Morrow 2020: 90). As Vernallis (2017: 2) concludes: 'Perhaps all we can say about music video is it's a relationship between music and image we recognize as such'. However, there is a range of useful approaches to analysis developed by various scholars. For example, Goodwin (1992: 86–88) proposes a three-part model to broadly explain the relationship between sound and visuals: illustration, whereby 'the visual narrative tells the story of the song lyric'; amplification, when the visuals 'add layers of meaning'; and disjuncture, which occurs when the visuals have 'no apparent bearing on the lyrics'. Focusing on the details of the audio-visual relationship, Korsgaard (2017: 65–69) identifies specific ways in which 'vision is musicalized in music video' (Korsgaard 2017: 65). For example, camera movements and movements of objects within the frame can be cut 'on the beat' (Korsgaard 2017: 66). There can be a relationship between musical and visual textures (Korsgaard 2017: 66–67) and, in relation to intensity and loudness, 'visuals are capable of expressing the rising and falling in musical dynamics' (Korsgaard 2017: 67). Similarly, with tempo, 'just as "loud" music often means "loud" imagery, a "fast" musical tempo often means "fast" imagery' (ibid.). Structurally, 'different parts of the song [can] take place in different settings or spaces' (ibid.) and musical loops and repetition can be accompanied by visual loops and repetition (Korsgaard 2017: 68).

So far, in relation to students' own promotional materials, analysis of music video takes place less often than analysis of images and performance. This is due not only to the complexity of analysis but also to the fact that student musicians are more likely to have created images and given performances than they have produced a music video. Nonetheless, more student musicians are now creating short form visuals using, for example, Spotify Canvas, and TikTok, and so it will be interesting to see how well the existing analytical approaches work with these new forms, and how they could be developed.

Conclusion

The responses of IASPM mailing list members to the notion that music-related discussion should be primarily focused on 'the music itself' is a timely reminder that extra-musical elements are integral to music. Their importance is clear, not only in scholarly discussion, but in research and education. This chapter has argued that including the study of visual aspects of music in vocational, practice-focused PMHE courses is both necessary and justified, and students can benefit greatly by focusing such study on their own promotional materials and performances. Outlining the approach taken in a module taught on the BA Music course at LIPA, the chapter has discussed key aspects of an analytical toolkit for student musicians, which incorporates consideration of musician persona, images, dress and costuming, performance, and music video. This approach enables students to identify and potentially subvert dominant visual discourses in popular music, providing not only an opportunity for professional development, but a critical and change-making tool. The approaches outlined are inevitably subject to changes brought about by developments in research, technology, industry, society and culture, and must continue to evolve to remain relevant and useful. Whatever the future holds, the ability to analyse and interpret visual aspects of both their own and others' musical creativity is essential for musicians to answer the question 'How do I look?'

References

Auslander, P. 2009. 'The physical performance of popular music'. In *The Ashgate Research Companion to Popular Musicology*, edited by D. B. Scott, 303–15. Farnham: Ashgate.

Auslander, P. 2021. *In Concert: Performing Musical Persona*. Ann Arbor: University of Michigan Press.

Auslander, P. 2023. *Liveness: Performance in a Mediatized Culture*. 3rd edn. London: Routledge.

Bailey, J., ed. 2014. *The Cultural Impact of Kanye West*. New York: Palgrave Macmillan.

Baym, N. K. 2018. *Playing to the Crowd: Musicians, Audiences, and the Intimate Work of Connection*. New York: New York University Press.

Bestley, R., A. Ogg, and Z. Howe. 2022. *The Art of Punk: Posters + Flyers + Fanzines + Record Sleeves*. Atglen, PA: Schiffer.

Cambridge Dictionary. 2023. 'Persona'. https://dictionary.cambridge.org/dictionary/english/persona (accessed 6 February 2023).

Cannon, J., and T. Thomas. 2015. *Get More Fans: The DIY Guide to the New Music Business. 2015 edition*. Union City, NJ: Musformation.

Ceci, L. 2022. 'TikTok – Statistics & Facts'. *Statista*, 23 November. https://www.statista.com/topics/6077/tiktok/#topicOverview (accessed 6 February 2023).

Chertkow, R., and J. Feehan. 2019. 'Define your persona, find your voice, and build your artist brand'. *Disc Makers Blog*, 1 May. https://blog.discmakers.com/2019/05/define-your-persona-build-your-artist-brand/?utm_campaign=EA1919&utm_source=DMAudio&utm_medium=Email (accessed 6 February 2023).

Chion, M. 2019. *Audio-Vision: Sound on Screen*. 2nd edn. New York: Columbia University Press.

Dodds, S. 2015. 'Dancing the popular: The expressive interface of bodies, sound and motion'. In *The Sage Handbook of Popular Music*, edited by A. Bennett and S. Waksman, 401–17. London: Sage.

Duffett, M. 2020. *Elvis: Roots, Image, Comeback, Phenomenon*. Sheffield: Equinox Publishing.

Eicher, J. B., and S. L. Evenson. 2015. *The Visible Self: Global Perspectives on Dress, Culture, and Society*. 4th edn. New York: Fairchild Books.

Fast, S. 2001. *In the Houses of the Holy: Led Zeppelin and the Power of Rock Music*. Oxford: Oxford University Press.

Forde Thompson, W., P. Graham, and F. A. Russo. 2005. 'Seeing music performance: Visual influences on perception and experience'. *Semiotica* 156, no. 1–4: 203–27. http://eprints.qut.edu.au/26430/1/26430.pdf

Goffman, E. 1959. *The Presentation of Self in Everyday Life*. New York: Doubleday.

Goodwin, A. 1992. *Dancing in the Distraction Factory: Music Television and Popular Culture*. Minneapolis: University of Minnesota Press.

Gotting, M. C. 2023. 'Live music industry in the United Kingdom (UK) – statistics and facts'. *Statista*, 6 January. https://www.statista.com/topics/6065/live-music-industry-in-the-uk/ (accessed 6 February 2022).

Gregory, G. 2019. *Boy Bands and the Performance of Masculinity*. New York: Routledge.

Haferkorn, J., B. Kavanagh, and S. Leak. 2021. *Livestreaming Music in the UK: A Report for Musicians. May 2021*. https://livestreamingmusic.uk/report/ (accessed 6 February 2022).

Hansen, K. A. 2019. '(Re)Reading pop personae: A transmedial approach to studying the multiple construction of artist identities'. *Twentieth-Century Music* 16, no. 3: 501–529. https://doi.org/10.1017/S1478572219000276

Harrison, A. 2017. *Music: the Business. The Essential Guide to the Law and the Deals*. 7th edn. London: Virgin Books.

Hawkins, S. 2016. *Queerness in Pop Music: Aesthetics, Gender Norms and Temporality*. New York: Routledge.

Hawkins, S. 2017. *The British Pop Dandy: Masculinity, Popular Music and Culture*. Abingdon: Routledge.

Holt, F. 2011. 'Is music becoming more visual? Online video content in the music industry'. *Visual Studies* 26, no. 1: 51–62.

Hooper, E. 2017. 'Do the stars know why they shine? An argument for including cultural theory in popular music programmes'. In *The Routledge Research Companion to Popular Music Education*, edited by G. D. Smith, Z. Moir, M. Brennan, S. Rambarran, and P. Kirkman, 153–65. London: Routledge.

Iddon, M., and M. L. Marshall, eds. 2013. *Lady Gaga and Popular Music: Performing Gender, Fashion, and Culture*. New York: Routledge.

IFPI. 2022. *Engaging with Music*. https://www.ifpi.org/wp-content/uploads/2022/11/Engaging-with-Music-2022_full-report-1.pdf (accessed 6 February 2022).

Jennings, R., and A. Gardner, eds. 2012. *'Rock on': Women, Ageing and Popular Music*. Farnham: Ashgate.

Jones, S., and M. Sorger. 1999. 'Covering music: A brief history and analysis of album cover design'. *Journal of Popular Music Studies* 11–12, no. 1: 68–102. https://doi.org/10.1111/j.1533-1598.1999.tb00004.x

Kearney, M. C. 2017. *Gender and Rock*. Oxford: Oxford University Press.

Korsgaard, M. B. 2013. 'Music video transformed'. In *The Oxford Handbook of New Audiovisual Aesthetics*, edited by J. Richardson, C. Gorbman, and C. Vernallis, 501–21. Oxford: Oxford University Press.

Korsgaard, M. B. 2017. *Music Video After MTV: Audiovisual Studies, New Media, and Popular Music*. London: Routledge.

Krivine, A. 2021. *Reversing into the Future: New Wave Graphics 1977–1990*. London: Pavilion Books.

Lavine, M., and T. Moore. 2009. *Grunge: Photographs by Michael Lavine*. New York: Abrams Image.

Leonard, M. 2007. *Gender in the Music Industry: Rock, Discourse and Girl Power*. Abingdon: Routledge.

Libeks, J., and D. Turnbull. 2011. 'You can judge an artist by an album cover: Using images for music annotation'. *IEEE Multimedia* 18, no. 4: 30–37. https://doi.org/10.1109/MMUL.2011.1

Littleton, D. J. 2023. 'How to get noticed by a record label'. *Music Gateway*, 24 January. https://www.musicgateway.com/blog/how-to/getting-noticed-in-the-music-industry-as-a-singer-or-artist (accessed 6 February 2023).

Machin, D. 2010. *Analysing Popular Music: Image, Sound, Text*. London: Sage.

Morrow, G. 2020. *Designing the Music Business: Design Culture, Music Video and Virtual Reality*. Cham: Springer Nature Switzerland AG.

Paine, A. 2023. 'Vinyl destination: Can the format's sales growth continue in 2023?' *Music Week*, 6 February. https://www.musicweek.com/labels/read/vinyl-destination-can-the-format-s-sales-growth-continue-in-2023/087370 (accessed 6 February 2023).

Quality Assurance Agency for Higher Education. 2019. *Subject Benchmark Statement: Music*. https://www.qaa.ac.uk/docs/qaa/subject-benchmark-statements/subject-benchmark-statement-music.pdf?sfvrsn=61e2cb81_4 (accessed 6 February 2023).

Reilly, A., and B. Barry. 2020. 'Introduction'. In *Crossing Gender Boundaries: Fashion to Create, Disrupt and Transcend*, edited by A. Reilly and B. Barry, 1–20. Bristol: Intellect.

Richardson, J., ed. 2015. *The Oxford Handbook of New Audiovisual Aesthetics*. New York: Oxford University Press.

Rose, G. 2016. *Visual Methodologies: An Introduction to Researching with visual materials*. 4th edn. London: Sage Publications.

Sexton, J. 2009. 'Digital music: Production, distribution and consumption'. In *Digital Cultures: Understanding New Media*, edited by G. Creeber and R. Martin, 92–106. Maidenhead: Open University Press.

Stassen, M. 2022. 'YouTube Music and Premium surpass 80m paid subscribers'. *Music Business Worldwide*, 9 November. https://www.musicbusinessworldwide.com/youtube-music-and-premium-surpass-80m-paid-subscribers/ (accessed 6 February 2023).

Tate, J., ed. 2005. *The Art and Music of Radiohead*. Farnham: Ashgate.

UCAS. 2023. www.ucas.com (accessed 6 February 2023).

UK Music. 2022. *This Is Music 2022*. https://www.ukmusic.org/research-reports/report-archive/this-is-music-2022/ (accessed 6 February 2023).

Vernallis, C. 2017. 'Beyoncé's overwhelming opus; or, the past and future of music video'. *Film Criticism* 41, no. 1. https://doi.org/10.3998/fc.13761232.0041.105

Warner, S. 2017. 'Where to now? The current condition and future trajectory of popular music studies in British universities'. In *The Routledge Research Companion to Popular Music Education*, edited by G. D. Smith, Z. Moir, M. Brennan, S. Rambarran, and P. Kirkman, 127–38. London: Routledge.

Warwick, J. 2015. 'Midnight ramblers and material girls: Gender and stardom in rock and pop'. In *The Sage Handbook of Popular Music*, edited by A. Bennett and S. Waksman, 332–45. London: Sage.

Author biography

Helen Elizabeth Davies is Subject Leader of Popular Music Studies at the Liverpool Institute for Performing Arts, UK. Her key research interests are popular music and gender, popular music visuals, music education, music in everyday life, and ethnographic research. She has published research into musicians in vocational popular music higher education and graduates working in the music industry, focusing on gender-related experiences and issues. Since 2019, she has carried out research with the organization UK Music on diversity in the UK music industry workforce for their biennial diversity report. She is currently writing a book on popular music visuals.

6 Songwriting, Visuality, and Technological Determinism: Exploring Artistic Responses to Perceived Negative Effects of Streaming on Songwriting and Production

Hussein Boon

Introduction

This chapter examines intersections between songwriting and visual musical outputs, primarily video, and the tensions around claims of technologies' deleterious influence on popular music practitioners. Arguments concerning technology's effect in and on music, particularly songwriting, will be discussed as well as how these developments could be viewed more positively. A generally less well-considered factor in these debates is the diversity of stakeholder interests in the music ecosystem. This means that some practitioners might not value the same aspects or continuities valued by previous generations, or even between disparate groups of music practitioners, which is an important mitigating factor.

The use of video forms a significant discussion point for this chapter which challenges the idea of audio as the pre-eminent format building on the work of Meier (2017). In discussions on songwriting, video tends to be an overlooked or neglected artefact in respect to its role in meaning making. In some instances, video provides a layer of meaning making not present in lyrics or audio alone, which I refer to as their visuality. This shift to video is further confirmed by platforms such as Spotify adopting a visual component to their streaming audio service (Lipshutz 2023).

This chapter contributes an articulation and understanding of these issues within the field of songwriting, how these are discussed (especially by academics and journalists), and how these various issues might also affect the development of a curriculum of study in a higher education institution. This conflict corresponds with previous generations of music makers where 'their main characteristic ... opposed all the models of musical consumption of other generations' (Fabbri 1982: 76). This opposition must be kept in mind when considering creator dissonance between various groups. My aim here is to contrast this dissonance with what has been facilitated. I draw attention to what Freire refers to as the 'dynamic present' (Friere 2000: 84). This is an increased representation that reveals a form of power exercised for their practitioners when '*mediating* musical and visual meanings to a global public' (du Gay et al. 1997: 23, original emphasis). Thus, individual music creators' use of YouTube to disseminate their work and to develop audiences is 'not as a means of escaping from the world but of acting upon it' (Fiske 2010: 321).

Chapter Outline

There are three main areas of concern for this chapter. Songwriting and technological determinism are the first and second closely linked terms. Popular music has generally been driven by technological developments, either as production, or as dissemination and consumption. As will be discussed, the medium does have an effect in shaping outputs, but this need not be viewed negatively. Questions of negative effect are a well-researched and recurring debate since Edison's invention of the phonograph and the development of vinyl records, in an industry that is driven to exploit commercial opportunities derived from new technologies.

The definition of songwriting used for this chapter is broadly framed, acknowledging that songs can be written using a multitude of instruments and technological devices, utilizing various vocal and instrumental expressive forms (Isherwood 2014: 2). Songs can also make use of numerous chords or none, and observations such as Everett's 'The bridge usually ends on the dominant ...' (Everett 1999: 16), is recognized as advice that works in certain songwriting settings or traditions and, therefore, not of universal applicability.

The third term, visuality, is the song and image presented in visual outputs as the twin cultural revolutions of the visual and sound (du Gay et al. 1997: 19). These are opportunities to create a connection that reaches beyond audio alone.

The larger context for this chapter includes those of Black Lives Matter and #MeToo, which several videos featured in this chapter address or speak directly to. The challenges of the creative working context include 100,000 tracks uploaded daily to Spotify (Ingham 2022), increasing levels of job precarity (Canham 2021), misogyny in music (Dredge 2023b), an ongoing cost of living crisis, and a wide-ranging mental health crisis in the music profession (Gross and Musgrave 2020), with Artificial Intelligence encroaching in artistic domains (Clancy 2022; Donahue 2023).

Video Examples

Videos selected for this chapter are suitable examples to illustrate extensions of the audio track. They are by no means a definitive selection but do display sufficient diversity in the mix of video methods. For educators the diversity of video options can be used to stimulate discussion with students, especially when engaging in creating this extensible work, as part of their digital strategy. Almost all selected artists started within the era of streaming with most releasing their music post-2010.

As will be seen with the discussion of Vulfpeck, artists are able to build quite successful ventures using video without the intervention of a large or even medium-sized record label (see Daniels 2022 for a TikTok and Spotify study; Edlom 2020: 132). Therefore, video is also a form of mediatization as 'accumulable value' (Auslander 2008: 28). This accumulable value is possible via advertising-supported platforms such as YouTube (still developing for TikTok), which can prove useful in generating income, for some, within challenging surveillance economies (Zuboff 2019).

The absence of major labels also brings another aspect to the discussion of artist independence. For example, the UK artist Little Simz has always worked independently via AWAL and resisted attempts to sign to a large major record label. Subsequent to the release of Simz's fourth album *Sometimes I Might Be Introvert* (Music Week 2021b), AWAL was acquired by Sony (CMA 2022a). This highlights difficulties for independent artists to maintain *their* independence when major labels seek to control or dominate the market, particularly if they are losing market share due to independent artist activities (Dredge 2023a).

Visuality

Traditionally, music video has tended to be considered within the context of MTV and primarily as marketing. Some consider that YouTube 'provides record labels with the opportunity to augment the reach of MTV' (Rogers 2023: 8). Yet, my argument is for a reorientation. Video, when controlled by the artist rather than by a controlling media entity (or record label), can be used as a vehicle for 'seeing' and enabling difference to be foregrounded. Different pockets of resistance, i.e. to marginalization, to exclusion, to a lack of visibility, to having a presence, can be detected in visual statements which might not be immediately obvious in audio recordings alone and not catered for in the MTV-centric approach. Therefore, visuality comprises those elements not audible in an audio recording, extended in the visual domain, adding meaning and value to the song, which results in an expansion of material expressions. My definition refers to the work of Foster (1988), building upon Carlyle's earlier, though controversial formulation (1993[1841]). Carlyle's ideas are controversial due to their 'strongman' focus, which leads to a favouring of (white) authoritarian male-dominated structures with an emphasis on the 'heroic', that has some crossover with 'the white-savior industrial complex' (Cole 2012). Mirzoeff (2006), however, also indicates that some rethinking of Carlyle's position is possibly in order. Despite these concerns, many relevant ideas around strength and resistance are revealed 'among how we see, how we are able, allowed, or made to see, and how we see this seeing or the unseen therein' (Foster, cited in Mirzoeff 2006: 55).

Many of the videos selected for this chapter have a human-centredness aspect to them, connecting as a powerful argument for visuality. Video outputs range from those achievable by anyone to bigger budget releases. Sometimes all that is needed is a green screen and a message (Figure 6.1). Drillminister's *Nouveau Riche* is an example of this as part of the 'vital forms of culture from the margins of societies' (Hesmondhalgh and Saha 2013: 180).

Figure 6.1 *Nouveau Riche* (Drillminister 2020 used by kind permission of the artist), timestamp: 2'14"

Artists from the margins, like Drillminister, are able to communicate these statements of resistance via their visuality as an important means of representation and the amplification of difference in video, challenging notions of fixed identities, truth, and the purpose of music (Wall 2003: 158). Resistance is utilized by these artists in varied ways, which can be identified as resistance to the status quo; social and/or market conditions; or a lack of representation and exclusion.

Formulating Video

I propose that music videos posted on services such as YouTube function in a number of ways:

1. Video operates as an extension of audio, foregrounding the 'recording artist personality' (Meier 2017: 10), and that video can be considered the primary discovery mechanism for potential listeners (IFPI 2019: 9) and the largest mode of music consumption at 82% (IFPI 2022: 13).
2. Video can function as both a document of the lived experience of the artist, even if as dramatized event, exhibiting what Fiske terms social power – 'the power to construct meanings, pleasures, and social identities' (Fiske 2010: 319).
3. Video can be understood as a form of resistance (Grossberg 1993: 159), particularly for artists and communities underrepresented or historically marginalized by the music industry and hegemonic practices of media channels such as MTV.

Video from any or all of these perspectives extends audio-meaning into a domain that improves connection with potential audiences. These areas of connection function in the domains of the social, of representation, and the passing of knowledge (see PacmanTV 2020). Types of knowledge include wisdom, folklore, history, tradition, values, and conventions. These videos document aspects of life not found in everyday news and media channels (see Mashrou' Leila 2019) and, therefore, are capable of addressing important issues within the selected visual aesthetic for the song. This reveals that 'music becomes a space for promoting – or conversely, resisting or subverting – particular ideologies or positions of authority' (Nooshin 2009: 3), as in *Hijabi* (*Wrap My Hijab*) (Figure 6.2) by highlighting a point of tension.

114 The Handbook on Music Business and Creative Industries in Education

Figure 6.2 Mona Haydar's *Hijabi (Wrap my Hijab)* (Haydar 2017 used by kind permission of the artist), timestamp: 0'09"

Videos, like Pa Salieu's *B***k* (Salieu 2020), have a pedagogical and community empowerment focus, exploring contemporary, historical, and cultural themes of the African diaspora, contrasted with the perilous nature of contemporary life for young, black men.

Figure 6.3 Pa Salieu, *B***k* (Salieu 2020 used by kind permission of Warner Music Group), timestamp: 1'12"

Others explore a Freirean-like pedagogy, such as calling into question neoliberalism's trickle-down economics and the demonizing and targeting of certain communities by ethnicity and class (Drillminister 2020). Communities not traditionally able to gain access to mainstream media channels are enabled to create their own responses to dominant cultural logics (Fiske 2010: 313), with Haydar and Drillminister being examples of 'active resistance' (Fiske 2010: 321). All of these examples address the 'dynamic present' (Freire 2000: 84), and the lived experience of the artist as a part of their community. Building on Freire's work, Nemer suggests that what needs to be understood is how tools like video 'can be appropriated by the oppressed in their pursuit of freedom' (Nemer 2022: 5). These videos provide audiences with moments of recognition, and potentially an opportunity to critique their own conditions. It cannot be understated that these sorts of vehicles act as a powerful (auto)ethnographic account.

Videos disseminated via platforms such as YouTube may also offer entrepreneurial opportunities for music styles or practitioners perhaps not deemed to be commercially viable by record labels, which is considered in the next section.

Vulfpeck – An Entrepreneurial Case

The group Vulfpeck showcased their take on funk in video performances to build a large, global fanbase. Through their activities and consistent approach, they were able to sell out Madison Square Garden (Knopper 2019; Vulf 2019), without a hit or being signed to a major record label. Vulfpeck's entrepreneurial opportunity illustrates a bottom-up approach, built one fan at a time. They are also an example of working against a dominant cultural logic characterized as 'non-commercial viability' that is demonstrative of the 'power of YouTube's musical communities to generate interest in certain events' (Rogers 2023: 9). Whilst I have described the band as 'non-viable', at least to large record labels, this does not mean that an audience cannot be found. In many ways their example underscores the general trend of building profitable niches (Mulligan 2021a). Their approach shows that 'Musicians who make original music become the owners of property that is of potential value. Because performances of the works they create can be exchanged for money, but only if customers can be found' (Jones 2012: 66).

Vulfpeck found their customers via YouTube, in what some commentators refer to as 'the rise of creator culture' (Mulligan 2021b). Their video performances are a marketplace activity, enabling them to establish dialogue with an appreciative audience. This market is also an informal one due to few, if any, barriers to entry and the relative ease to use available tools. Vulfpeck might not be as revolutionary as Haydar or Drillminister, but their actions can also be thought of as a form of resistance (Grossberg 1993: 159), one that is anti-record labels, and against 'fashionability' as a necessary ingredient or predicate for 'success'. The message here is that styles of music considered outmoded need to generate and sustain sufficient public interest to be signed (Music Week 2021a). Given this imperative, and the inextricable link with technology, the next section considers technological determinism and its claimed effects on music, in particular songwriting.

Songwriting and Technological Determinism

Bimber highlights that 'technological determinism' is quite an elusive term (Bimber 1990: 332), which some have interpreted as a 'pervasive, yet controversial, theory about the relationship between technology and society' (Kline 2015: 109). Dafoe, in a bid to reclaim technological determinism from being a 'critic's term and straw position' (Dafoe 2015: 1049), suggests that the research focus should concern two areas. These are '(1) the autonomy of technological change and (2) the technological shaping of society' (Dafoe 2015: 1052).

Any declaration of technology's effect on music can be viewed from three general classifications: normative, nomological, and unintended consequences. A normative critique can be summed as a 'relinquishing of control' (Bimber 1990: 337) thereby robbing users of agency, revealing its 'implication in modern relations of power' (Taylor 2009: 46). Nomological is where technology develops autonomously according to an internal logic and forces a 'prescribed social change' (Bimber 1990: 334), such as shifts from ownership to subscription-based models. Unintended consequences produce results that 'even wilful interveners are unable to anticipate and control' (Bimber 1990: 339), which also forms an interesting area for music practice and pedagogy. Some influential popular music practices have 'used technology in ways unintended by those who manufacture it' (Théberge 2001: 3), where 'the explicit rejection of various technologies are thus instrumental in defining a particular "sound"' (Théberge 2001: 4). Katz suggests that in a musical context 'it is not simply the technology but the relationship between the technology and its users that determines the impact' (Katz 2004: 3).

More recently, many of the negative arguments concerning the technological impact on songwriting tend to be focused upon streaming and remuneration rates. These observations emerge from a number of sources: academic, music industry press, streaming technology companies as well as from personal blogs, newspaper articles and YouTube channels, as parts of the cultural circuit (du Gay et al. 1997: 5).

One recurring argument is that a focus on getting paid leads to audience attention deficit which encourages skipping (Hesmondhalgh 2022: 13;

Lamere 2014; Montecchio et al. 2020), bringing about an overall deterioration in songwriting quality. Some identify this deterioration as pleasing the algorithm, which is claimed to be a songwriting approach calculated to be picked up by an algorithm. This approach is described by some as the Spotify 'sound that has practically become synonymous with the platform' (Pelly 2018). This type of trend was reported as impacting upon two areas where 'the average hit song is getting shorter, while longer songs are becoming hits less often' (Bemrose 2019). Léveillé Gauvin's research project of 303 top 10 singles between 1986 and 2015 identified song lengths as experiencing 'an 80 per cent decrease in 30 years' (Sumanac-Johnson 2019), yet Bennett's earlier research reveals different results due to a longer timeframe and different song selection (Bennett 2012: 142). However, producer Dr. Luke observed that 'My problem with eighties songs is they take too long to get to the chorus' (Seabrook 2015: 239). Willis identified that singles 'lasted for only 2½ minutes' (Willis 1990: 39), while Hennion suggests 'the pop song is "a little three-minute novel"' (Hennion 1990: 188). Despite these competing ideas, Gauvin observed that artists 'can make their songs as long or as short as they like' (Bemrose 2019).

If songs can be any length, then the argument that streaming diminishes songwriting practice by 'forcing' (Zeger 2020) both normative and nomological practitioner responses is highly contestable. This position ignores a variety of possible social contexts as also having influence, where the 'creative trajectory for the musician/ producer ... are always positioned in relationship to the individual's wider social and personal trajectories' (Strachan 2020: 91). Song length, therefore, is routinely identified as one of these forced response indicators. Yet the quality of a song, such as a hit (in the charts or not), might also be impacted by the mix which reveals an 'ambiguity about whether it is the song or the mix of the song that is actually "great"' (Percival 2011: 468). Therefore, relying upon a quantitative measure (i.e., song length), to establish the qualitative nature of the work is a flawed mechanism, especially where changes are brought about by shifts in culture.

Song length as affected negatively by streaming's impact upon songwriting can be summarized thus:

1. Streaming pay outs only occur once a stream is active for 30 seconds or more. Therefore, to get to 30 seconds, songs and their productions must make compromises to reach this target by avoiding structuring elements such as intros, middle 8s, bridges, and codas.

2. To meet these conditions, practitioners render all musical sections effectively as if they were a chorus, viewed as direct evidence of the algorithm's cause and effect upon songwriting.
3. Therefore, there is no requirement for songs to be much longer.

Some commentators (Brown 2019; Pelly 2018) point to the role that Spotify's algorithm has in song recommendation (see Hesmondhalgh 2022: 7 for an extended discussion). However, the algorithm is also influenced by specific user actions, such as saving the track, i.e. not just casually listening to it, and by users incorporating it into their own playlists (consider Barack Obama's Summer playlist).

In the UK, a recent government investigation found that 'The single largest mechanism through which music was streamed was '"user curated" playlists at 42%' (CMA 2022b: 43–44). Additional evidence from UK DSPs (Digital Service Providers) shows that '70% of listens continue to be user led' (CDEI 2023). The algorithm cannot be thought of as a stable mechanism as it is also constantly being tweaked by streaming companies. In fact, users can also tweak the algorithm (Tiffany 2018). Given the potential for algorithmic variation between streaming platforms, the variety of playlists, combined with differences in user behaviour around the world, it becomes more difficult to assert that there is a stable and predictable songwriting approach that could be comprehensively applied in songwriting situations to 'game' the algorithm. Finally, there is a clear gap in the research on how music recommender systems work, noted by Hesmondhalgh and colleagues, which is contrasted with the more well-researched, though anecdotal and sentiment-based research 'on how musicians and music professionals think [recommender systems] operate' (Hesmondhalgh et al. 2023). This can be expanded to include a variety of commentators such as journalists, bloggers and vloggers, contributing to the perception that algorithms are the single influential cause of changes to songwriting approaches. In the next section I foreground some of the reasons why songwriting has always been a point of tension.

Songwriting as a Site of Tension

The phrase 'Don't bore us, get to the chorus' used by Dave Grohl (MacMillan 2016) is attributed to Motown boss Berry Gordy (Turkel 2020) and is one that predates the introduction of streaming. This reveals songwriting as perhaps always being a site of tension, where songs are required to be both 'exciting' and to maintain listener interest (Seabrook 2015: 194, 239).

If songwriters are expected and encouraged to experiment in a number of areas of their practice, should this automatically imply that songs should be longer or remain at the same idealized single length? Could songs go in the opposite direction? Could they become shorter or adapt to new formats similar to Stravinsky's *Serenade in A* (Katz 2004: 3) with each movement the length of one side of a 78rpm record or a collection like Tierra Whack's 15-minute visual album (Whack 2018)? Some of Bob Dylan's songs are shorter than or equal in length to many of the songs made today, yet *Subterranean Homesick Blues* (Dylan 2015) is not considered deficient. A view of song length as indicator of quality is therefore a questionable proposition.

Moore suggests that musical expectations will vary depending upon differing value-based systems and that songs using repeating sequences 'seem to have quite a degree of freedom in terms of the[ir] lengths' (Moore 2001: 58). Therefore, songs with a dominant requirement of form reveal the importance and reliance upon harmonic changes (Moore 2001: 58). This leads to important questions of whether the expressive vehicle of songwriting is being adversely impacted if this tradition is adapted, altered, or even ignored.

A conclusion that could be arrived at from these various discussion points is that contemporary songwriting by a younger generation is buffeted by the twin poles of quantitative and qualitative judgements. Many of these judgements are generally voiced by previous and older generational practitioners who deem this younger generation to be somehow inadequate (Beato 2021). Further evidence of this, such as the resurgence of older, and generally well-established music, draws attention to the domination of catalogue, where new artists compete not only with their contemporaries but also with the weight of the past (Savage 2021). Therefore, video, as an extension of audio, is one active solution to this very real issue.

The songs and artists discussed in this chapter can be best described as displaying a form of relative autonomy while being influenced by their respective cultural dynamics. This is practised within and in relation to the various constraints and opportunities brought about by new technology and/or by new cultural forms in the creation of expressive musical pieces. Rather than a single strand, these can be considered as 'a variety of currents of innovation moving in a number of directions toward highly uncertain destinations' (Winner 1978: 88). Winner's observation is directly applicable to songwriting because there is not really a single extant model in use; just a multiplicity of variations and differences.

Video Examples

Table 6.1 highlights some video examples to be considered within the range of formats deployed by artists and, in some instances, by fans.

Table 6.1 Video examples

Video type	Description	Additional notes	Example(s)
Still image	The use of still image, possibly distressed using post-processing. Image not necessarily of the artist but does capture atmosphere.	Useful for limited budgets.	The Weeknd (2011) (Rogers 2023: 11)
Visualizer	Motion graphics, mandalas and sound waves, reacting to the music. Assets can also be generated using AI (RunwayML 2023).	Tends to favour music where drums and bass are more prominent though not exclusively.	Ocean (2016)
Lyric	Varies from placing lyrics over a static image background, still montage, animations, line drawings, time lapse, and so on. Lyrics can appear on screen in blocks, or per sentence, or rhythmically sync'd to the music.	Peters's lyric video demonstrates the use of journal entries, as a variation on Bob Dylan's cue cards. Note the dressing-table setting and 'clutter' of life.	Peters (2020a)
		Peters demonstrates a variation on the lyric theme utilizing images sent in by fans as an example of co-creation and fan engagement.	Peters (2020b)
		Parks demonstrates how short segments, combined with a disjunct editing style, can assist in underscoring the song theme.	Parks (2020)
Translation	Additional content item, appreciated by non-native speakers.	Translations need to be accurate. Language societies, local University and college departments are good sources to find those willing to work on this type of project.	França (2020)
Perspective video	Drone footage, cameras tied to shoelace or knee, mounted on motorized toy or skateboard.	Taliable's example incorporates elements of CGI and live action, with clothes and artworks sourced from upcoming London-based designers and artists.	Taliable (2020)

Music video	Can run from big budget productions to using a phone. Can be performances, choreographed, to camera, single shot, situational, bizarre, and political. Need not be expensive, but does require planning!	Kyan (2018), starting at 2:17, where the artist is stripped of their external representation, which is subsequently appropriated by others. This is a powerful message and one that cannot be communicated by words and audio alone.	Kyan (2018)
		Carter addresses growing up trying to make sense of her parents' divorce and rejection by her father.	Carter (2018)
		Bree Runway tackles the subject of #MeToo and the video contains some difficult scenes. There is a sense of triumphalism in the closing scenes, starting at 3:34, especially the use of twerking as a symbol of self-ownership and reclaiming power and strength. Some might find the video disturbing, but it deals with a subject that the entertainment and creative industries find difficult to confront.	Runway (2017)
Narrative drama	The narrative drama is an extension of the song, told through either personal or fictionalized accounts and is generally, though not exclusively, episodic. It is advisable to find a good director of photography, and/or creative director.	Rapman (2018) presents an episodic drama akin to a soap opera, in three parts.	Rapman (2018)
		Whack World is a rich, at times David Lynch-like, cinematic experience.	Whack (2018)
		Nines presents a drama to accompany their album release. Shifts between various settings from home, council estate, relationship problems, bereavement, on tour. Interspersed with questions and responses during a counselling session discussing the aftermath of a violent attack.	Nines (2020)

Discussion

The video examples highlighted in this chapter are more than mere marketing. Arguably they constitute the 'symbolic good' (Jones 2012: 67, 200), reinforcing that 'Musicians are text-makers more than they are musicians' (Jones 2012: 66). Therefore, video offers opportunities to create a rich intersection between the artist, the song, recorded performance, ideation, and audiences. Therefore, this is not just about songwriting and production approaches but also the development of audiences and markets.

We no longer live in a time where there is a dominant musical practice in respect of harmony, melody, form, or subject. What becomes clear is that there are 'a proliferation of textual practices in which highly rigid formal structures coexist with a radical pluralism or eclecticism' (Straw 1993: 11). Therefore, it is difficult to assert that music that addresses this radicality and eclecticism, which is also empowering and emancipating for its communities, minorities in particular, is also somehow technologically determined and, therefore, inferior. In many ways the opposite has occurred: technology has increased the number of expressive outputs, not reduced them.

Technology is a double-edged sword, embraced and vilified, potentially leading to double standards. Those who use technology to mediate their songs encounter varying amounts of praise and criticism which should be an area of concern for higher education programmes endeavouring to decolonize and reduce canon formation in their curricula (Boon 2022: 264–65). Where technology becomes perceived as cause for the deterioration of song quality, especially songwriting, then the gulf between student and teacher life worlds increases (Boon 2022: 263). Music has always been prone to a thread of nostalgia (Jakubowski 2021), especially in an industry that thrives on long-term licensing revenue by exploiting catalogue, but, as Dylan advises, songs can become 'some different republic' (Dylan 2004: 34). Are we brave enough to allow them to be so?

Conclusion

This chapter discussed songwriting combined with visual representation and the various concerns about the impact of technology on songwriting quality. This contributes to an understanding from a variety of perspectives which includes those less well-represented voices and practitioners in songwriting literature. My contribution in this debate is to ground the work within a number of theoretical positions and to highlight why video extends the audio recording. Despite the various negative positions discussed in this chapter, the minimum requirement to access YouTube or TikTok is a 'video'. I use quotation marks here because there are many potential variations, but with two important points to be considered. The first is that the artist must have control as the authorial voice (Straw 1993: 9) and secondly, that the barrier to entry continues to remain low. A low barrier does not mean inferior or low-quality work.

Through the various video examples, I have attempted to show this shift to authorial voice as broadly as possible, highlighting practitioners who embody some or all of these ideas. The examples of resistance referred to throughout this chapter address issues of cultural change and legacy. For some artists, video also addresses a historic lack of representation in traditional media channels. As an overall approach this can best be described as one that does not require anyone's permission to make something and publish it anyway. Above all, these practitioners represent a passion to make a difference.

If there is anything to be understood about songwriting, it is that it has always been a site of tension and one that is highly contested. For education, this spectrum of disagreement becomes magnified when academics also express an opinion on what constitutes 'good' songwriting. When educators express a preference for melody and harmony then how do they make a space in their curriculum for other modes of expression that do not follow an explicitly Western-European model?

Understanding the delicate balancing act required of practitioners managing issues between the autonomous and heteronomous poles of choice, i.e. creative decision-making and markets, is a necessity. Audio recordings are not and need not be considered as standalone items, nor even the end product. Whilst there is a desire to privilege audio for analytical purposes, it should also be understood that for many new and establishing artists – many 'discovered' on platforms such as YouTube and TikTok – this discovery process requires some form of meaningful visual artefact, which should not be immediately dismissed nor considered as mere marketing or an extension of MTV. In this sense, music videos discussed in this chapter 'are not simply "standardized" returns to commercial straitjackets' (Straw 1993: 11). Meier argues that 'Recorded music, though still essential, is now just one music product among many, connected to a different product: "the artist-brand"' (Meier 2017: 4), and for many listeners, video is *the* primary source of discovery and engagement with the artist brand.

References

Auslander, P. 2008. *Liveness: Performance in a Mediatized Culture*. New York: Routledge.
Beato, R. 2021. 'Is today's music just a laptop and a celebrity?' YouTube, 3 January. Video, 28:33. https://youtu.be/IO-2I8b3Ngo?t=308

Bemrose, B. 2019. 'Song length: The Spotify effect'. *PRS for Music*, 20 May. https://www.prsformusic.com/m-magazine/features/song-length-the-spotify-effect/

Bennett, J. 2012. 'Constraint, collaboration and creativity in popular songwriting teams'. In *The Act of Musical Composition: Studies in the Creative Process. SEMPRE Studies in the Psychology of Music*, edited by D. Collins, 139–69. Farnham: Ashgate.

Bimber, B. 1990. 'Karl Marx and the three faces of technological determinism'. *Social Studies of Science* 20, no. 2: 333–51. https://doi.org/10.1177/030631290020002006

Boon, H. 2022. 'Student and tutor life worlds and impossible standards in higher popular music education'. In *Purposes and Places of Popular Music*, edited by G. D. Smith and B. Powell, 261–66. Bristol: Intellect.

Brown, R. 2019. 'How music algorithms know your taste better than you do'. *The Spinoff*, 4 December. https://thespinoff.co.nz/partner/microsoft/04-12-2019/why-bossy-algorithms-make-the-best-dj/

Canham, N. 2021. *Preparing Musicians for Precarious Work*. New York: Routledge.

Carlyle, Thomas. 1993[1841]. *The Norman and Charlotte Strouse Edition of the Writings of Thomas Carlyle: On Heroes, Hero-Worship and the Heroic in History*. Berkeley: University of California Press.

Carter, G. 2018. 'Why Her Not Me'. Directed by James Slater. YouTube, 27 September. Music video, 3:53. https://youtu.be/dtWzfRc6uUs

CDEI. 2023. 'The impact of recommendation algorithms on the UK's music industry'. *Centre for Data Ethics and Innovation*, 9 February. https://www.gov.uk/government/publications/research-into-the-impact-of-streaming-services-algorithms-on-music-consumption/the-impact-of-recommendation-algorithms-on-the-uks-music-industry

Clancy, M. 2022. *Artificial Intelligence and Music Ecosystem*. Abingdon: Routledge.

CMA. 2022a. 'CMA clears Sony's acquisition of AWAL'. *Competition and Markets Authority*, 15 March. https://www.gov.uk/government/news/cma-clears-sony-s-acquisition-of-awal

CMA. 2022b. 'Music and streaming market study: Update paper'. *Competition and Markets Authority*, 26 July. https://assets.publishing.service.gov.uk/government/uploads/system/uploads/attachment_data/file/1093698/220726_Music_and_streaming_-_update_paper.pdf

Cole, T. 2012. 'The white-savior industrial complex'. *The Atlantic*, 21 March. https://www.theatlantic.com/international/archive/2012/03/the-white-savior-industrial-complex/254843/

Dafoe, A. 2015. 'On technological determinism: A typology, scope conditions, and a mechanism'. *Science, Technology, & Human Values* 40, no. 6: 1047–1076. https://doi.org/10.1177/0162243915579283

Daniels, M. 2022. 'The unlikely odds of making it big on TikTok'. *The Pudding*, June. https://pudding.cool/2022/07/tiktok-story/

Donahue, B. 2023. 'Universal Music asks streaming services to block AI companies from accessing its songs'. *Billboard*, 12 April. https://www.billboard.com/pro/universal-music-asks-spotify-apple-stop-ai-access-songs/#!

Dredge, S. 2023a. 'DIY and non major/Merlin music now accounts for a quarter of Spotify streams'. *Music Ally*, 3 February. https://musically.com/2023/02/03/diy-artists-now-account-for-a-quarter-of-spotifys-music-streams/

Dredge, S. 2023b. 'Misogyny in music: "The imposter syndrome is created by the systems"'. *Music Ally*, 8 February. https://musically.com/2023/02/08/misogyny-in-music-imposter-syndrome-systems/?utm_source=substack&utm_medium=email

Drillminister. 2020. 'Nouveau Riche'. YouTube, 28 February. Video, 3:09. https://youtu.be/SuowvWMGRbk

du Gay, P., S. Hall, L. Janes, H. Mackay, and K. Negus. 1997. *Doing Cultural Studies: The Story of the Sony Walkman*. London: Sage Publications.

Dylan, B. 2004. *Chronicles: Vol. 1*. London: Simon & Schuster.

Dylan, B. 2015. 'Subterranean Homesick Blues'. Directed by D. A. Pennebaker. YouTube, 9 October. Music video, 2:18. https://youtu.be/MGxjIBEZvx0

Edlom, J. 2020. 'Authenticity and digital popular music brands'. In *Popular Music, Technology, and the Changing Media Ecosystem: From Cassettes to Stream*, edited by T. Tofalvy and E. Barna, 129–48. London: Palgrave.

Everett, W. 1999. *The Beatles as Musicians: Revolver through the Anthology*. Oxford: Oxford University Press.

Fabbri, F. 1982. 'A theory of musical genres: Two applications'. In *Popular Music Perspectives*, edited by D. Horn and P. Tagg, 52–81. Göteborg and London: IASPM.

Fiske, J. 2010. *Television Culture*. London: Taylor & Francis Group.

Foster, Hal, ed. 1988. *Vision and Visuality*. Seattle, WA: Bay Press.

França, L. 2020. 'Bree Runway – What Do I Tell My Friends? (Tradução/Pt-Br)'. YouTube, 28 May. Music video, 3:25. https://youtu.be/skXV0HHz4fo

Freire, P. 2000. *Pedagogy of the Oppressed: 50th Anniversary Edition*. New York: Bloomsbury Academic.

Gross, S., and G. Musgrave. 2020. *Can Music Make You Sick? Measuring the Price of Musical Ambition*. London: University of Westminster Press.

Grossberg, L. 1993. 'The media economy of rock culture: Cinema, post-modernity and authenticity'. In *Sound and Vision: The Music Video Reader*, edited by S. Frith, A. Goodwin, and L. Grossberg, 159–79. London: Routledge.

Haydar, M. 2017. 'Hijabi (Wrap my Hijab)'. Directed by Tunde Olaniran and Mona Haydar. YouTube, 27 March. Music video, 3:43. https://youtu.be/XOX9O_kVPeo

Hennion, A. 1990. 'The production of success: An antimusicology of the pop song'. In *On Record*, edited by S. Frith and A. Goodwin, 184–206. London: Routledge.

Hesmondhalgh, D. 2022. 'Streaming's effects on music culture: Old anxieties and new simplifications'. *Cultural Sociology* 16, no. 1: 3–24. https://doi.org/10.1177/17499755211019974

Hesmondhalgh, D., and A. Saha. 2013. 'Race, ethnicity, and cultural production'. *Popular Communication* 11, no. 3: 179–95. https://doi.org/10.1080/15405702.2013.810068

Hesmondhalgh, D., R. Campos Valverde, D. Bondy Valdovinos Kaye, and Z. Li. 2023. 'The impact of algorithmically driven recommendation systems on music consumption and production – a literature review'. *Centre for Data Ethics and Innovation*. https://www.gov.uk/government/publications/research-into-the-impact-of-streaming-services-algorithms-on-music-consumption/the-impact-of-algorithmically-driven-recommendation-systems-on-music-consumption-and-production-a-literature-review

IFPI. 2019. 'IFPI Music Listening 2019'. *IFPI*. https://www.ifpi.org/wp-content/uploads/2020/07/Music-Listening-2019-1.pdf

IFPI. 2022. 'IFPI Music Listening 2022'. *IFPI*. https://www.ifpi.org/wp-content/uploads/2022/11/Engaging-with-Music-2022_full-report-1.pdf

Ingham, T. 2022. 'It's happened: 100,000 tracks are now being uploaded to streaming services like Spotify each day'. *Music Business Worldwide*, 2 October. https://www.musicbusinessworldwide.com/its-happened-100000-tracks-are-now-being-uploaded/

Isherwood, M. 2014. 'Sounding out songwriting: An investigation into the teaching and assessment of songwriting in higher education'. *Higher Education Academy Report*. https://www.researchgate.net/publication/312136002_Sounding_out_songwriting_An_investigation_into_the_teaching_and_assessment_of_songwriting_in_Higher_Education

Jakubowski, K. 2021. 'Why we're obsessed with music from our youth'. *The Conversation*, 11 February. https://theconversation.com/why-were-obsessed-with-music-from-our-youth-154864

Jones, M. 2012. *The Music Industries: From Conception to Consumption*. London: Palgrave Macmillan UK.

Katz, M. 2004. *Capturing Sound: How Technology Has Changed Music*. Berkeley: University of California Press.

Kline, R. R. 2015. 'Technological determinism'. In *International Encyclopedia of the Social & Behavioral Sciences*, edited by J. D. Wright, 2nd edn, 109–12. Amsterdam: Elsevier.

Knopper, S. 2019. 'How funk band Vulfpeck sold out Madison Square Garden without a manager or big label'. *Billboard*, 10 March. https://www.billboard.com/pro/how-vulfpeck-sold-out-madison-square-garden-without-manager-label/

Kyan. 2018. 'Lonely River'. Directed by Ukweli Roach & Kyan. 5 December. Music video, 3:26. https://youtu.be/dE1o9AnT7No

Lamere, P. 2014. 'The Skip'. *Music Machinery*, 2 May. http://musicmachinery.com/2014/05/02/the-skip/

Lipshutz, J. 2023. 'Daniel Ek on Spotify's next step: It's a chance for artists to "build connection"'. *Billboard*, 8 March. https://www.billboard.com/pro/daniel-ek-interview-spotify-redesign-new-artists-fans/

MacMillan, J. 2016. 'DAVE GROHL "DON'T BORE US! GET TO THE CHORUS!"' YouTube, 25 September. Video, 2:46. https://www.youtube.com/watch?v=eQV95ehUU4s

Mashrou' Leila. 2019. 'Cavalry'. 11 June. Music video, 3:26. https://youtu.be/2L_alOo4G3s

Meier, L. M. 2017. *Popular Music as Promotion: Music and Branding in the Digital Age*. Cambridge: Polity Press.

Mirzoeff, N. 2006. 'On visuality'. *Journal of Visual Culture* 5, no. 1: 53–79. https://doi.org/10.1177/1470412906062285

Montecchio, N., P. Roy, and F. Pachet. 2020. 'The skipping behavior of users of music streaming services and its relation to musical structure'. *PLoS ONE* 15, no. 9: e0239418. https://doi.org/10.1371/journal.pone.0239418

Moore, A. F. 2001. *Rock, the Primary Text: Developing a Musicology of Rock*. 2nd edn. Burlington, VT: Ashgate.

Mulligan, M. 2021a. '"Middle class" artists need niche, not scale'. *Music Industry Blog*, 17 September. https://musicindustryblog.wordpress.com/2021/09/17/middle-class-artists-need-niche-not-scale/

Mulligan, M. 2021b. 'The paradox of small'. *Music Industry Blog*, 18 June. https://musicindustryblog.wordpress.com/2021/06/18/the-paradox-of-small/

Music Week. 2021a. 'Nathan Evans unveils his plan to turn sea shanty success into pop stardom'. *Music Week*, 25 June. https://www.musicweek.com/talent/read/nathan-evans-unveils-his-plan-to-turn-sea-shanty-success-into-pop-stardom/083574

Music Week. 2021b. 'Little Simz on life outside the major label system'. *Music Week*, 7 September. https://www.musicweek.com/talent/read/little-simz-on-life-outside-the-major-label-system/084079

Nemer, D. 2022. *Technology of the Oppressed: Inequity and the Digital Mundane in Favelas of Brazil*. Massachusetts: MIT Press.

Nines. 2020. 'Crabs In A Bucket'. Directed by Nines and Charlie Di Placido. 27 August. Video, 27:17. https://youtu.be/nYNmS305_VQ

Nooshin, L. 2009. 'Prelude: Power and the play of music'. In *Music and the Play of Power in the Middle East, North Africa and Central Asia*, edited by L. Nooshin, 1–31. Surrey: Ashgate.

Ocean, D. 2016. 'Me Rehúso'. 18 September. Music video, 3:25. https://youtu.be/aDCcLQto5BM

PacmanTV. 2020. 'Roadworks: Beyond the Road (Documentary) | @PacmanTV'. YouTube, 5 January. Video, 12:49. https://youtu.be/OGF_WtV1Ki8

Parks, A. 2020. 'Black Dog'. 23 June. Music video, 3:41. https://youtu.be/CEKXONzXrE0

Pelly, L. 2018. 'Streambait pop'. *The Baffler*, 11 December. https://thebaffler.com/downstream/streambait-pop-pelly

Percival, J. M. 2011. 'Music radio and the record industry: Songs, sounds, and power'. *Popular Music and Society* 34, no. 4: 455–73. https://doi.org/10.1080/03007766.2011.601598

Peters, M. 2020a. 'Daydreams'. 27 March. Music video, 3:07. https://youtu.be/5Jm7tdhz37s

Peters, M. 2020b. 'The List'. 19 May. Music video, 3:24. https://youtu.be/Is7T3ebwGxM

Rapman. 2018. 'Shiro's Story'. Directed by Andrew Onwubolu, 8 April. Video, 10:15. https://youtu.be/H_6ZJrg-E3Q

Rogers, H. 2023. '"Welcome to your world": YouTube and the reconfiguration of music's gatekeepers'. In *YouTube and Music Online Culture and Everyday Life*, edited by H. Rogers, J. Freitas, and J. F. Porfírio, 1–38. London: Bloomsbury Academic.

Runway, B. 2017. 'Bree Runway – What Do I Tell My Friends?'. Directed by Fred Rowson. 21 September. Music video, 4:24. https://youtu.be/qL24u7qyyiw

RunwayML. 2023. 'Everything you need to make anything you want'. https://runwayml.com/

Salieu, P. 2020. 'B***k'. Directed by Meeks and Frost. 20 October. Music video, 1:54. https://youtu.be/UFNtxlEKgFM

Savage, M. 2021. 'Classic bands accused of crowding out new music on streaming services'. *BBC News*, 19 January. https://www.bbc.co.uk/news/entertainment-arts-55717156

Seabrook, J. 2015. *The Song Machine: How to Make a Hit*. London: Jonathan Cape.

Strachan, R. 2020. *Sonic Technologies: Popular Music, Digital Culture and the Creative Process*. London: Bloomsbury Academic.

Straw, W. 1993. 'Popular music and post-modernism in the 1980s'. In *Sound and Vision: The Music Video Reader*, edited by S. Frith, A. Goodwin, and L. Grossberg, 2–17. London: Routledge.
Sumanac-Johnson, D. 2019. 'Don't bore us, get to the chorus? How streaming is changing songs'. *CBC*, 9 February. https://www.cbc.ca/news/entertainment/streaming-songs-changes-1.5002748
Taliable. 2020. 'Muzzled Butterfly'. Directed by z_bleach and Taliable. 8 October. Music video, 2:27. https://youtu.be/jEdrLk969oM
Taylor, D. 2009. 'Normativity and normalization'. *Foucault Studies* 7: 45–63. https://doi.org/10.22439/fs.v0i7.2636
Théberge, P. 2001. '"Plugged in": Technology and popular music'. In *The Cambridge Companion to Pop and Rock*, edited by S. Frith, W. Straw, and J. Street, 1–25. Cambridge: Cambridge University Press.
The Weeknd, 2011. 'High For This'. 20 March. Music video, 4:14. https://youtu.be/sX9DgavXiN4
Tiffany, K. 2018. 'You can now play with Spotify's recommendation algorithm in your browser'. *The Verge*, 5 February. https://www.theverge.com/tldr/2018/2/5/16974194/spotify-recommendation-algorithm-playlist-hack-nelson
Turkel, B. 2020. 'Don't Bore Us. Get to the Chorus'. *Linked In*, 1 July. https://www.linkedin.com/pulse/dont-bore-us-get-chorus-bruce-turkel/
Vulf. 2019. 'Vulfpeck Live at Madison Square Garden'. 19 December. Music video, 1:43:57. https://youtu.be/rv4wf7bzfFE
Wall, T. 2003. *Studying Popular Music Culture*. London: Hodder & Stoughton Educational.
Whack, T. 2018. 'Whack World'. Directed by Thibaut Duverneix. 30 May. Music video, 15:47. https://youtu.be/EOTebhPy04g
Willis, P. 1990. 'The Golden Age'. In *On Record: Rock, Pop, and the Written Word*, edited by Simon Frith and Andrew Goodwin, 35–45. London: Routledge.
Winner, L. 1978. *Autonomous Technology: Technics-out-of-Control as a Theme in Political Thought*. Massachusetts: MIT Press.
Zeger, E. 2020. 'Alt rock by algorithm'. *Frieze*, 28 August. https://www.frieze.com/article/alt-rock-algorithm
Zuboff, S. 2019. *The Age of Surveillance Capitalism*. London: Profile Books.

Author biography

Hussein Boon is a principal lecturer at the University of Westminster and member of the Black Music Research Unit. His teaching areas include music production, performance technologies, songwriting, modular synthesis, live coding, music business and Artificial Intelligence. He was part of the team that established Rockschool's popular music exams and has worked for various artists, including Beats International, Billy Ocean and De La Soul. His recent publications include using shift registers for semi-improvised songwriting, several short fiction stories about AI and music, reimagining the DAW as a design tool, and the role of the anti-aesthetic in music production education.

7 Anyone Can be a Musician: Art School Pedagogy and the Rise of the Non-Musician

Simon Strange

> I'm an anti-musician. I don't think the craft of music is relevant to the art of music. (Eno, in Davy 1975)

> [P]unk was the biggest influence at the time, and with our musical abilities, what other options did we have? I certainly couldn't say I was a musician. (Grey, in Neate 2008: 24)

Introduction

Conceptually, anyone can be a musician – this was a critical position within punk (Laing 1985; Savage 1991; Albertine 2014), post punk (Reynolds 2005) and new wave (Cateforis 2011) popular music genres which developed from the mid-1970s. In this chapter, I argue that this position of non-musicianship connected to radical UK art school pedagogy from the 1960s and 70s, infusing those who studied and were indirectly connected to an art education ethos, where a concentration on the artistic self – in addition to philosophies of attitude and experimentation – were valued over technique.

Twentieth-century art education reflected changing art worlds, where visual replication of the romantic period was replaced by conceptually developed work, facilitating 'high' and 'low' art to become diffused through postmodern ideals. The idea of what it meant to be an artist became deconstructed, at a point where art and popular music were being redefined. Originating from bands such as the Velvet Underground and Roxy Music, the non-musician was prominent in UK socio-cultural worlds through the 1970s, leading to an array of music genres thereafter including hip hop, jungle, and indie for example (Strange 2022). I suggest that lessons can be learnt from art pedagogy for current higher popular music education (HPME) and creative exploration, to help address what Mark Fisher (2018: 321) defined as a period of cultural deceleration. His concept of popular modernism called for a re-examination related to original post-punk ideals infused by an art school aesthetic. For this I concentrate on the non-musician.

UK art education consisted of fine art and design, adding a necessary quotient of cultural and historical studies through the 1960 Coldstream Report. A conundrum existed in that art colleges were given stricter adherences for new degree level DipAD but a level of autonomy in pedagogical processes. Many courses retained traditional elements, but experimental courses emerged in some UK art schools (such as Newcastle, Leeds, Hornsey, and Ipswich for example) which concentrated on non-hierarchical, non-linear concepts such as cybernetics (Cybernetic Serendipity 1968) alongside philosophies of the Situationist International and Art and Language movements. Art school musicians often explored conceptual, process-led, and experimental practices (exemplified through the extraordinary work of the Portsmouth Sinfonia), providing an example of art and music combining to redefine assumptions. The impact of the non-musician as an individual artist and part of a self-evolving scene, or scenius (Eno 1996), is explored. Utilizing a connected ethos following a postmodern approach, I undertook art pedagogical research via free-flowing interviews, co-creating meaning with participants who intersected between art college and popular music. Interviewees included an array of key people who crossed the artistic divide, including Roy Ascott, Brian Eno, Gavin Bryars, Dexter Dalwood, Stephen Mallinder (Cabaret Voltaire), Lester Square (the Monochrome Set), Gina Birch and Ana da Silva (the Raincoats), Keith Levene (PiL), Gaye Black (the Adverts), and Bill Drummond (the KLF).

Conceptual Art – Popular Music

Some art schools and art worlds were aligned through the ideals of postmodernism and conceptual art, which became prominent in the 1960s and 70s (Huyssen 1984; Best and Kellner 1997). Art concentrated on something greater than just moving paint across a canvas, but instead related to thought processes and an aesthetic of living, style and fashion becoming prominent in some of the more radical art courses. Artistic processes were re-evaluated as conceptual development held greater prominence than learning traditional technique (Osborne 2002), and barriers between artforms faded. Sensing the changing scene, Brian Eno (interview with author, December 2017) highlighted how art education could provide a foundation for multi-subject art explorations, stating:

> If having ideas is being an artist then I can have ideas about music, just as I can about film, or about sculpture or anything else. Suddenly it seemed that this new idea that we could move from one

art form to another was completely possible; if it wasn't craft based, if it wasn't dependent upon years of experience of actually making something, then hey why shouldn't I be able to do it.

Conceptual and eclectic ideals seeped into popular music with an artistic aesthetic. Examples included Bill Drummond of the KLF who devoured philosophies brought forward by Gavin Bryars at the Liverpool College of Art, coexisting alongside the revivalist Ska/RnB sounds of Prince Buster. Gina Birch and Ana da Silva's art education collided with the influences of the Velvet Underground and conceptual art into post-punk band The Raincoats, producing an innovative sonic.

Postmodern blurring of boundaries between the perceiver and creator defines conceptual ideals and can be related to Christopher Small's (1998) *Musicking* or Eno's (1996) *scenius*, as collective expression is more than just the creation of a product but an assimilation of lived lives, where everyone can be an artist.

The Roadmap for Art School Connections with Non-musicianship

Breaking open traditional art education, UK art school philosophies led from ideas forged at the Bauhaus, through Black Mountain College to the New York School of artists and musicians. Within Black Mountain, tutor John Cage and student Robert Rauschenberg explored similar avenues of expression towards silence and white paintings, respectively (Jones 1993; Molesworth 2015). Simple ideas, exemplified by Eric Satie's Furniture Music and formulated in Cage's silent piece, 4'33', elucidated a reimagining of musical creation in line with conceptual ideas in art, where thought processes took precedence, and the perceiver became embedded in the art piece.

Philosophies incubated in the New York School led to conceptual ideas and new forms of music which flowed through the Cage-inspired avant-garde Fluxus movement. Interconnections between visual and auditory creatives flourished, excited by emerging concepts which challenged art forms, exemplified through the abstract expressionism of Jackson Pollock and the indeterminate music of Morton Feldman. The utilization of graphic scores or paint being thrown on a canvas upset traditional Western conceptions, breaking open processes of creation and the role of the artist. It was the minimal compositions of US composers Philip Glass, La Monte Young, Steve Reich, and Terry Riley alongside Pauline Oliveros and Alison Knowles which cemented conceptual ideals into popular music making, where technical musicianship was less of a necessity. Conclusively, the Velvet Underground brought Minimalist ideas and an artistic aesthetic, defining the Duchamp-Cage-Warhol axis where anyone could be an artist (or a musician).

Leading from Marcel Duchamp's readymade art pieces to the Xerox photocopier, ideas and technological advancement brought self-sufficiency to the fore: the everyday could be both utilized and reproduced. The art school-infused, playful, postmodern-style amateurism of the music and DIY industry around punk was a feature for Laing (1985), and conceptual, personal, and innovative methods became central to artistic creation. For art students, popular music was an industry where they could see a commercial space for their artistic endeavours whilst maintaining creative experimentation, as visual genres including Dada, Futurism, and Surrealism influenced an intersection between art and life.

Musicians within emerging popular music genres of the mid-1970s were unconstrained by technical abilities, embracing the interchangeability of performers and audience due to a reduction in the idea of the creative genius (Reynolds 2005: 114; Allen in Young 2006: 93), and a redefining of what it meant to be an artist. UK schools ignored popular music in their curriculum until the late 1960s and, even then, the pedagogical processes relied on classical music concepts, featuring scores and an exact replication of the composer's artistic direction. Extolling individualism, educationalist Lucy Green (2001) highlighted that popular musicians learned in a less formalized manner, so art schools were a natural preserve, encouraging self-direction of skills through listening and mimicking. Aspiring popular musicians explored the craft by playing along to records, jamming with friends, experimenting with instruments, vocals and lyric writing, as informal learning practices leant a correlation to concepts apparent within experimental art pedagogy, where traditional technique was eschewed.

Unlearning

Unlearning as a pedagogical philosophy relates to the non-musician, introducing ideas of freedom, concentrating on experimental creative processes unencumbered by previous education. Originating from Johannes Itten on the introductory Bauhaus *Vorkurs* before becoming a key element in some of the more radical UK art schools in the 1960s and 70s, unlearning freed students from following the representative romantic tradition of the visual artist. In reference, Bauhaus director Walter Gropius stated that,

> [E]very new student arrives encumbered with a mass of accumulated information which he (*sic*) must abandon before he can achieve perception and knowledge that are really his own... The

preliminary course concerns the students' whole personality since it seeks to liberate. (quoted in Goldstein 1996: 263)

Unlearning inherently connects to artists' interests in child art (Singerman 1999: 106) and the punk ethos of inhibition and returning to year zero. Bauhaus masters, Kandinsky and Klee, explored the phenomenon, discovering creative advantages in an earlier time or state before the burden of the adult mind, concentrating on the 'inner tone' of child-based art (Kandinsky quoted in Fineberg 1998: 87). Similarities existed with the utilization of 'child-like' practices (Johnstone 1941) employed at the London Central School as a way of facilitating students to remain in their original creative state, with education 'not an end but a process'; phrases such as 'blank state' and 'tabula rasa' defined the purity of a child's response to early education (Westley in Llewellyn et al. 2015: 28). Musically, ethnomusicologist John Blacking discovered an inherent creativity within humans when researching the Venda people of South Africa, equating to a creative naturalness (Spitzer 2021).

The first year of UK fine art courses in the 1960s and 70s was often devoted to a reconditioning of 'previous training and experience' (Frith and Horne 1987: 28); a year zero in art found equivalence in the reboot of popular music as assumed by punk, exemplified in *The Blank Generation*, the name of Richard Hell and the Voidoids' first album or the 1976 film of New York new wave punks.

Experimental Pedagogy

Not all UK art colleges were conceptually or politically inclined, but some of the most well-known which embraced the concept of unlearning were *The Locked Room* (St Martin's), *Art Theory* (Coventry), *The White Room* (Reading), and *The Groundcourse* (Ipswich), in particular.

Originating at Ealing (1961–64) and then Ipswich (1964–67), Roy Ascott's *Groundcourse* focused on philosophies and practices of unlearning achieved by disorientation, challenging, and confusing students through explorations into human behaviour (Scoates 2013: 23), experimenting with the 'concept of power, the will to shape and change' (Ascott in Allen 2011: 51). Ascott's pedagogy focused on the discovery of an artist's place within the world, with Eno (interview with author, December 2017) confirming that 'part of the deal was that you were what you believed in'. The use of problem-solving and personality games, employed on the *Groundcourse*, intrigued Eno. 'So that was really, really interesting, this idea that you are not a fixed thing, you can change things about yourself, you can see what it is like to be somebody else'. Ascott (interview with author, October 2017) also remarked, 'I try to get them to understand that they aren't who they think they are', but communal constructs, akin to existing within a cybernetic organism.

Meanwhile at St Martin's School of Art, *The Locked Room* or *'A' Course* (1969) supported first-year students to unlearn habits by containing a group in a white room, providing random materials without instruction for eight hours per day, in silence, and bereft of time details. The aim was to reduce 'habitual practice. They were trained to see with un-habitual eyes' (Westley 2007; Tickner 2008: 9), putting them in a position of 'existence before essence' (Kardia in Westley 2007). Containing a similar emphasis and influenced by her Newcastle Fine Art education, Rita Donagh (1970) veered away from the traditional life room focus in developing the *White Room* (Westley in Llewellyn et al. 2015: 54); encouraged by the avant-garde, her teaching was more closely linked to popular music than the University of Reading's own music department (Bracewell 2007). Consisting of marked grids, the workspace changed into a performance area over the course of a few weeks, exhibiting the possible multifaceted nature of an art studio reflecting art, life, and ideas of collaboration (Bracewell 2007: 260). Pedagogy included blindfolded life drawing, with the model being a dynamic central element, inspiring students such as The Moodies, a performance art glam music group who preceded iconic punk group The Slits (Bracewell 2007: 219).

Worlds revolved around key art courses, in subcultural milieu, within specific times and places, relating to the concept of scenius – a self-evolving eco-system or collective genius (Eno 1996). The 1960s and 70s were a certain point in time where students embraced experimental concepts and engaged with political and philosophical theorizing. A self-evolving cybernetic horizontal non-hierarchical manifestation existed, where the group aesthetic was key to break through conditioning. Likewise, K-Punk (Fisher 2018) recognized interconnections between the producers of music and their audience as a self-evolving 'scenius' (a term Eno (1996) coined to connect the concept of genius through group collaborations rather than individual endeavour), existing through the post-punk era (and subsequent dance music genres).

Situationist International/Art and Language

Breaking connections with traditional concepts of creativity were the Situationist International and Art and Language movements, whose revolutionary ideas found a space in art pedagogy, connecting to the mainstream through popular music. Interactions with their philosophies within some art departments in the 1970s supported the generation of scenii (pl), with trainee artists and popular musicians connecting through socio-political commonalities.

The ethos of the Situationist International reflected a realignment of previously assumed hierarchies or concepts. These included constructing situations which maximized creative play; 'detournement', featuring the reconfiguring and rerouting of materials to create new meaning; to be unemployed; critiquing the 'society of the spectacle', based on changing the perceptions of consumer culture; and recommending offensive, disruptive behaviour, aimed at the bourgeoisie (Walker 1987: 120; Knabb 2006; Gorman et al. 2015). Educator T. J. Clarke encouraged Leeds University students towards deconstruction (Dettmar 2014), whilst punk managers Malcolm McLaren and Bernie Rhodes utilized Situationist ideals in the visual and auditory development of the Sex Pistols and The Clash (Gilbert 2009), respectively. McLaren, like Jeff Nuttall at Leeds Polytechnic (Charnley 2015), believed in deconstructing artforms, that all forms of dullness should be avoided, calling art schools the 'islands of the dispossessed', and stressing that 'unemployment should be embraced as liberation; kids should dress up, fuck, steal and have fun' (Rambali in Worley 2017: 99). An equivalent emancipatory philosophy suggested by Fisher (2014), was previously supported by pop artist Richard Hamilton (1982: 180; Frith and Horne 1987: 36) and Eno (BBC Radio 6 Music, 2015), directing artistic needs for time and space without financial pressure.

The Art and Language movement was formulated towards the end of the 1960s, with the main protagonists based at Leeds (Polytechnic and University), Coventry, Nottingham, and Watford art departments. The aims of the group were summarized by Harrison (1991: 14) as combining intellect and practice featuring 'expression and spontaneity not as existential modes but as conventions', influenced by avant-garde philosophies, 'testing the mainstream' (Harrison 1991: 20). Art and Language interconnected artistic mediums concentrated on language or 'conversations' (Osborne 2002: 33), with philosophies centred on the critique of art and a blurring of artistic process boundaries (Crippa in Llewellyn et al. 2015: 137). Most directly, the Coventry-based *Art Theory* course (1969–71) contained a radical nature taught through the group's philosophies (Salaman 2015: 170), often shocking and confusing students as well as governing bodies, resulting in quite short-lived programmes (Harrison 1991; Salaman 2015: 166).

New wave and post-punk bands such as Gang of Four and Talking Heads were directed by the experimental and radical nature of the Art and Language movement through their art education (Reynolds 2005; Steenstra 2010). 'Gang of Four thrived on friction', which was reflected in the angular and stark nature of their music, especially within Gill's guitar sound (Reynolds

2005: 113; Dooley 2018), including an undercurrent that was more internal and theoretical than punk. Fellow Leeds graduates, The Mekons, explored 'a kind of meta-rock, radically self-critical and vigilant' arena (Reynolds 2005: 112). Personalized and anti-rock minimalist ideals inhabited post punk (Laing 1985: 128), while Byrne (2013) aimed to strip elements away and generate a Minimalist ethos in the music of Talking Heads. The band's Rhodes Island School of Design education informed 'a performance style defined by negatives' – there were no guitar solos, 'no rock moves or poses, no pomp or drama, no rock hair, no rock lights, no rehearsed stage patter ... [T]he lyrics too were stripped bare' (46).

Simplicity to Complexity

Non-musicianship centred on deconstructing traditional ideas, often through embracing Minimalist ideals. Bryars (interview with author, November 2017), for example, was searching for creative processes which were 'technically simple, conceptually very clean', while Eno (interview with author, December 2017) stated that, 'simplicity for me is the magic'.

At home in his Notting Hill studio, Eno (interview with author, December 2017) demonstrated the interaction between a simple idea and resultant complexity using a small double pendulum model. Gently manipulating one arm resulted in an unlimited variety of movement in the conjoining one, reflecting 'a phase shift, a complete step difference' evident in cybernetics and non-linear processes. Likewise, Eno's *Ambient 1: Music for Airports* provides an auditory cybernetic organism, transporting the listener through self-propelled randomized piano and bell toned resonance, generating kinetic energy which transfers from one note left hanging in reverberant space, informing the timbre and direction of the next.

In a more abrasive form, post-punk band Wire were influenced by Eno's ethos of non-musicianship and the minimalist elements of the avant-garde, within a guitar shredding viscerality. Singer Newman mentioned how on his first day at art college one of his tutors played *Piano Phase* by Reich, which for him connected composers Riley, Cale, and Eno (Neate 2008: 19). Wire also explored art-based philosophies reflected in the band's shortened song lengths, pursuit of the new, Dada-influenced random lyric writing, and even their minimal band name itself (Reynolds 2005: 143). Like US art graduates Devo, whose first album was produced featuring Eno's fluid cybernetic process of 'interlocking parts', their acknowledged aim was to create music that was anti-rock, with minimalism replacing any attempt at 'a wall of sound' (Cateforis 2011: 41). A minimalist aesthetic provides opportunities for engagement from both less technically inclined musicians and the audience, enhanced through the dawning of innovative technologies.

Technology and the Non-musician

Simplicity of concept was possible with the emergent technology of the twentieth century, supporting the development of new art forms, and providing the possibility for artists to reduce their impact on the artistic process (Cage 1961; Reichardt 1968; Shanken 2015). Modern technology was in early evidence from artists like Malevich (Groys 2018: 101) and Moholy-Nagy (Kostelanetz 1970), who preceded Cage as the first proponent of turntablism (Cox and Warner 2017: 483). Moholy-Nagy had previously explored the new dimensional potential of photography, reducing the provision of painted representation and encouraging explorations into cut-up techniques. For the popular musician 'it was recording technology itself that gave them artistic status' as new technologies provided an opportunity for musicians to reconfigure and review their work (Frith and Horne 1987: 172). The advent of tape allowed explorations into audio collage or cut ups (Nyman 1999), finally matching artists' use of film. Crossing post punk and new wave divides, Cabaret Voltaire were inspired by cut-up techniques, using technology to bypass previous technical music requirements and create music that was strident and electronic; as Stephen Mallinder noted, they 'weren't interested in learning music but just wanted to use these tools to create unusual sounds'. Cabaret Voltaire acquired industrial-sized tape machines from secondhand shops, which, according to Mallinder, 'allow[ed] ordinary people to make music in whatever way, which democratised things and was really a precursor to punk' (Mallinder 2018).

Ascott introduced cybernetic and systems-based principles into art education (Shanken in Ascott 2003: 1), excited by modern technologies and thought processes (Shanken 2015: 66). These ideals filtered into the mainstream, as the *Cybernetic Serendipity* exhibition at the ICA in 1968 signalled a shift in the interactions between technology and art, combining automated processes, computers, and music (Reichardt 1968). Video and film were utilized by some art departments where an increased portability, reduced price and reproductive potential, redefined creative processes (Strand 1987; Craig-Martin 2015: 67; Banks and Oakley 2016: 46).

Eno (interview with author, December 2017) amplified the importance of technology in connecting art schools with popular music, utilizing early tape machines at Winchester School of Art and the EMS synth in Roxy Music.

> You have to think that this was a particular time for music and first of all there was a whole new medium: that was electronics, which

were just starting to appear, and it was a medium for which nobody knew the rules, least of all musicians.

It was the working musicians of the time, within established traditions, who had a one-dimensional view of music. Popular musicians started to embrace electronic effects and overdubbing recording techniques whilst classical musicians tended to remain in their cloistered environs. Contrarily, although some art schools embraced new technologies, Eno (interview with author, December 2017) believed that not many artists were as forward-thinking, exclaiming: 'I just think it is insane that most of the art world didn't really pick up on the understanding of what a revolution that was; to have a communitarian art form that was technologically very, very savvy'. A couple of art colleges notably embraced music technology. At Hornsey, Lester Square noted the musical nature of the cohort fed by the light/sound workshop while Watford contained a bespoke studio, rehearsal spaces, and a Ferrograph tape machine, fired up to record the Portsmouth Sinfonia and post-punk band Wire, amongst others (Callomon, interview with author, February 2021).

Recording technology facilitated placing the medium of sound in a space rather than time dimension as defined by Eno, utilized within dub production techniques and areas such as Pauline Oliveros' Deep Listening (Von Gunden 1980). Replicating art, the canvas is confined within vertical and horizontal elements, whilst the freely suspended reliefs of Victor Pasmore (1963) exemplified possibilities to view the artwork from multiple dimensions. Employing the same concept (transmitted from Pasmore through to Ascott), Eno (1996; interview with author, December 2017) explored process-centred simplicity within his work, allowing ambient music pieces to evolve organically or highlighting the spaciousness in his contrasting work with bands such as Talking Heads, U2, and more recently the indie collective Super Organism. The focus was upon granular simplicity, concentrating on the space between the notes and effect-based ambience, such as reverb tails or delay timings. Using the studio as a compositional tool, Eno (1979) developed constantly evolving organic sounds, most notably in the regenerating *Reflections* album from 2017.

Sonic palettes unfurled through the development of production techniques. Art-infused bands such as the Velvet Underground, Talking Heads, Wire, and Gang of Four explored conceptual ideas featuring a minimalist aesthetic (Hegarty 2007). As the new wave scene emerged into the 1980s, production refinement brought these spaces into sharper focus. Examples include the work of producer Martin Rushent, well-known for working with the Human League, embracing silence and space in music (Reynolds 2005: 332), specifically the remixed League Unlimited Orchestra release, where reverb and delay are accentuated instead of the original vocal-led tracks. Producers Martin Hammett with Joy Division and Trevor Horn redefining Frankie Goes to Hollywood and the Art of Noise, showed similar inclinations and a reimagining of the medium where production was the spectacle. Joy Division's *Atmosphere* features a dronal spaciousness with ambience replicating the lyrics' message ('walk in silence'). Instruments are placed in their own distinct space, provided by directional panning and spatial placement, whilst the use of tom drums rather than the whole drum kit provides depth and a dark aesthetic. Bass and guitar provide linear motifs with occasional chords left to chime and glistening bells cascade, parts that were simple to play but resonated with a taut visual and sonic depth.

The Worst Orchestra in the World

Originating as an art school scenius, the Portsmouth Sinfonia (1973) aimed to play as expertly as possible. Containing a fluid cohort of around thirty lapsed or uncommitted classical musicians, the results were in part stunningly discordant with moments of extreme beauty, and buckets of humour. Formulated by Bryars, members included Eno on clarinet, flute-playing fellow interviewee Clive Langer from Deaf School, in addition to avant-garde composer Michael Nyman on Cello. They recorded and released works with Eno's support, so the Sinfonia had a wider impact than would normally have been the case.

The random nature and mistakes of the Sinfonia reflected an art school aesthetic, through childlike play in addition to a punk and DIY attitude. Organic motion was one feature which artistic bands like The Velvets or The Raincoats explored (Pelly 2017), amid a realization that exact timing wasn't necessary, something also reflected in the imperfections of 1980s music technology (the Akai MPC sampler, Roland TR808 drum machine, or the Atari 1040 computer, for example). Renowned hip hop producer J Dilla (Charnas 2022) later added perfection to imperfection in a slew of beats whose out-of-kilter timings revolutionized contemporary popular music. Previously for the Sinfonia, by pushing the boundaries of preconceived concepts of the orchestra it was possible to randomize, as Langer recalled:

> Sometimes musically, it also really worked: it was a bit like being on a roller coaster instead of being on a drag track. The music was being pushed and pulled in tempo and in pitch, which at times sounded really good.

Experimental and conceptual artistic philosophies were evident in the pedagogy at Portsmouth, with Bryars (interview with author, November 2017) recollecting: 'We did work on experimental pieces that had text notation or instructions so they could develop ideas and create things'. The conceptual nature of his course attracted more experimentally focused students, who were interested in exploring the latest ideas within art. This seemed inevitable for Bryars as '[I]n a way, it was always the case the freer students would gravitate towards us as they wouldn't get such a historically informed thing like why aren't you doing painting, that kind of stuff'.

As part of the Beethoven Bicentenary event held by the Scratch Orchestra in 1970, the Portsmouth Sinfonia displayed art education influences based on rearranging hierarchical ideas of the orchestra, in an even more dramatic and irreverent manner. As Bryars (interview with author, November 2017) recollects:

> Some very curious things were done there: John White did the complete piano sonatas on the tuba; basically he played the first and last note of every one so it was an index. Someone else played the Diabelli variations inside a big glass bubble, and 4 double basses played the slow movement from the string quartet. The Sinfonia played Beethoven's 5th, well at least bits we recognised we played, so it was about 5 minutes long.

Reconceptualizing music as defined by the Portsmouth Sinfonia reflected concepts of the Situationists, whilst the filing system signified above mirrored the artistic direction taken by the Art and Language exhibit *index 01*, *Documenta 5* (Osborne 2002: 34).

Non-musicianship in Punk, Post Punk and New Wave

Many art college and popular music connections devolved from an aesthetic awareness related to an eclectic mix of sonics and anti-rock aesthetic (Bracewell 2007; Frith and Horne 1987; Walker 1987; Reynolds 2005). Roxy Music exhibited 'pop music, astonishingly, more shaped by Duchamp than Bo Diddley' (Fisher 2018: 280). Punk also contained links to conceptual art (Marcus 2011) and extra non-musicianship (White 2011: 189); Wire arrived unskilled before improving and developing those 'skills or approaches to being in a situation where you don't know what the fuck's going on and you don't know what to do' (Lewis in Neate 2008: 73).

As singer Newman suggested: they 'were doing fucking art. Punk was art. It was all art' (Reynolds 2005: 129). Public Image Limited (PiL) guitarist Keith Levene (interview with author, March 2018) injected an art school spirit, mentoring The Slits' Viv Albertine's piercing sonic who also connected to Dada and Surrealist philosophies instilled through her history of art studies at Chelsea College of Art and Design. Levene openly sought non-musicianship so when hitting 'a wrong note, he'd immediately repeat the error to see if the wrongness could become a new kind of rightness' (Reynolds 2005: 8). Levene challenged musical preconceptions as 'the idea was to break through conditioning' (ibid.). Reflecting cybernetic ideals of systemized simplicity, The Slits producer Dennis Bovell worked to contain their sound (Reynolds 2005: 80), a role he had also undertaken with The Pop Group (Reynolds 2005: 78).

Emerging from Leeds University, the Gang of Four experimented with playing fewer notes (Langford in Dooley 2018: 80) in reverence to the spatial sounds of dub and reggae. Neighbours Scritti Politti often consisted of non-musicians, a collective concentrating on Art and Language and other artistic review techniques: contextualizing and critiquing. As Reynolds (2005) noted about the group's philosophies of creative practice, 'to choose one path implicitly entailed repudiating others, so why not be explicit and (self-)conscious about the process' (Reynolds 2005: 199). Discussing violinist Vicky Aspinall, The Raincoats' Gina Birch (interview with author, June 2018) recounted: 'We used to say to her, oh we like that noise when you drop the bow on the strings, that's a really good noise. All those noises she would have probably been trained out of from early childhood'. Dexter Dalwood likewise avoided constraints through a lack of technical knowledge, recalling an audition for New Wave band Squeeze: Jools Holland said to me, 'let's do a funk jam in D. It was at that moment I thought, I am going to go to art school. I didn't really know what he meant' (interview with author, May 2018).

Higher Popular Music Education (HPME)

It is key to ask whether art school pedagogy and the connected concept of non-musicianship can be translated to contemporary music worlds. HPME can be a lifeline for creatives from a range of socio-cultural backgrounds, breaking through barriers imposed by grades or qualifications, where an interest and dedication to music can provide an avenue into academic advancement. The political landscape of higher education in the UK contains embedded neoliberalism; art school pedagogical elements of attitude, trust, daring, exploration, and invention can help aspiring creatives break through glass ceilings. Reflecting on British historical periods such as the Coldstream influenced 1960s and New Labour in the late 1990s provides templates where creativity was fostered by government structures, tracing beacons of light for future higher education generations.

The twenty-first-century music market is a different animal to that which existed in the second half of the 1900s. Is it possible to translate the concept of the non-musician into this time and place? Saturation of the popular music market through an expanded DIY aesthetic has provided an emancipated but unregulated morass, which seems to both favour and hinder the expressive non-musician. UK DJ John Peel encouraged the non-musician, acting as a gatekeeper with an eclectic set of keys. As Tom Robinson (2022) suggests, Peel only needed to please himself 'rather than be fair and balanced', an anarchic attitude reflected in the variety of music which filtered through. In Peel, the non-musician had a champion with influence, which is sadly lacking in the current mainstream. HPME is effective in delivering well-rehearsed technical musicians with a deep knowledge of their market, developing a generation of savvy, well-intentioned, often bland derivative musicians. Consider the impact of a seemingly anarchic band like Idles from Bristol, UK, who in the 1970s would have been considered punk lite.

The art school dance continues for the non-musician. Brian Eno's beautiful, immersive electronic soundscapes or Gina Birch's quirky angst remain highlights of the current music and arts scene, whilst art school renegades Lester Square and Helen Reddington remain active within art, music, film, and activist arenas, continuing the non-musicians' statement of intent. Hip hop contains its own array of art school graduates who vetoed traditional music education, including Chuck D, Mobb Deep, Ice Cube, and MIA, with deep connections to street art and an alternative music voice.

Conclusion

Art school pedagogy was connected to popular music development with an experimental and attitudinal approach, from the Bauhaus onwards, where eradicating preconceptions of previous learning was a key pedagogical philosophy and practice. When art could be anything, simplicity of concept, assimilated in the Duchamp-Cage-Warhol-Eno axis, spun philosophies from the avant-garde to the mainstream across artforms. Simplicity of process connected to a minimalist aesthetic, made possible by new technology which offered an exploratory and emancipatory aspect across the visual and auditory arts. From the emergence of reproductive technologies to the birth of synthesizers and personal recording studios, naïve DIY possibilities fostered a punk ethos which bled into post punk, new wave, and future music genres. Concepts originating from a variety of art colleges exemplified the postmodern spirit, where through the 1960s and 1970s, concepts of radical groups such as Art and Language and the Situationist International encouraged a re-evaluation of preconceived ideals, embracing interconnections between art and life of the embedded artist. Arising from this viewpoint, anyone could be an artist: everyone could be a musician.

For twenty-first-century musicians and educators, revisiting the interconnection that existed between art schools and popular musicians from the 1970s could expand creative horizons, a necessity for innovative work to break through the increasingly over-saturated popular music industry. By introducing art pedagogical concepts, I suggest that HPME define a less technically centred and commercially embraced ethos, towards a broader education concentrated on the creative self, allowing for experimentation and individuality within a collaborative dynamic. Exploring concepts of scenius, where the collective creates something greater than the individual, will be important for future research, to examine how art school concepts of non-musicianship and scenius manifest within contemporary popular music genres such as hip hop, jungle, techno, grime, indie, and new jazz, for example.

References

Albertine, V. 2014. *Clothes Clothes Clothes, Music Music Music, Boys Boys Boys*. London: Faber and Faber.
Allen, F., ed. 2011. *Education: Documents of Contemporary Art*. London: Whitechapel and MIT Press.
Ascott, R. 2003. *Telematic Embrace: Visionary Theories of Art, Technology, and Consciousness*. Edited by E. Shanken. Berkeley, CA: University of California Press.
Ascott, R. 2017. Interview with Roy Ascott by Simon Strange, Bristol, 27 October.
Banks, M., and K. Oakley. 2016. 'The dance goes on forever? Art schools, class, and higher education'. *International Journal of Cultural Policy* 22, no. 1: 41–57. https://doi.org/10.1080/10286632.2015.1101082
BBC Radio 6 Music. 2015. *Brian Eno: John Peel Lecture*. http://www.bbc.co.uk/programmes/p033smwp (accessed 2 February 2017).
Best, S., and D. Kellner. 1997. *The Postmodern Turn: Critical Perspectives*. New York: The Guilford Press.
Birch, G. 2018. Interview with Gina Birch by Simon Strange, London, 15 June.
Bracewell, M. 2007. *Re-make, Re-model: Becoming Roxy Music*. Cambridge, MA: DaCapo Press.
Bryars, G. 2017. Interview with Gavin Byars by Simon Strange, London, 15 November.
Byrne, D. 2013. *How Music Works*. Edinburgh: Canongate Books.
Cage, J. 1961. *Silence: Lectures and Writings*. Middletown, CT: Wesleyan University Press.
Callomon, C. 2021. Interview with Cally Callomon by Simon Strange, London, 12 February.
Cateforis, T. 2011. *Are We Not New Wave? Modern Pop at the Turn of the 1980s*. Ann Arbor: University of Michigan Press.
Charnas, D. 2022. *Dilla Time: The Life and Afterlife of J Dilla*. London: Swift Press.
Charnley, J. 2015. *Creative License: From Leeds College of Art to Leeds Polytechnic 1963–1973*. Cambridge: The Lutterworth Press.

Cox, C., and D. Warner. 2017. *Audio Culture: Readings in Modern Music*. London: Bloomsbury.
Craig-Martin, M. 2015. *On Being an Artist*. London: Art Books.
Cybernetic Serendipity. 1968. *Cybernetic Serendipity Music*. https://cyberneticserendipity.net/ (accessed 3 March 2019).
Dalwood, D. 2018. Interview with Dexter Dalwood by Simon Strange, Bath, 9 May.
Davy, S. 1975. *Bubbly, Bubbly Eno*. Available at: http://www.moredarkthanshark.org/eno_int_beet-jan75.html (accessed 19 December 2018).
Dettmar, K. J. H. 2014. *Gang of Four: Entertainment!* 33 1/3. London: Continuum.
Donagh, R. 1970. *White Room*. Available at: https://annebeanarchive.com/1970-white-room/ (accessed 1 May 2020).
Dooley, J. 2018. *Red Set: A History of Gang of Four*. London: Repeater Books.
Eno, B. 1979. 'The studio as a composition tool'. Republished in *Audio Culture: Readings in Modern Music*, edited by C. Cox and D. Warner, 127–31. London: Bloomsbury, 2017.
Eno, B. 1996. *A Year with Swollen Appendices: Brian Eno's Diary*. London: Faber and Faber.
Eno, B. 2017. Interview with Brian Eno by Simon Strange, London, 1 December.
Fineberg, J. 1998. *Discovering Child Art: Essays on Childhood, Primitivism and Modernism*. Princeton, NJ: Princeton University Press.
Fisher, M. 2014. *Writings on Depression, Hauntology and Lost Futures*. London: Zero Books.
Fisher, M. 2018. *K-punk: The Collected and Unpublished Writings of Mark Fisher (2004–2016)*. London: Repeater.
Frith, S., and H. Horne. 1987. *Art into Pop*. London: Routledge.
Gilbert, P. 2009. *Passion is a Fashion: The Real Story of The Clash*. London: Aurum Press.
Goldstein, C. 1996. *Teaching Art: Academies and Schools from Vasari to Albers*. Cambridge: Cambridge University Press.
Gorman, P., D. Thorp, and F. Vermorel. 2015. *Eyes for Blowing up Bridges: Joining the Dots from the Situationist International to Malcolm McLaren*. Southampton: John Hansard Gallery.
Green, L. 2001. *How Popular Musicians Learn*. Aldershot: Ashgate.
Groys, B. 2018. *In the Flow*. London: Verso.
Hamilton, R. 1982. *Collected Words*. London: Thames and Hudson.
Harrison, C. 1991. *Essays on Art and Language*. Oxford: Basil Blackwell.
Hegarty, P. 2007. *Noise/Music: A History*. New York: Continuum.
Huyssen, A. 1984. 'Mapping the postmodern'. *New German Critique* 33: 5–52. https://doi.org/10.2307/488352
Johnstone, W. 1941. *Child Art to Man Art*. London: Macmillan.
Jones, C. A. 1993. 'Finishing school: John Cage and the abstract expressionist ego'. *Critical Enquiry* 19, no. 4: 628–65. https://doi.org/10.1086/448691
Knabb, K., ed. 2006. *Situationist International Anthology*. Revised edn. Berkeley, CA: Bureau of Public Secrets.
Kostelanetz, R. 1970. *Moholy-Nagy*. London: The Penguin Press.
Laing, D. 1985. *One Chord Wonders*. Milton Keynes: Open University Press.
Levene, K. 2018. Interview with Keith Levene by Simon Strange, 7 March. Video conference.
Llewellyn, N., B. Williamson, H. Westley, E. Crippa, et al. 2015. *The London Art Schools: Reforming the Art World, 1960 to now*. London: Tate.

Mallinder, S. 2018. Video conference with Simon Strange, 18 February.
Marcus, G. 2011. *Lipstick Traces: A Secret History of the Twentieth Century*. London: Faber and Faber.
Molesworth, H. 2015. *Leap Before You Look: Black Mountain College, 1933–1957*. New Haven: Yale University Press.
Neate, W. 2008. *Wire's Pink Flag*. 33 1/3. New York: Continuum.
Nyman, M. 1999. *Experimental Music: Cage and Beyond*. 2nd edn. Cambridge: Cambridge University Press.
Osborne, P. 2002. *Conceptual Art*. London: Phaidon.
Pasmore, V. 1963. *Abstract in White, Green, Blue, Red, Grey and Pink*. Tate.
Pelly, J. 2017. *The Raincoats: The Raincoats*. 33 1/3. London: Continuum.
Portsmouth Sinfonia. 1973. *Portsmouth Sinfonia: Plays the Popular Classics* [LP]. Transatlantic Records.
Reichardt, J., ed. 1968. 'Cybernetic serendipity: The computer and the arts'. *Studio International*. Special edition September 1968.
Reynolds, S. 2005. *Rip It Up and Start Again: Post Punk 1978–84*. London: Faber and Faber.
Robinson, T. 2022. 'The relevance of John Peel to the development of music scenes'. *Twitter*, 2 November. https://twitter.com/freshnet/status/1587914105956048898 (accessed February 2022).
Salaman, N. 2015. 'Art theory: Handmaiden of neoliberalism?' *Journal of Visual Art Practice* 14, no. 2: 162–73.
Savage, J. 1991. *England's Dreaming: Sex Pistols and Punk Rock*. London: Faber and Faber.
Scoates, C. 2013. *Brian Eno: Visual Music*. San Francisco: Chronicle Books.
Shanken, E. A., ed. 2015. *Documents of Contemporary Art: Systems*. London: Whitechapel and MIT Press.
Singerman, H. 1999. *Art Subjects: Making Artists in the American University*. Berkeley: University of California Press.
Small, C. 1998. *Musicking: The Meanings of Performing and Listening*. Hanover: University Press of New England.
Spitzer, M. 2021. *The Musical Human: A History of Life on Earth*. London: Bloomsbury.
Steenstra, S. 2010. *Song and Circumstance: The Work of David Byrne from Talking Heads to the Present*. London: Continuum.
Strand, R. 1987. *A Good Deal of Freedom: Art and Design in the Public Sector of Higher Education, 1960–1982*. London: CNAA.
Strange, S. 2022. *Blank Canvas: Art School Creativity and the Development of Punk, Post Punk and New Wave Music*. Bristol: Intellect Publishing.
Tickner, L. 2008. *Hornsey 1968: The Art School Revolution*. London: Francis Lincoln.
Von Gunden, H. 1980. 'The theory of sonic awareness in *The Greeting* by Pauline Oliveros'. *Perspectives of New Music* 19, no. 1–2: 409–16. https://doi.org/10.2307/832602
Walker, J. A. 1987. *Cross-Overs: Art into Pop/Pop into Art*. London: Routledge.
Westley, H. 2007. *The Year of the Locked Room*. Available at: https://www.tate.org.uk/tate-etc/issue-9-spring-2007/year-locked-room (accessed May 1, 2023).
White, G. 2011. 'The Ians in the audience: Punk attitude and the influence of the avant-garde'. In *Avant-garde Performance and Material Exchange: Vectors of the Radical*, edited by M. Sell, 188–206. New York: Palgrave Macmillan.

Worley, M. 2017. *No Future: Punk, Politics and British Youth Culture 1976–84*. Cambridge: Cambridge University Press.

Young, R. 2006. *Rough Trade: Labels Unlimited*. London: Black Dog.

Author biography

Simon Strange is a multidimensional creative, spanning the academic and creative industries, a trombone player, music producer, photographer and socio-cultural academic. Simon has performed around the world and curates the Sidmouth International Jazz and Blues Festival. Strange is Research Programme Manager at Bath Spa University, overseeing an AHRC funded project related to the concept of story. He leads a team who are exploring the use of Story Skills within a range of organizations. His first book, *Blank Canvas*, based on pedagogical connections between UK art schools and popular music, was released by Intellect Publishing in 2022, looking at the creative connection between art and music. Simon has written articles for the *Journal of Popular Music Education* as well as presenting at various conferences of the IASPM, KISMIF, and the Punk Scholars Network.

8 Scaling Up: Teaching Contemporary Music through Repertoire Structures

Sean Foran, Jade O'Regan, Vincent Perry, and Tom O'Halloran

Introduction

In Western popular music, learning to play effectively in an ensemble context requires knowledge and understanding of music structures and skill acquisition through self-discovery and peer learning (Schippers 2009). Tertiary music study often gives students the space and encouragement to learn these vital skills in various contexts, from replicating covers through historical analysis of classic popular music repertoire, genre re-interpretation, songwriting and performing original student material, improvisation, and the use of stage technology. Research on rehearsal and performance techniques in tertiary music contexts has identified creativity, communication, balance, technique, and sharing as crucial skills when assessing musical groups (Blom and Encarnacao 2012: 40). Cashman and Garrido explain the importance of personal practice and group rehearsal in preparing for memorable live performances, identifying four contemporary music performance categories, 'reading gigs, improvising gigs, rock gigs and folk gigs' (Cashman and Garrido 2019: 68), while Chandler (2014) provides clear criteria for teaching popular singing, with a wide knowledge of repertoire and understanding of stylistic differences in genres being a critical part of authentic delivery. Pulman (2014) researched popular music rehearsals, investigating perceptions by tutors and students of the activities and dynamics within band programmes at seven universities and conservatories in the United Kingdom.

For contemporary musicians studying at Australian tertiary institutions, an ensemble performance programme is often a core part of the curriculum, and this research compares the experiences of 42 current students, alumni, and music teaching staff across ensemble programmes at three Australian institutions: the Sydney Conservatorium of Music, JMC Academy Brisbane, and Edith Cowan University in Perth.

This chapter contributes to the field of research in contemporary music ensemble instruction, investigating how selected tertiary institutions in Australia develop performance skill learning in their ensemble programmes. Through three case studies of current degree programmes, we compare approaches, using feedback from learners, instructors, and alumni to ascertain the value of the learning activities in their respective ensemble curricula. Whilst the exact context varied minimally between each of these institutions, an expanded concept of *repertoire* was found to be the driving force – encompassing the importance of soft skills, stagecraft, music cognition, and developing original repertoire or songwriting. By engaging current students (who are actively learning), alumni (who can critically reflect on their previous learning in light of emerging careers), and staff (who can give insight into their own performance and teaching experience), this study gives a multi-faceted insight into the rich learning outcomes within these ensemble programmes.[1]

Context to Study

There are several studies examjining popular music teaching at tertiary institutions in Australia. Harrison et al. (2013) and Lebler (2013) observe assessment practices, investigating the benefits of peer assessment, transparency of grading systems, and feedback mechanisms. Blom and Encarnacao (2012) explore the kinds of hard and soft skills that music students in rock ensembles choose as important in rehearsal and performance contexts. A continuum of these skills is evident, with concepts including 'communication to the audience' and 'incorporating each other's playing' (Blom and Encarnacao 2012: 40) – both blending hard and soft skill sets. Encarnacao and Blom's (2020) book *Teaching and Evaluating Music Performance at University: Beyond the Conservatory Model* approaches Australian tertiary-level music teaching from a variety of angles – student experiences, teaching approaches, professional development, and evaluating performance across a variety of popular, classical, and improvisatory music. Donna Weston has discussed the importance of critical listening and analysis when evaluating student musicianship (Weston and Byron 2015), the significance of popular music performance within popular music studies (Weston 2017), and the usefulness of soft skills in the careers of alumni students from Griffith University (Weston 2020). The latter

1. All data pertaining to student, alumni, and lecturers' short-term and long-term reflections were analysed equally.

of these is particularly relevant to this study as we also discovered that soft skills including communication, managing expectations, friendship-forming and confidence were important to our interviewees.

In the United Kingdom, Creech et al. (2008) investigated how classical and popular musicians learn about performance, finding that contemporary musicians 'attached greater importance to non-notational musical skills such as memorizing and improvising' (Creech et al. 2008: 230). Mark Pulman (2014) highlights the importance of group work in higher education popular music practice, noting that small group teamwork is typical of both industry activity and in undergraduate studies. Our approach is similar to Kokotsaki and Hallam's (2007) study of popular music performers, which uncovered themes of music making as a musical act, a social act and making to influence the self. However, to build on this, we have included the views of teaching staff, and of students' experience with live performance music technology, to gather an understanding of how each party engages with repertoire in popular music ensemble activity.

Case Studies

The undergraduate degrees presented in this chapter are from three Australian institutions: a two-year Bachelor of Music from JMC Academy, taught at the Brisbane campus; a four-year Bachelor of Music (Contemporary Music Major) taught at the Sydney Conservatorium of Music at the University of Sydney; and the four-year Bachelor of Music from the Western Australian Academy of Performing Arts (WAAPA) at Edith Cowan University, taught from the Mount Lawley campus.

Sydney Conservatorium of Music (University of Sydney)

The Bachelor of Music (Contemporary Music Major) at the Sydney Conservatorium is a 4-year degree that focuses on writing, producing, and performing original music. Through units in music skills, history and cultural studies, and electives chosen from the broader offerings at the University of Sydney, students can explore music from a variety of angles. Expected learning outcomes of this degree require that students demonstrate a broad range of skills including writing, producing, mixing, and performing original music in both studio and live contexts.

In the ensemble part of the degree there are two strands – the first is based around original music, where each week a student in the class brings in an original song, teaches it to the ensemble, and acts as a musical director while the other students perform as 'session musicians'.[2] The second, an elective called *Popular Music Ensemble*, is based around performing cover songs, and students meet a new guest lecturer each week who guides them through learning new songs in a variety of popular music styles. The thread through both units is to play 'for the good of the song', to turn up prepared, and with a professional attitude towards the task. It is the experience in these two subjects, which current students, alumni, and staff drew from in the interviews and conversations.

JMC Academy Brisbane

The JMC Academy Bachelor of Music programme is a six-trimester programme with students completing 24 credit points per trimester over two years. The ensemble units are core to the curriculum with students completing six ensemble units that follow a sequenced development programme. Student learning outcomes include applying technical and creative skills, communication skills, planning and implementing a rehearsal and performance schedule, and using creative and technical skills to conceive and create original material for performance and recording.

Alongside these ensemble units in the degree programme, students also complete foundational studies in music theory, ear training, music technology, and music industry. Along with the student's principal study – of either performance, songwriting, or production – the ensemble unit stream is the primary place where students engage in collaborative music creation, developing performance and songwriting skills for future career work. This design is supported by what Hitchcock (2008) highlights as the importance of knowledge sharing, mentoring, and the various forms of communication and feedback in this complex collaborative endeavour. The assessment for these units is designed for praxial learning, with the students completing public performance tasks, live and studio recordings to help simulate industry activity and connect them with performance venues, producers, and sound engineers. These performance events are designed to mirror professional musical activities (Harrison et al. 2013).

2. Grove Music (2002) defines a session musician (sometimes referred to as a 'studio musician' or 'sideman') in popular music as 'a player who works exclusively in recording studios, whether as a freelance or as the employee of a recording or film company'; however, this limited definition doesn't include the specifics of the job, such as exceptional proficiency on an instrument or vocals, ability to play a wide repertoire of styles, performing and recording quickly and efficiently, suggesting musical ideas, communicating with other players, writing and distributing lead sheets and charts, and so forth.

Broadly, the ensemble programme at JMC reinforces the repertoire structures that Cashman and Garrido (2019) identify, with selected repertoire incorporating reading of chord charts and lead sheets, requiring student improvisation and performance of rock and folk style material. This repertoire requires them to use the processes that Conkling (2016) notes – analysis, exploration, performance, and recording. In the first two trimesters, there is a greater emphasis on analysing and exploring familiar repertoire in the popular music canon, with students learning the frameworks and content of this material. The varied performance and recording scenarios require the students to demonstrate their musicianship skills and ability to work coherently and consistently as a group.

Western Australian Academy of Performing Arts (WAAPA), Edith Cowan University

The Contemporary Music major is one of five streams of available majors within the four-year Bachelor of Music degree at the Western Australian Academy of Performing Arts, at Edith Cowan University. The Contemporary Ensemble units are in each semester of the degree (1 through 8), and attribute 15 credit points each within a normal 60-credit point full-time semester load. Students study vocals, guitar, drums, bass, or keyboards in the Contemporary Music major – with around half a typical cohort intake consisting of vocal students. The Contemporary Ensemble units exist alongside various music technique and professional music career units (not unlike other institutions) which attract a lower credit point rating of five, indicating WAAPA's emphasis on small group repertoire development and associated performance outcomes. Typical activities include small ensemble groups of three to eight members (effectively bands) led by a tutor. The bands focus on learning, arranging, and rehearsing songs creatively. These groups also write original compositions within the third and fourth year of the degree and apply advanced improvisation and interaction methods by forming small instrumental groups, which perform at recitals and public concerts.

Elite performance is supported by interactions and exchanges between the major music streams: Classical, Jazz, Composition and Music Technology, and Contemporary Music/Music Artist students. These project-based exchanges take many diverse forms of musical outcomes and/or performances, each fostering a hands-on learning approach – complete with corresponding requirements of negotiation between musical styles and problem-solving through communication skills. These interactions add to a student's broader 'portfolio' of industry-relevant or transferable skills, as they broaden students' notions and experience of what is possible within their own musical ecosystem. This widening of musical focus and exchange of skills outside the siloed music major is now often acknowledged as a baseline expectation for a constantly evolving music industry (Strong 2019: 293–94).

Methodology

This study focuses on ensemble courses across all three institutions, and participants selected for this research consisted of a cross-section of students (15), alumni (15), and staff/instructors (12). Student participants were music students at varied levels of their program of study, and alumni consisted of a mix of graduates within a timeframe of 1–5 years since programme completion. Each institution completed individual semi-structured interviews during January 2021 and their individual participant groups are outlined in Table 8.1.

Table 8.1 Interview numbers across three institutions showing participant groups

Institution	Interviews conducted
Sydney Conservatorium of Music	6 current students, 6 alumni, 3 staff
JMC Academy Brisbane	5 current students, 5 alumni, 5 staff
Western Australian Academy of Performing Arts (WAAPA)	4 current students, 4 alumni, 4 staff

This method echoes the research of Hauser et al. (2017), who interviewed songwriters in varying stages of their careers to create a useful group of 'core competencies' of the songwriting process within popular music. Our 'core competencies' are instead focused on performance and repertoire, rather than original songwriting entirely. The questions posed in the interviews are shown in Table 8.2.

The semi-structured interviews utilized grounded theory to enable the 'actions, interactions and processes of the people involved' (Robson 2011: 147) and assisted in formulating theory into the research. Theoretical sampling was utilized; the participant interviewees were not taken at random but chosen in this case to give a cross-section of experiences in the performance programmes. At each institution, a written invitation was extended to current students, lecturers, and alumni to participate in the study, volunteers registered their interest, and effort was made to select interviewees that enabled a mix of major study areas and industry experience. These interviews took place in person, over the telephone or on Zoom, depending on the suitability for the interviewee. Ethics approval was granted, and all interviewees were anonymized to ensure privacy and were given the opportunity to check that their responses were accurately represented.

Table 8.2 Lists of questions for students, alumni, and staff across all three institutions

Current student question	Lecturer question	Alumni question
Can you give some examples of skills you have learned throughout this ensemble programme and how you've used them in your own music, songwriting and performing?	How did you learn your ensemble performance craft? Were there formal study elements and/or industry experiences?	Can you give some examples of skills you have learned throughout this ensemble programme and how you've used them in your own music, songwriting and performing?
What material are you currently performing? Can you describe the process for developing it?	Can you give some examples of how you create opportunities for students to acquire music performance skills in the ensemble setting?	What material are you currently performing? Can you describe the process for developing it?
Do you conceptualize music differently after working with an ensemble in this programme? If so, how?	What parts of the music performance skill set do you work on with students?	Do you conceptualize music differently after working with an ensemble in this programme? If so, how?
How important are the band dynamic and interactions throughout this programme? What do you like best and least about the process?	What is the musical tool you feel most comfortable with, or are the best at teaching?	How important are the band dynamic and interactions throughout this programme? What do you like best and least about the process?
What do you like best about playing music with others?	Can you talk about the way your industry experience contributes to your ensemble teaching?	What do you like best about playing music with others?
Has preparing and performing original and/or covers repertoire helped you learn to play better in an ensemble context? In what way/s?	Do your current industry experiences further influence your role with the students?	Has preparing and performing original and/or covers repertoire helped you learn to play better in an ensemble context? In what way/s?
What on-stage technology have you embraced through the course? Do you see this as an important component of a live music career?	Do you approach teaching performing cover songs and original songwriting differently? How?	What on-stage technology have you embraced through the course? Do you see this as an important component of a live music career?

What do you wish you had learned when you were the age of your students? What do you think they need to know in the current music industry?	After completing this course, have you implemented some of the performance skills developed throughout your study? Which ones and why?
Is there a set of skills that you believe are most beneficial to possess for an ensemble supervisor in these kinds of programmes?	Do you think studying original songwriting skills or advanced compositional tools have proved helpful in your music career so far? Do you think any aspects need to be emphasized or changed?

The interview data were engaged using an open coding method, where the responses were given indicative labels. Axial coding was then used to create subcategories that consistently defined terms across all 34 JMC Academy (JMC), University of Sydney (USYD), and Western Australian Academy of Performing Arts (WAAPA) interview transcripts, and that also merged common concepts and phenomena.

Data in the form of mentions are presented at the broader participant group level, the participant group plus institution level, and finally presented and interpreted at the wider subcategory level – producing key themes for discussion.

Findings

There were several recurring concepts that resonated across the student, staff, and alumni participant groups from the three institutions. Table 8.3 lists these concepts (the results from the open and indicative coding stages), and therefore exhibits areas of emphasis from all participant groups engaging with the programmes. Subcategories and their concept definitions were drawn from resolving these initial labels and aligning concepts, uniting all three institutions in like terms (see Table 8.3).

When considering the participant groups across all three institutions, the interview subcategories can be viewed by the number of mentions from all students, staff, or alumni (see Figure 8.1).

Table 8.3 Subcategories and their definitions drawn from resolving labels and aligning concepts within the JMC, USYD, and WAAPA interviews

Subcategory type	Concepts identified within interviews
Performance skills	Stagecraft, connection to audience, confidence, understanding the musical material, microphone techniques, control over musical elements in performance, technical execution of musical parts.
Group dynamics	Group and individual communication styles, interpersonal relationships, tutor–student dynamic, sense of fun, collaborative skills, negotiating ideas, listening, sharing, articulating musical intent, efficiently facilitating ensemble activities.
Developing repertoire – Covers/standards	Skills in performing covers. The value of this repertoire. Identifying musical elements in songs.
	Ideas about musical style, shape, and musical influences.
	Music theory.
	Skills of arrangement: re-imagining, reharmonization or other specific musical techniques. Learning and replicating repertoire.
Developing repertoire – Originals	Artistic identity, ability to perform original music.
	Generating pop/rock/folk songs, generating original jazz/fusion compositions.
	Processes in songwriting as a group or individually, general songwriting strategies. Arrangements, lyrics, structure, dynamics, melody, harmony.
	Changed conceptualizations of music.
	Writing and reading charts.
Technology in performance	Technologies including laptops, backing tracks, pedals, microphones, PA systems, in-ear monitoring, amplifiers and mixers, hardware and software.
	Setting up, packing down.
Industry experience	Opportunities that staff, current students, and alumni have/had, performances, mentoring, business skills.
	How industry experience is shaping teaching approaches.
Teaching strategies	Pedagogical strategies used towards ensemble skills and technical facility when developing covers and original repertoire.
	The role of academic, performance, and industry experience within ensemble pedagogy.
	Pedagogy of stage performance technique.

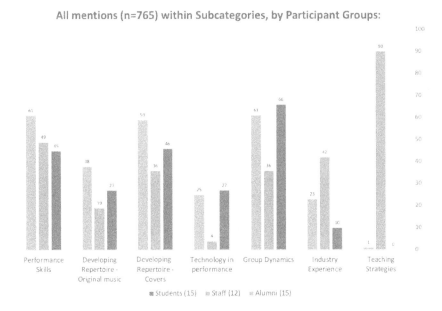

Figure 8.1 All mentions within subcategories, by the combined participant groups from each institution

When focusing on each separate institution, the subcategory mentions can be compared by the local participant groups (see Figures 8.2–8.4).

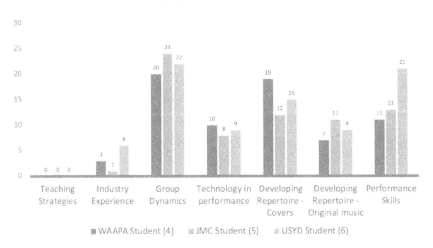

Figure 8.2 Student participant group; mentions per subcategory at the individual institution level

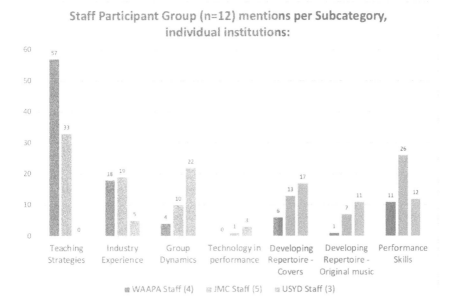

Figure 8.3 Staff participant group; mentions per subcategory at the individual institution level

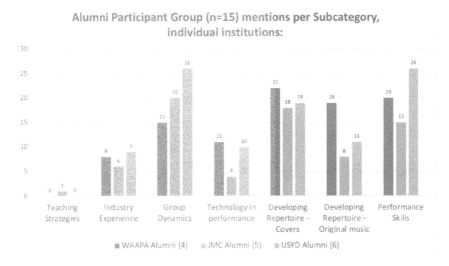

Figure 8.4 Alumni participant group; mentions per subcategory at the individual institution level

When moving to interpret our subcategories, we first considered the corresponding number of mentions and their percentage of total interview quotations. This may be seen (descending clockwise) in Figure 8.5.

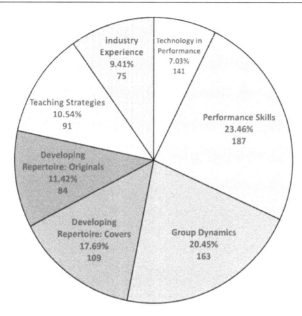

Figure 8.5 Axial coding of all interviews (3 music institutions, 34 participants, 765 total quotations)

We found axial coding of these sub-categories suggested the overarching trend and orientation of all 34 participant interviews toward four themes: 'soft skills', 'stagecraft', 'music cognition', and 'songwriting'. Further selective coding revealed a core theme of *repertoire*, which was often seen as a prime motivator and way to structure these ensemble activities and understand how those themes have been actualized. This axial and selective coding is illustrated in Figure 8.6.

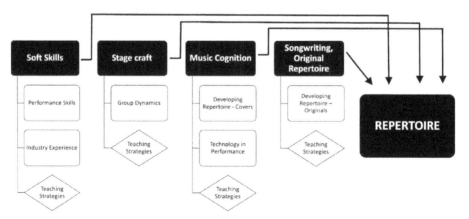

Figure 8.6 Axial coding produces four themes, while selective coding suggests the core theme of 'Repertoire'

While the positionality of the interviewees is varied (students in training, students at the start of their careers, and educators who are experienced musicians), their multifaceted ideas and experiences help define their understanding of ensemble 'repertoire'. These perspectives are heard through the interviews at both the sub-category and broader themes level.

The following section will discuss the four main themes that emerged from the participants, each connecting to the overarching concept of repertoire.

Theme 1: Soft Skills

One of the strongest realizations made by the current students interviewed was recognizing the importance of 'group dynamic' as an element that was required for the ensemble group to function effectively. For these students, positive group dynamics and communication helped develop enjoyable repertoire experiences and outcomes. What was clear through the conversations at all institutions was that students, staff, and alumni placed equal importance on such 'soft skills', i.e., managing group dynamics, friendship forming, professional attitude and confidence. These themes were particularly strong in discussions with alumni as they reflected on their studies within the context of their growing careers in music, aligning well with the previous research of Blom and Encarnacao (2012) and Weston (2020) within an Australian university context. Lecturers stressed the importance of working with students to craft a positive group dynamic so that the group creates self-identity, trust, and a cohesive working environment.

As Student A highlights, it is not always positive, but the challenging group experiences prepare them for industry work:

> Even though there's been clashing things happen, I actually think it's character development, and also really important before you get fully into the industry to actually know what it's like to kind of work with different creatives. ... it gives you a really good insight into, like, the actual troubles of working with different creative people.

The troubles that Student A (and many others) referred to included personality clashes, variance in individual musical competency, and differences when understanding musical styles and repertoire. However, these differences do foster development, as other current students explained that challenging group dynamics can allow individuals to grow via peer learning occurring within ensemble sessions, and noticing how each member of the group is crucial for ensemble success.

These conversations also crossed over into ideas about friendship and camaraderie. Many alumni students met and formed bands within their respective degrees and have remained performing together since graduation. Accordingly, a strong theme that resonated throughout every related conversation was performance attitude. One alumni student noted:

> I'd say [attitude] is more important [than skill]. I would much rather do a gig with someone who knows four chords on a guitar and is lovely and easy to get along with than someone who knows a guitar inside out, but you just can't connect with any day of the week.

Alumni musicians are now currently performing and releasing their own original music, and have wider musical experiences beyond those at university, yet they remarked that they did develop as practitioners through tackling and negotiating different attitudes to ensemble performance in their tertiary study. These findings mirror Weston's (2020) detailed study of the Queensland Conservatorium of Music's (Griffith University) Bachelor of Popular Music programme, which found that soft skills such as these are 'as equal to, sometimes more important than, hard skills such as musical, technical and business knowledge' for students who have completed popular music study at university, and that these skills are of 'critical importance to the degree and the success of its graduates' (Weston 2020: 535). Similarly, there was also a connection to Kokotsaki and Hallam's (2007) findings around the social effects of performance, such as 'sense of belonging', 'working with like-minded people', and 'making friends' (Kokotsaki and Hallam 2007: 100).

These positive experiences and group dynamics were contrasted with student experiences that were at times challenging and had undesirable implications for all participants. At least two students said they found it perplexing when placed in ensembles where other students either did not adequately learn the required repertoire or had less comparable skills. Student D answered:

> I've been in similar situations where people have consistently not learnt repertoire, for whatever reasons. And, you know, that's something that can weigh an ensemble down. But that's few and far between.

When asked if their unit marks suffered because of this group dynamic around repertoire, Alumni B confirmed this was the case:

> So yeah, I didn't practice as hard and I didn't care, because I was bitter. Which, at the end of the day, it just affected me, it didn't

affect anybody else, which I learnt the hard way. But yeah, it did. My marks weren't as great.

The responses from staff and students illuminated the importance of an ensemble working together for 'the good of the song', rather than focusing on individual performance skills. It appears students often remember how it *felt* to play together even more than the notes that were played, stressing the importance of attitude, friendship, group dynamic, and the common experience of performance anxiety for students during their ensemble performance classes.

Theme 2: Stagecraft

Students and alumni interviewees mentioned that the ensemble units they participated in required them to learn how to perform in front of an audience; as Alumni E says, 'in ensemble, you are not only learning about making the music, [but] you are also learning how to make the whole performance'.

The various activities involved in preparing repertoire for live performance were found to drive these multiple areas of stagecraft skills acquisition; and included instrumental facility and technique. Current student and alumni interviews repeatedly mention various other skills gained as a direct consequence of this particular suite of units, including: 'interacting with an audience', 'how to front a band', 'how to move and look' (as a vocalist appropriate to the musical setting), memorizing repertoire quickly, group interplay, accompanying vocals, dynamics, and changing keys. Accordingly, staff validated the benefits of authentic or 'real' assessment activities (playing in industry venues or simulated settings etc.) when performing repertoire.

Some current students mentioned that they had often not performed professionally as part of a band before attending university, and the performance units gave them the opportunity to extend their skills by performing publicly – often with instruments, styles, and genres that were out of their 'comfort zone' of previous experience. Student C explained how their realizations changed throughout live performance classes, noting that thinking about what performance was like and actually doing it were two different things, the latter requiring specialized practice:

> When I came to [university] I had never performed and I just thought, like, I would just be able to do it if I got up on stage ... and I slowly realized that I'm not comfortable on stage whatsoever ... I had to basically tackle performance anxiety for so long. Even now, I'm still doing that.

The use of technology in performance – including the use of laptops, hardware effect units, and an understanding of live sound technology such as microphone and venue sound systems – was under-represented in the interview data, which suggests that there is a lack of emphasis on this element in these programmes.

Further, most alumni felt that the use of technology in performance of repertoire was somewhat secondary, or not particularly relevant to what their audiences or clients wanted. They did, however, feel that knowledge of in-ear monitors, setting up PA equipment, click tracks, triggering, pedal boards, and looping were partially relevant and could have been taught more within these ensemble units.

Theme 3: Music Cognition

Live performance ensemble units require students to engage with a large and varied repertoire, which was viewed positively by all respondents. The challenge of understanding many kinds of music is reported to help develop various specific musical skills which can potentially be re-applied to the creation of new original repertoire or other projects. Student D comments on how they now musically adapt and benefit from:

> just having that opportunity to explore other musicians' repertoire … there's been such a diverse … range of repertoire as well … it's just been great in applying … those harmonic and rhythmic concepts … I don't think I'd be able to compose fusion-oriented music without having that kind of foundation.

Even though interviewees cited the varied repertoire structures as a critical part of the programme, the development of increased music cognition skills and the ability to apply these in a variety of ways was also a central response in this research across all students, staff, and alumni.

Alumni respondents reflected on how their ability to listen to the varied instrumental parts significantly increased during their study. Through understanding music theory concepts and then applying them in a band situation, it gave them a greater appreciation of balance within a song. For example, Alumni D mentions listening to the bass part from a new perspective:

> But to be able to, like you know, listen to what the bass is doing, and what the drums are doing, and kind of have an idea from a musical theory standpoint why they chose to do that stuff.

All respondent groups highlighted the relationship between critical listening, music theory, and the connection to live music creation. To extend this notion further, a comment by Alumni C suggests that the large variety of musical skills embedded within this set repertoire (such as the detailed analysis of musical parts) could be positively contributing to their portfolio career, keeping an emphasis on live performing work.

> I feel I just listen to way more detail and listen to what parts go with what ... I didn't want to do full-time teaching, because I do lots of gigs during the weekend and stuff, so I wanted to kind of have a nice balance. Which is good, it's what I've now got.

Staff with high levels of musical skill and experience were perceived desirable – if not required – to facilitate this learning due to the high level of specificity involved. Staff C also mentioned the positive impactful pedagogical results when demonstrating the live performance of repertoire:

> I think it's understanding the roles of all of the instruments ... Because I've had some experience playing most instruments, but particularly playing drums, bass, and guitar ... I feel pretty comfortable and pretty confident ... giving technical advice and instructions.

Lecturers placed importance on using their industry skills to teach students the ability to be more aware of the core elements of music such as rhythm, harmony, melody, and form; hearing music in real-time, and transferring ideas from the rehearsal room to the stage with an understanding of what they're trying to achieve and why they're doing it. Further, it was found that staff selected repertoire informed by their current professional practice, as Staff A articulates:

> The original music component ... there's much more creativity in the course [now], especially from the end of second year onwards ... creative arrangements and original songs in ensemble ... And they now have a composition and production class. So, these kinds of changes have been implemented because of my current practices in the industry.

One staff member expressed the observation that education institutions are in fact changing the way repertoire is now learnt and experienced in the industry, as a larger proportion of musicians are now emerging from them, and wonders if something has been lost in the process:

> ... there's probably less and less of them these days, it's more common for people to do a music degree. But when I first started doing gigs, most of the people I worked with had never studied formally ... but [we learnt] to be able to roll with a more oral tradition, or people that have very different ways of working. You know, some people might want to rehearse all day and sing in a rehearsal room playing 12-bar blues for a whole day, which is, on the surface, very simple music. But as we all know ... like any music ... there's depth to it, and to do it *well* is a certain ... other skillset ... I learnt a lot from just hanging out with people that were far more experienced than I was. And some of the lessons were the most brutal lessons along the way, but they're the best lessons. [Laughs]

Theme 4: Songwriting and Original Repertoire

Students, alumni, and staff reflected on the different skills students need when performing original music in class together, as opposed to cover songs. All three groups stressed the arrangement as being particularly important during these ensemble sessions, more so than any individual performance skill as a vocalist or instrumentalist.

Many students admitted a great deal of anxiety when first playing their original songs to their class, as Student E explains:

> Like, I was ... I cannot even explain how nervous I was to play with people I'd never met before. Oh, and bring a song you've written, I was like, oh, my God, this is so personal!

While this was a strong theme throughout many of the conversations in this study, there were some reflections that noted a change in these anxious feelings over time. They explained that the more they were asked to perform, the easier it was to let go of some of the feelings of shyness and lack of confidence. Student B explained:

> Just playing with people, you sort of understand a bit about them. And that's probably what helped getting through it.

Student A also touched on similar feelings:

> I think the most that I got out of that class, though, was confidence. Like, it was nice to work with other people. And there was a little sense of, like, people had to step up and work together ... swap[ping] vocal parts ... doing harmonies. That was great practice for me.

Hall (2015) acknowledges this 'fear of failure' phenomenon in an ensemble context and suggests that 'to be prepared to be wrong requires a learning environment in which there exists a high level of trust, mutual respect and good relationship between staff and student' (Hall 2015: 105). Staff B also acknowledged this in their conversation:

> Some people, already, even when they're really young, have a set of ideas of who they want to be and what they want to do and how they want to define their music. If you're talking about something that's not related to that, they just shut off. I try and encourage people to come to that point of throwing in some ideas and be knocked back, but still being creatively engaged.

Along with building trust and developing a positive relationship between teachers and students, creating a 'safe' rehearsal space to learn is paramount. Hunter (2008) acknowledges the literal and metaphorical meanings of a 'safe space' in the context of theatre studies in Australia, and these frameworks similarly apply to the band rehearsal room as they do to a theatre stage. Hunter outlines the different ways a space may feel safe in a creative and supportive environment: Firstly, ensuring that the physical qualities of the space are 'safe' and those working in it are not at risk of injury (e.g., tripping on leads, excessive volume levels of instruments, and so forth). Secondly, and more aligned with the feminist and educational discourses on the 'safe space' (see Ludlow 2004), it can mean 'a space bordered by temporal dimensions (such as a workshop or rehearsal time/space) in which discriminatory activities, expressions of intolerance or policies of inequity are barred' (Hunter 2008: 8). And thirdly, that a space can become a safe one through the comfort of familiarity; 'The space becomes safe as it becomes known' (2008: 8).

In the classroom, these descriptions of a safe space resonate with the research of Hendricks et al. (2014), who outline a teacher-led approach to the creation of a safe space, which demonstrates kind and constructive feedback:

> ... students can sense the genuineness of a caring teacher whose focus and mental investment is demonstrated through specific constructive feedback regarding musical improvements and effort. In addition to being mentally present with students, being emotionally present allows teachers to be sensitive to how students are responding to feedback, thereby allowing them to better gauge the level of pacing, praise, and/or challenge. (38)

For students to be 'knocked back' and still maintain resilience requires a 'safe space', as Staff B actively tries to provide. Staff, who involved in developing students' original material within an ensemble context, experience challenges related to imparting musical direction, and how to teach students to develop their own material and arrive at their own ideas or musical decisions. Staff expressed how, at times, pedagogy may potentially blur into the roles of co-creator, and even potential issues of authorship, as Staff C remarks:

> I remember a couple of years ago … they got up at some performance and said, like, 'Oh, this is a song I wrote with this band', and didn't mention me at all, which is, like, I guess fine, but … a bit weird, too. I was like, 'Man, this song really didn't have … you know, it didn't have anything until I put it all together like this'. Not that it didn't have anything, that's too harsh! [Laughs] … Yeah, I have [more of] a clear idea of the full picture than they do, and *because* I have a clearer picture, maybe it's easier for them to jump on that because it makes sense. But what I don't know is how to translate that, you know, [in] the years of music that I've learnt for them so they can make those decisions on their own. And perhaps it is just [about] … taking my hands off the steering wheel and just letting them direct a little bit more.

Interviewees also noted how working with repertoire that included covers had a positive impact on their development of original material. As Alumni C notes:

> I guess it ultimately requires you to have a deeper understanding of the things that you're playing rather than just kind of rote learning it.

Similarly, Alumni D noted that performing cover material in an ensemble helped them to gain the confidence to start their own originals band:

> It was a really safe environment for me to try [ensemble playing] for the first time and build a bit of confidence in that area – enough confidence that I was happy to ask two people to play in my [originals] band with me and that's been going for two years now.

Further to this, Staff D passionately noted,

> … you've gotta learn vernacular! you've got to [develop] creative vocabulary, you do this by standing on the shoulders of giants … who definitely stood on the shoulders of people before them.

By exposing aspiring songwriters to a variety of genres and eras, it helps them build their musical vernacular and vocabulary. Yet, the added value of these songwriting/original music units – beyond practising performance and songwriting skills – appears to be the fostering of confidence in students to enable them to have the agency to advocate for their own ideas and musical choices during and outside of class.

Conclusion

What began as an investigation into repertoire across three institutions ended up being a discussion of much wider and interconnected issues for students, alumni, and staff, with participants commenting on the importance of playing 'for the good of the song' rather than focusing on individual performance skills.

The other themes that resonated most with participants were stagecraft – focusing on the 'whole performance' not just the notes played – and music cognition, which enabled improvements to performance and arrangement skills. It was also found that by exposing aspiring songwriters to a variety of genres and eras, they can build their musical vernacular, and add to their musical 'toolkit' from which to express their own creativity. However, the broader notion that threaded all the ideas together was emphatically *repertoire*, where performing both original and cover songs can enhance a student's understanding of ensemble playing and songwriting and yield wider personal skills like confidence and tackling performance anxiety.

Our conversations with staff reflected that, at times, being an effective teacher for a contemporary ensemble requires you to not tell the students the answer to every question, as they can be better prepared for a career in music by learning more general problem-solving skills. This may need to be more explicitly taught. Based on our findings, when approaching ensemble teaching, providing students with an opportunity to develop appropriate soft skills – such as open communication, giving and receiving kind feedback, and negotiating different creative ideas – through engaging with a large amount of varied repertoire, can and should be a focal point for ensemble programmes. Furthermore, our discussions with both students and teachers noted the importance of creating a safe rehearsal space to learn and experiment with new musical ideas. Also, by developing trust between teachers and students, we the educators are more capable of providing better feedback within a performance context. For our alumni students, soft skills, in addition to the performing experiences learned through ensemble playing at university, have proved particularly useful in their burgeoning music careers.

Drawing from the interviews with staff, alumni, and student participants from these three institutions, there were commonalities observed between the way teaching staff work collaboratively (i.e., learning not only from each other but from students), and using repertoire formats to enhance the student's ability to successfully collaborate. This research has been a mirror of this collaborative learning, in that institutions with similar interests in music performance outcomes can surely benefit from one another. We found it extended our notions of pedagogy and believe that it could potentially create a more thoughtful and rewarding music programme experience for staff and students at each music institution involved in such dialogue and conversation.

References

Blom, D., and J. Encarnacao. 2012. 'Student-chosen criteria for peer assessment of tertiary rock groups in rehearsal and performance: What's important?' *British Journal of Music Education* 29, no. 1: 25–43. https://doi.org/10.1017/S0265051711000362

Cashman, D., and W. Garrido. 2020. *Performing Popular Music: The Art of Creating Memorable and Successful Performances*. New York: Routledge.

Chandler, K. 2014. 'Teaching popular music styles'. In *Teaching Singing in the 21st Century*, Landscapes: the Arts, Aesthetics, and Education, vol. 14, edited by S. Harrison and J. O'Bryan. Dordrecht: Springer.

Conkling, S. 2016. 'Looking in on music: Challenges and opportunities for the scholarship of teaching and learning'. *Teaching and Learning Inquiry* 4, no. 1: 1–13. https://doi.org/10.20343/teachlearninqu.4.1.11

Creech, A., I. Papageorgi, C. Duffy, F. Morton, E. Hadden, J. Potter, C. De Bezenac, T. Whyton, E. Himonides, and G. Welch. 2008. 'Investigating musical performance: Commonality and diversity among classical and non-classical musicians'. *Music Education Research* 10, no. 2: 215–34. https://doi.org/10.1080/14613800802079080

Encarnacao, J., and D. Blom. 2020. *Teaching and Evaluating Music Performance at University: Beyond the Conservatory Model*. London: Routledge.

Grove Music Online. 2002. 'Session (i)'. https://www.oxfordmusiconline.com/grovemusic/view/10.1093/gmo/9781561592630.001.0001/omo-9781561592630-e-2000403100 (accessed 3 June 2021).

Hall, R. 2015. 'Enhancing the popular music ensemble workshop and maximising student potential through the integration of creativity'. *International Journal of Music Education* 33, no. 1: 103–12. https://doi.org/10.1177/0255761414533310

Harrison, S. D., D. Lebler, G. Carey, M. Hitchcock, and J. O'Bryan. 2013. 'Making music or gaining grades? Assessment practices in tertiary music ensembles'. *British Journal of Music Education* 30, no. 1: 27–42. https://doi.org/10.1017/S0265051712000253

Hauser, C. V., D. R. Tomal, R. S. Rajan, J. Peterik, and B. Thomas. 2017. *Songwriting: Strategies for Musical Self-Expression and Creativity*. London: Rowman & Littlefield.

Hendricks, K. S., T. D. Smith, and J. Stanuch. 2014. 'Creating safe spaces for music learning'. *Music Educators Journal* 101, no. 1: 35–40. https://doi.org/10.1177/0027432114540337

Hitchcock, M. 2008. 'Making music together: The blending of an on-line learning environment for music artistic practice'. Paper presented at the Creating Value: Between Commerce and Commons, Brisbane, Australia, June 25–27.

Hunter, M. A. 2008. 'Cultivating the art of safe space'. *Research in Drama Education* 13, no. 1: 5–21. https://doi.org/10.1080/13569780701825195

Kokotsaki, D., and S. Hallam. 2007. 'Higher education music students' perceptions of the benefits of participative music making'. *Music Education Research* 9, no. 1: 93–109. https://doi.org/10.1080/14613800601127577

Lebler, D. 2013. 'Using formal self and peer-assessment as a proactive tool in building a collaborative learning environment: Theory into practice in a popular music programme'. In *Collaborative Learning in Higher Music Education: Why, What and How?*, edited by H. Gaunt and H. Westerlund, 111–21. London: Routledge. https://doi.org/10.4324/9781315572642

Ludlow, J. 2004. 'Safe space to contested space in the feminist classroom'. *Transformations: The Journal of Inclusive Scholarship and Pedagogy* 15, no. 1: 40–56.

Pulman, M. 2014. 'Popular music pedagogy: Band rehearsals at British universities'. *International Journal of Music Education* 32, no. 3: 296–310. https://doi.org/10.1177/0255761413491207

Robson, C. 2011. *Real World Research*. 3rd edn. Chichester: John Wiley & Sons.

Schippers, H. 2009. *Facing the Music: Shaping Music Education from a Global Perspective*. Oxford: Oxford University Press.

Strong, C., S. Brunt, F. Cannizzo, E. Montano, I. Rogers, and G. Shill. 2019. 'Adapting the studio model for the Australian popular music education context'. *Journal of Popular Music Education* 3, no. 2: 293–308. https://doi.org/10.1386/jpme.3.2.293_1

Weston, D. 2017. 'The place of practice in tertiary popular music studies: An epistemology'. *Journal of Popular Music Education* 1, no. 1: 101–16. https://doi.org/10.1386/jpme.1.1.101_1

Weston, D. 2020. 'The value of "soft skills" in popular music education in nurturing musical livelihoods'. *Music Education Research* 22, no. 5: 527–40. https://doi.org/10.1080/14613808.2020.1841132

Weston, D., and T. Byron. 2015. 'Killing the muse: Listening creativities and the journey to creative mastery'. In *Activating Diverse Musical Creativities: Teaching and Learning in Higher Music Education*, edited by P. Burnard and E. Haddon, 57–74. London: Bloomsbury.

Author biographies

Sean Foran is a Brisbane-based composer, pianist, and improvising musician. An ARIA nominated artist he has received the prestigious Brisbane City Council's Lord Mayors Emerging Artist Fellowship, AMC/APRA Award for Excellence in Jazz, APRA Professional Development Award for Jazz, and the QLD Music Award multiple times. His research investigates improvisation with technology, contemporary music career strategies, and jazz industry practices. He is currently performing with acclaimed improvising trio 'Trichotomy', is Course Director for Audio and Music at SAE University College, co-director of the publishing company 'Prepared Sounds', and associate artist of the Australian Music Centre.

Jade O'Regan is a Lecturer in Contemporary Music Practice at the Sydney Conservatorium of Music (University of Sydney). She is the co-author of *Hooks in Popular Music* (2022) with Dr Tim Byron, which combines pop musicology and music psychology to understand pop music in an interdisciplinary way. Her research interests include the musical analysis of pop music, genres, songwriting, and creativity. She is an experienced music communicator who has been featured as a speaker at SxSW, Splendour in the Grass, on ABC News, and Triple J. She is also a performing musician and songwriter.

Vincent Perry is a Darwin-based drummer, record producer, and avid collector of vintage instruments and recording gear. Vincent draws his musical inspiration from the house bands of the 1960s recording industry, especially Phil Spector's Wrecking Crew and Motown's Funk Brothers. He is currently a percussionist for the Darwin Symphony Orchestra, drummer for the Hot and Cold Big Band, and a lecturer at Charles Darwin University, where he delivers higher education and Vocational Education and Training (VET) music units.

Tom O'Halloran is a Senior Lecturer at the Western Australian Academy of Performing Arts (WAAPA) at Edith Cowan University, where he is the academic coordinator of the jazz performance major within the Bachelor of Music degree. In 2017 he won the APRA Art Music Award for Jazz Work of the Year, and he is a regularly commissioned composer, pianist, and improviser. He gained a Master of Music (composition) from the Sydney Conservatorium of Music and holds a Bachelor of Music (jazz performance) from WAAPA, and is currently completing the PhD. His future research interests are hybridity and multi-disciplined approaches, technology within jazz, and assimilating techniques of modernism within jazz.

9 'How NOT to land an internship': A Case Study of Experiential Learning in Sound Recording and Music Production Education

Kirk McNally

Introduction

The title for this chapter is borrowed from a 2007 internet forum post for would-be interns in the field of sound recording and the music business. The author of the post rants about an email he received from an individual seeking an internship and presents the many errors and missteps he believes the would-be intern committed. Though wildly problematic for a number of reasons, the original post and the comments it has since garnered do an excellent job of highlighting the prevailing attitudes towards internship opportunities held by both music-industry professionals and the students who seek to engage with them and their businesses. Music-industry professionals point to the knowledge, experience, proximity, and potential credits that interns will obtain, while internship seekers show both reverence and resistance to the perceived internship experience. In true fairy-tale fashion, the forum thread concludes with a post by an individual who outs themselves as the hapless writer of the original email.[1] The story told is that following their initial blunder, this person completed a successful internship at another 'big' studio and has gone on to a highly successful career in 'the business'.

---

1. The original discussion forum thread can be found here: https://gearspace.com/board/rap-hip-hop-engineering-and-production/143994-how-not-land-internship.html. And a 2013–16 follow-up: https://gearspace.com/board/rap-hip-hop-engineering-and-production/814307-how-not-land-internship-part-2-a.html.

A desire to land a starring role, mirroring this individual's story and becoming part of the internship fairy tale, is something I have consistently heard from students over my 15+ years as a teacher in music-industry postsecondary education. Ultimately, my goal of rewriting this story, with a focus on student learning and in response to changes observed in the field, is what led to this chapter. The learning activity detailed here is an example of community-engaged learning, an umbrella term for various action-oriented and participatory approaches to research. A case study is used to examine the value students associate with this type of activity as well as the learning outcomes we can expect from implementing this type of learning opportunity in our courses.

Background

The music industry, and recording studios in particular, have historically relied on the apprenticeship model to train and educate new recruits to the field. This training method has been theorized as 'situated learning' by Lave and Wenger (1991). In this method, the trainee or apprentice, with the support of a master practitioner, moves through a series of key steps, including observation, modelling, scaffolding, fading, and coaching (Pratt 1998). Although the apprenticeship model is still evident today, formal sound-recording programmes offered by academic institutions, whose roots trace back to the foundation of the first training institute at the Hochschüle fur Musik in Detmold, Germany, in 1946 (Borwick 1973), are now the prevalent means of training students interested in pursuing careers in this part of the music industry. A range of outcomes is possible from these contemporary programmes. The University of Surrey (United Kingdom), for example, advertises that its graduates have gone on to positions in recording and mastering, film sound and post-production, studio management, technical support, live-sound-system specification, installation, or operation, and composition for film and television or audio for games.[2]

The desire for the 'situatedness' that the apprenticeship model is built upon has not waned within the field, however: music-industry programmes have created institutional facilities and structures that mirror the industry. Professional-level recording studios, institutional record labels, and

---

2. The University of Surrey is home to the prestigious BMus/Bsc (Hons) Music and Sound Recording course. An overview, including 'Career and Graduate Prospects', can be found here: https://www.surrey.ac.uk/undergraduate/music-and-sound-recording-tonmeister

music-management 'companies' are relatively common as part of these formal academic programmes.[3]

Despite these in-house opportunities for students, there remains a desire for a genuine connection to the field via internships, particularly for post-secondary students in specialized music-business degrees (Rolston and Herrera 2000). In his study of audio-engineering curricula, Dave Tough reports that 'audio engineering technology (AET) students must be offered several internship and mentorship opportunities to develop competencies' (Tough 2010: 5). Data from the same study reveals that both traditional business and music business competencies are important for AET students. Doug Bielmeier, an audio-education researcher and scholar, argues that internships should be *required* for degree-granting audio-education programmes (Bielmeier 2020). The promise of what internship opportunities afford students – proximity to professional practice, networking opportunities, and development of interpersonal, technological, leadership, and entrepreneurial skills (Frenette et al. 2015) – clearly makes them attractive, and these opportunities are strongly advocated within music-industry education programmes.

But who are these internship opportunities benefiting, and is the internship model still valid in a post-COVID-19 pandemic world? The arts economy as a whole has previously been identified as having a significant surplus of workers with regard to both demand and opportunity (Becker 1982; Faulkner 1983; Miège 1989). This reality is compounded by the presence of internship opportunities, or the so-called intern economy, whereby student workers are ready and willing to work without remuneration (Frenette 2013). In this situation, the music industry is supported by unpaid labour and lacks the resources to provide sustainable careers for those who hope to use the internship as a pathway, or *springboard*, to full-time employment. Playing on this springboard analogy, Jacobson and Shade (2018: 331–32) present a typology of internships that they label a *stringtern*, which describes a 'system of sequential – or string – of internships' that rarely results in full-time employment. The implications of this practice clearly illustrate the benefits for the employer, with internships being used as a free trial, as conveyor-belt labour, and as displacement of paid employment.

Looking at the demographics of internships in North America, a special report on internships in the arts, authored by Alexandre Frenette, found that

3. For example, Drexel University is home to Mad Dragon Music, an independent, student-run record label; HUBB Records was launched in 2019 at BIMM (British and Irish Modern Music Institute) in Bristol, UK; and Vermilion Records is a not-for-profit, student-run record label based out of Queensland University of Technology in Brisbane, Australia.

'Black and Hispanic/Latino alumni were less likely to have done internships than their White and Asian counterparts', and when they had done internships, they were more likely to be unpaid (Frenette et al. 2015). Two recent ethnographic studies (Wolfe 2019; Reddington 2021) illustrate how the systemic gendering and heteropatriarchal culture of the commercial recording studio excludes women and gender-non-conforming people (WGNCP) and other representatives of minority social groups. This is supported by the fact that the Audio Engineering Society (AES), the largest international professional organization in the field of audio, has a WGNCP membership of only 7%. Given the diversity, equity, and inclusion initiatives present on-campus today, these facts raise serious questions about the value of promoting traditional internship opportunities within higher education.

Internship opportunities within the music industry are also governed by the geographical location of the student's institution. In their study of the geography of the music industry, Florida and Jackson (2010) show that the industry in the United States has become increasingly concentrated, with the major centres being New York, Los Angeles, and Nashville. While regional opportunities may exist, the companies that offer them are often smaller than those in the major centres, which limits the number of internship opportunities available. This finding is supported by the work of Frenette et al. (2015) and their study of internships in the arts, in which they identify the role of geography in the intern economy. Not surprisingly, areas with high-density populations have greater internship opportunities, which creates competition for the available positions and contributes to a greater number of unpaid internships in these regions. This becomes more problematic when viewed in light of their finding that 'women, Black, Hispanic/Latino, and first-generation college graduates all appear to hold a disproportionate number of unpaid internships' (Frenette et al. 2015: 8). Internships have been identified as perpetuating inequalities within our society and limiting class mobility (Thompson 2012). The simple fact that many students may not have either the resources or the ability to move to a major centre for an unpaid internship creates further questions about their inclusion within post-secondary programmes.

Now almost two decades old, the concept of the *network studio* (Théberge 2004) has been amplified by the COVID-19 pandemic; where it was once a choice to collaborate and work remotely, it has now become a necessity. Running parallel to this development is the ongoing growth of online communities, social networks, and forums that allow students and professionals from the music industry to meet virtually to discuss and share information about all factors of their studies and work. Building a social network, which can be undertaken during higher education, offers students some aspects of a traditional internship – specifically, the opportunity to network and practise interpersonal skills – and has been shown to have long-lasting effects on careers (Frenette and Dowd 2019). Echoes of what a traditional apprenticeship offers students are found in these online communities. However, as Gaston-Bird et al. (2021) report, we are reminded that even these virtual spaces continue to be extremely gendered, are not inclusive, and perpetuate the social and societal barriers that prevent greater diversity within the audio field.

Henson and Zagorski-Thomas (2019: 14) contend that there is a 'need to turn traditional learning approaches inside out'. The research presented here is an example of doing just that. This approach bridges the gap between student expectations of traditional internship models and a more equitable learning approach by using community-engaged learning as a component of a fourth-year sound-recording course at University of Victoria (UVic). The project was funded by a community-engaged learning grant through the Learning and Teaching Support and Innovation (LTSI) centre at UVic. The case study received a certificate of approval from the University of Victoria Human Research Ethics Board.

Context

The University of Victoria is a research-intensive post-secondary institution located on the west coast of Canada. With a population of ~86,000 residents, the city serves as the metropolitan core for a region of 360,000,[4] with a provincial population currently estimated at 5.1 million. A recent study of the music-industry labour market in the province of British Columbia identifies a mere 6,600 people whose main form of employment is in the music industry. While regional high-school and post-secondary education and training provide pathways into the industry, the study also finds that a 'majority (80%) of music professionals have not participated in an internship or work placement, primarily due to a lack of access or exposure to relevant opportunities' (Sound Diplomacy 2018). An equal majority (80%) of music businesses identified the need for professional development skills and support programmes to help them grow their businesses.

The students who participated in the project were all enrolled in a combined major programme in music and computer science (MUCS). In this degree programme, students study the fundamental topics of both disciplines, including music history, theory and musicianship, mathematics, fundamentals of programming, algorithms, data structures, and computer architecture. Graduates of the programme have found employment across a spectrum of

4. https://www.victoria.ca/

careers in the music industry, including sound recording, live sound venues, music-streaming platforms, performance, and video-game companies.

Community-Engaged Learning (CEL)

Where traditional internships have been shown to exclude minority and equity seeking groups, perpetuate social inequalities, and raise questions about labour systems and effective compensation (Frenette 2013; Frenette et al. 2015; Jacobson and Shade 2018), I identified community-engaged learning (CEL), a concept with roots in the broader field of service-learning and experiential education, as a way to emulate the internship experience and provide my students with the legitimate connection and 'situatedness' within the field they crave, but in a more equitable, balanced, and fair way. At UVic, CEL is defined as a form of experiential learning and community-engaged scholarship whereby students actively engage with course content through the combination of collaborations with community and facilitated reflection.[5] A core principle of CEL is reciprocity, with partnerships being mutually beneficial to all participants – community, faculty, and students. Through studies, CEL has been shown to increase student engagement with not only their specific course material but also their academic work in general (see, for example, Gallini and Moely 2003). The obvious benefit of this engagement is the improved academic performance observed in students who participate in CEL opportunities (Astin and Sax 1998; Vogelgesang and Astin 2000).

The CEL project presented here was centred within a fourth-year sound-recording course and in partnership with Cordova Bay Records (CBR),[6] a local independent record label. The overarching goal of the project was to support both the local Victoria music economy and expand the curricular scope of the course by adding elements of music business, music composition, and entrepreneurship. The expected outcome of this project was producing professional-level recordings of student compositions, to be distributed through a new subsidiary label or 'imprint' of CBR called Flood Tide Music (FTM). FTM is focused on streaming-only releases and curates everything from 'ambient and meditation music to post and neo-classical originals to chill down-tempo beats'.[7] Interviewed as part of this case study, the CBR president identifies the company's views of and experience with internships:

---

5. https://onlineacademiccommunity.uvic.ca/LearnAnywhere/cel/
6. http://www.cordovabay.com
7. This quote is taken from unpublished promotional materials shared by CBR with students in the class.

There are many unique aspects of the music industry that can only be learned through experience so this environment plays an important role in developing new talent. More often than not the situation is win-win. The industry has evolved so rapidly it has been key to have staff with fresh perspectives, which interns frequently offer. When mixed with more experienced team members this creates the growth needed to adapt.

Conceptual Framework

A useful model for designing the CEL activity of this study was found in the work of Thompson and McIntyre (2013). At the core of their work is the systems model of creativity developed by Csikszentmihalyi (1988, 1996, 1999) and further advanced by Kerrigan (2013) in the field of documentary filmmaking. Csikszentmihalyi's (1996: 6) model explains creative activity by using a system of three parts, connected through relationships and processes. The three parts are comprised of a 'domain' or culture that comprises a set of symbolic rules, guidelines, and practices, an 'individual' who brings novelty into the domain, and a 'field' of specialists or experts who identify and authenticate the novelty.

Thompson and McIntyre (2013) have used the systems model to produce a detailed mapping of the many categories and subcategories of the music industry that are contained within the 'field'. The field includes songwriting, performance, management, publishing, sound recording, live performance, and media. This mapping is used to isolate and identify community partners for CEL projects based on the nature of the specific area of study and/or the potential for reciprocity between the project partners. As already noted, Thompson and McIntyre also identify that the apprenticeship process – using the work of Meintjes (2005) and Horning (2004) – is the typical way individuals are exposed to the field and the interactions and relationships contained within it. Knowledge of the domain is necessary if students are to understand how decisions regarding the selection, adoption, or rejection of creative works or ideas are made within the field, as well as the mechanisms that guide these processes. Within a formal learning environment, this type of learning can be understood using an inquiry and analysis value rubric, as defined by the Association of American Colleges and Universities (AAC&U):

> Inquiry is a systematic process of exploring issues, objects or works through the collection and analysis of evidence that results in informed conclusions or judgments. Analysis is the process of breaking complex topics or issues into parts to gain a better understanding of them. (AAC&U 2009a)

While the field's structure and mechanisms can be taught within a formal learning environment, Thompson and McIntyre also identify that indirect knowledge of the field alone, without practical involvement and authentic connections to it, limits the value of this formal learning method. Turning to the work of Sawyer (2006), which highlights the role of collaboration in the making of many creative works, and the statement 'when members of the field contribute to the creative work they will invest their own reputations in that work' (Thompson and McIntyre 2013), we begin to see a way forward. This statement justifies the use of creative, collaborative projects to generate intrinsic motivation in students, and it directly links to the second learning outcome identified for the CEL project – lifelong learning. The AAC&U defines lifelong learning as 'all purposeful learning activity, undertaken on an ongoing basis with the aim of improving knowledge, skills and competence' (AAC&U 2009b).

McIntyre succinctly states that within the systems model of creativity, it is the role or task of the individual to make changes in the domain and then present these to the field. This CEL project models that task, and including CBR as the community partner provides an authentic exposure to the field. The opportunity for reflection, both within the class and individually, and the in-class feedback sessions with both peers and the community partner, are used to formalize learning of the field, including its processes and mechanisms. The CEL project can also be seen as working towards the learning outcome of creative thinking, the final identified learning outcome for this project. The following definition is again taken from the AAC&U:

> Creative thinking is both the capacity to combine or synthesize existing ideas, images or expertise in original ways and the experience of thinking, reacting and working in an imaginative way characterized by a high degree of innovation, divergent thinking, and risk taking. (AAC&U 2009c)

Case Study

This chapter uses an exploratory case-study design (Yin 2014) to evaluate a CEL project and understand the value students attribute to this type of activity and how the CEL approach improves learning outcomes. The materials used include course materials (assignments and creative works), student and instructor reflections, and semi-structured interviews with the project stakeholders. The project's assessment techniques and deliverables were all designed to facilitate student learning that is tied to the learning outcomes of inquiry and analysis, lifelong learning, and creative thinking – skills that are critical for students interested in a contemporary career in the music industry. The fourth-year course in which the project was delivered was composed of 10 students (3 female, 7 male). At 42%, the contributions by female students in the course far exceed those reported in the music industry. A recent University of Southern California Annenberg study (Smith et al. 2019), for example, shows that across 900 popular songs, women represented only 21.6% of the artists, 12.6% of the songwriters, and 2.6% of the producers.

At the beginning of the course, students were provided with a project brief and standard Flood Tide Music (FTM) new-artist onboarding. This included a list of target playlists and an FTM artist checklist for required deliverables (long bio, short bio, artist photo or images, artist logo, list of musical works, and songwriter shares). The CBR president gave two lectures as part of the course, introducing students to the CBR label and FTM imprint and providing an overview of the different revenue streams available to artists and the relevant copyright mechanisms. Students pitched their projects to the label president early in the semester, and in-progress works were critiqued mid-semester by the community partner. Regular in-class presentations and discussions promoted collaboration between students and allowed them to model aspects of the field. The CEL project was guided through the following three phases:

1. Project initiation, including the self-reporting of individual student learning goals and expectations of the project.
2. Works in progress, including the opportunity for peer feedback and discussion.
3. Project reporting, including a critical reflection on the learning experience, a self-assessment of the sound recording, and the self-reporting of independent research and skills development undertaken by the student.

Particular attention was paid to giving students the opportunity to reflect on their work – a key component of CEL – at the conclusion of each phase. This offered insight into the learning students perceived to be taking place over the course of the project. Case materials were analysed longitudinally and according to this phased timeline in order to identify patterns, both within individual phases and across the project experience. Semi-structured interview questions were developed in response to this analysis and used to explore the patterns observed and address rival interpretations of the case data (Yin 2014: 168).

Following the completion of the course, the AAC&U value rubrics for the previously identified learning outcomes were used to evaluate all course materials and to help guide the semi-structured interviews with study participants. These rubrics provide descriptions of student work associated with four levels of performance – benchmark (1), milestones (2 and 3), and capstone (4).[8]

Phase One: Project Initiation

Students were introduced to the CEL project, then asked to pitch a project that responded to the FTM brief. Accompanying their formal pitches were self-assessments in which students detailed their experience with the music business, their individual learning goals, and their expectations of the project experience. Many students accurately identified entities found within the mapping of the field of commercial record production. Their responses were weighted more heavily in sound recording and live performance, but their understanding of the landscape and actors was good as a baseline. To increase their knowledge in this area, the community partner gave a class that provided an overview of their business activity and background information about aspects of the music industry – copyright, contracts, and playlist curation, for example – that were relevant to the CEL project.

The analysis of these materials revealed two patterns of interest. The first was the high value that students attributed to having released their work on streaming platforms such as Spotify and Apple Music, and their subtle ranking of these different providers. This is illustrated in the following student response:

> Our first EP is on our Bandcamp page and the second one is available on Spotify and Apple Music. During the time we were active, we played a ton of shows and even recorded a couple music videos, one of which was a cover of 'Sorry' by Justin Bieber on YouTube.

A second pattern was that students distinguished between school-based, formal experiences and extracurricular, informal experiences. Several students indicated that they had significant experience recording on campus, but this activity was assigned a different status than experiences that involved 'commercial', 'professional', or 'actual' studios. Only two students illustrated their knowledge of the selection processes and mechanisms associated with the field of commercial record production. One student noted that their

8. The value rubrics for inquiry and analysis, lifelong learning, and creative thinking used in this study are freely available from the following website: https://www.aacu.org/initiatives/value-initiative/value-rubrics.

SoundCloud releases 'never found an audience'. Another student showed a more advanced understanding of contemporary selection processes, as illustrated in the following quote:

> Many released works are available on Apple Music, Spotify, Deeezer, Google Music, etc. via Universal Music's Spinnup distributor; released works on free sites including SoundCloud, Bandcamp, Datpiff, Audiomack, etc.; submitted music often to Curators and Blogs either directly, or via a submission site such as SubmitHub.

No students reported having registered their creative works with SOCAN (Society of Composers, Authors and Music Publishers of Canada) or indicated that gaining knowledge in this area of the music industry was one of their learning goals. The majority of students identified aspects of the CEL project that they perceived to be valuable, including the opportunity to

> showcase [my] composition and production skills to industry professionals with the aim to take my career further ... I'm very eager to see what the creative process is like when working with a label, as well as how one might get into this line of work.

Phase Two: Works in Progress

In the weeks following the initial project pitch, students began to realize their creative projects and make tangible the language, images, and concepts they had used to pitch their musical projects. Students had a second opportunity to meet the community partner and play excerpts from their creative works in progress to obtain feedback from the CBR label president.

Turning to the conceptual framework used for this project, this engagement with the community partner is a significant interaction between the 'individual' (student) and the 'field' (CBR label president). For the student, presenting their works in progress represents both evidence of technical and aesthetic ability and confirmation that their creative approach aligns with the label's positioning and goals. In other words, this was their opportunity to show their understanding of the 'domain' of record production. For the community partner, the activity models work that would normally be done by an artist and repertoire (A&R) representative – a person within a record company who is responsible for finding and signing talent. It also illustrates the role of the 'field' of record production, which has been defined as the 'social organization able to assess, reject and accept novel ideas, products or designs' (Thompson and McIntyre 2013: n.p.).

The materials used in analysing this phase of the project included the students' works in progress, their work plans for completion, and drafts of their band/artist bios. In the majority of cases, the students' written materials showed only a basic understanding of the positioning and goals of their projects and were limited with regards to answering *how* they would achieve them. The following statement is an example of the way students described their projects:

The goal of my piece is to provide atmosphere and ambience in a calming and melodic way. In comparison, the following statement – which represents the minority of student work – illustrates a greater level of engagement with the materials provided by the community partner and responds to the question of *how* it will be executed:

> The two Spotify playlists Instrumental Study and Peaceful Piano are the two main models for the style we are looking to create. Thus, it will be between 2–4 minutes in length, consist of mostly diatonic with some mixed modal harmony, and have at least two parts that will likely have an ABA form, with some sort of space or event before the 2nd A section.

Comparing these analyses with the students' self-assessments in phase one revealed that the more experience in the music business students had, the higher their level of engagement with the CBR materials and the more detailed their completion plans.

The transcripts of the students' in-class presentations and the critiques from the community partner were particularly important, providing insight into how students engaged with the community partner and the nature of the feedback they received. They were also a first indication of how well the students' projects matched CBR's expectations. Analysis of these materials revealed that the community partner chose to highlight and spotlight elements of the demos they liked but offered little explicit direction about what they felt wasn't working with the individual projects. The prevalent theme of their feedback was around listener engagement and a preference for works with elements that would create interest for the listener. Comments such as 'nice layering, [it] will keep the listener engaged' and 'There is a surprising amount of content in a relaxation piece of music' illustrate the focus upon this aspect of the students' work. The community partner was supportive of student work and in no instances indicated that work wasn't meeting their expectations.

Another theme from this analysis was that the students appeared unwilling to ask the community partner questions about their projects. As noted, the community partner's comments centred around highlighting aspects of student work that met with their expectations and aesthetics. Compared to a critique, this type of commentary provides less opportunity for dialogue. Still, given the opportunity for engagement that this session afforded, it was interesting to observe that students seemed reticent to ask questions of the community partner. My experience as their instructor for this course allows me to state that this is not the normal dynamic for this class, and therefore it was noted as significant. One potential explanation is that this resulted because of a perceived power imbalance and the positioning of the community partner within an academic setting. This was pursued through the semi-structured interviews, as the pedagogical value of being able to directly engage with, not simply experience the presence of, the community partner is important to the CEL project and therefore demands further exploration.

Phase Three: Project Reporting

The final phase of the CEL project was the delivery of the students' creative projects, including their pieces of music, artwork, and short and long bios, mirroring the list of materials CBR requires for any new artist being considered by the label. The projects were sent to the community partner for consideration, and students presented their projects in class for comments and critiques by their peers. The final component of the CEL project was student reflection, where they were asked to focus on the individual learning and skills development gained over the course of the project.

The analysis of these different components revealed a number of interesting themes. The first was the value students placed upon having their work signed, or picked up, by the label. Within a professional context – which this CEL project attempted to model – this would be the singular marker of success for a work. In this case the community partner ultimately did not choose any of their projects for release. However, in terms of the learning and skills development reported by students, the actual value of this project was the proximity to the community partner that it provided, and few mentioned any disappointment at not having their work signed by CBR. This is exemplified in a reflection provided by one student on the CEL project:

> I really liked how hands on and real world it was. So, the fact that it's kind of emulating what an artist would do. And that, I guess, is real world, we actually were doing that as artists, for Cordova Bay, writing up our bio, and thinking about all of the contexts that's involved with our music and how it's all going to reach its end point.

Another student directly identifies the value assigned to the proximity that the CEL project provided:

> And I had never really seen in general, people in the actual industry, and kind of, in a way, it made me think of the idea that jobs like that are out there.

And, finally, this student identifies how the proximity and insight into industry practices validated their educational experience, which is shown in their comparison of the two:

> I kind of felt that there was less separation than I would have thought.

It also became clear that while the project was seen as being 'real world', there was tension around its positioning as a class project, which affected how students ultimately approached it. Their comments echoed their self-reflections in phase one: they clearly saw this as a 'school project' and therefore an academic endeavour with a focus on their individual goals. It was interesting to hear how students saw themselves and their work within this context. The positioning of this as an academic project is evident in the following student comment:

> The project with CBR didn't feel like anything I had done as a professional, it was very much still a student project.

The use of *assignment* in the following comment again positions this as an academic activity, with the student also placing priority upon individual development and growth:

> I often like to make my own spin on whatever the assignment is. And sometimes it doesn't really line up with what they want. But it often ends up being better than if I just followed everything.

And, finally, here is another student's experience of this positioning of the work:

> Through doing that thing for Flood Tide Records, I felt like I wasn't in it for myself, there was a layer of separation between myself and my work. I could look at it more objectively. It's kind of like meditation, where you're trying to observe your thoughts rather than being in your thoughts. So yeah, I thought that also helped me to work on my own work and have that mindset going on.

Conclusion

The analysis above is useful in helping to develop an understanding of the value students placed upon the CEL project, and their experiences of participating in this project. It is clear that the community partner's position aligned with the students' understanding of the 'field' of record production, and the partnership was also seen as a legitimate opportunity to engage with the 'real world'. What is equally clear is that it would be unrealistic, given the geographic location and size of Victoria's music industry sector, that the same number of students would have been able to secure traditional internships. In this way, the CEL project structure multiplied what would otherwise have been a singular opportunity. In all the semi-structured interviews, which occurred following the conclusion of the course, students indicated that the project had been a positive experience and they had appreciated the opportunity to participate. Because the CEL project was embedded into a course it ensured that all students could participate, and with a currency of experience and academic credit, the problematic questions of inequity with regards to labour and compensation evident within the traditional internship structure are largely accounted for. Equally clear was the fact that the CEL project introduced a tension between school and professional work and that this affected the way students engaged with the project, which had interesting implications upon student learning. Returning to the motivation for this chapter – my desire to rewrite the 'internship' myth, with a focus upon student learning – I will now turn to the conclusions I have drawn about this project and attempt to answer how the CEL project functioned with regards to student learning outcomes.

Looking past the tension that the CEL project brought to the course, the most successful area with regards to student learning was in the category of lifelong learning, which aligns with one of the commonly referenced outcomes when using community-engaged learning approaches (Preston et al., n.d.; David M. Einhorn Center for Community Engagement, n.d.). In both the student self-reflections and semi-structured interviews, students routinely referenced the learning and skills developed over the course of the semester, and how this had changed their perspectives about both their academic and personal experiences. Using the AAC&U rubric, and evaluating student work in the subcategories of curiosity, initiative, independence, transfer, and reflection, the majority of students showed evidence of working at the second milestone or the capstone performance level. Importantly, with the semi-structured interviews occurring several months after the conclusion of this project, it was possible to see clues to how integrated the skills and dispositions involved in lifelong learning had become within the students. Concrete examples of this can be seen in their registering of creative works with SOCAN and forming new creative groups and projects.

In comparison, student learning in the areas of inquiry and analysis and creative thinking was observed and evaluated to be at lower performance levels. With regards to inquiry and analysis, the materials and resources provided to the students to help them develop their creative works were generally underutilized, and the process for achieving their creative goals didn't advance beyond benchmark or the first milestone performance levels. Creative thinking was somewhat more difficult to evaluate because of the different competencies and experience across the student cohort. Some students were very skilled with regards to sound engineering but had far less experience than their peers in composing music or working with composers, which was a component of this project. A longitudinal and individual approach was therefore employed to evaluate student work, using the self-reflections, samples of works in progress, and in-class critiques to evaluate their performance. This revealed that in the majority of cases, the students' ability to progress from benchmark performance levels was limited, regardless of their relative starting competencies.

The case-study data and analyses suggest that the limited learning observed in these categories is tied to the tension that the CEL project introduced into the course: students positioned school and professional activity as separate activities, and this affected the way they engaged with the project. This tension was pursued through the semi-structured interviews, revealing that in some cases the students' level of engagement, and how they approached their creative work, was based upon the activity being positioned as a school project. Students reported that because of this, they chose to work on their own learning goals; for example, recording techniques or mixing techniques. In essence they 'successfully reproduce[d] an appropriate exemplar' rather than 'evaluat[ing] creative process and product using domain-appropriate criteria'. These descriptions are taken from the AAC&U Creative Thinking Value Rubric and represent the benchmark versus capstone performance levels respectively.

The fact that the students had to complete the project but the community partner was under no obligation to use their creative works resulted in an assessment by one student that the community partner had no 'skin in the game'. This points to a key feature of a successful CEL project: genuine reciprocity between the community partner and the university and its students. The assessment above indicates that the value of the engagement *with* students by the community partner wasn't clear. The flow of information was viewed as being in one direction, similar to a standard lecture-based course, and the value of students' engaging with the partner, and empowering them to see the value of their contributions, was again not made clear. The CEL project ultimately was successful, and the engagement with the community partner significantly enhanced the course. However, I am left wondering how students would have engaged with this project had they known *their* value to the community partner and that this project provided the partner with:

> a way to reassess what's important within the industry and what we need to prioritize, and maybe what we even want to look at changing, because it's a very rapidly changing industry too. So, it's just sort of a great exercise to sit down and really sort of try and think about, okay, what are the important pieces here that we want future members of the industry to really, you know, drive home. (Interview with Cordova Bay Records president, 11 June 2021)

What is described here is a reciprocal relationship that is possible through a CEL project, one that provides significant value to both the student and community partner. The ability to structure and promote reciprocity between the students and community partner using the CEL framework is also very powerful with regards to student learning. If done effectively, it affords far greater control to educators than is possible when using traditional internships, and better models the 'real world' by ensuring the student has legitimate agency. This relationship is accounted for within the systems model of creativity – the basis of the conceptual framework used for this CEL project – whereby the individual, field, and domain of record production are shown as having an 'interrelationship between the system's elements, each one influenc[ing] each other through a dynamic system of causality' (Thompson 2019: 102). Future versions of this CEL project will reveal this interrelationship at the inception of the project and then be tested to see if this results in greater student learning and skills development in the areas of inquiry, analysis and creative thinking, and better prepares students for a future career in the music industry.

References

AAC&U (Association of American Colleges and Universities). 2009a. 'VALUE Rubrics – Inquiry and Analysis'. https://www.aacu.org/initiatives/value-initiative/value-rubrics/value-rubrics-inquiry-and-analysis

AAC&U (Association of American Colleges and Universities). 2009b. 'VALUE Rubrics – Foundations and Skills for Lifelong Learning'. https://www.aacu.org/initiatives/value-initiative/value-rubrics/value-rubrics-foundations-and-skills-for-lifelong-learning

AAC&U (Association of American Colleges and Universities). 2009c. 'VALUE Rubrics – Creative Thinking'. https://www.aacu.org/initiatives/value-initiative/value-rubrics/value-rubrics-creative-thinking

Astin, A. W., and L. J. Sax. 1998. 'How undergraduates are affected by service participation'. *Journal of College Studies Development* 39, no. 3: 251–63.

Becker, H. S. 1982. *Art Worlds*. Berkeley: University of California Press.

Bielmeier, D. 2020. 'Future educational goals and actionable items: Teaching communication skills for audio education institutions and educators'. In *Audio Education: Theory, Culture, and Practice*, 243–62. New York and Abingdon: Routledge.

Borwick, J. 1973. 'The Tönmeister concept'. Paper presented at Audio Engineering Society Convention 46, New York, 10–13 September.

Csikszentmihalyi, M. 1988. 'Society, culture, and person: A systems view of creativity'. In *The Nature of Creativity*, edited by R. Stenberg, 325–39. Cambridge: Cambridge University Press.

Csikszentmihalyi, M. 1996. *Creativity: Flow and the Psychology of Discovery and Invention*. New York: HarperCollins.

Csikszentmihalyi, M. 1999. 'Implications of a systems perspective for the study of creativity'. In *Handbook of Creativity*, edited by R. Stenberg, 313–35. Cambridge: Cambridge University Press.

David M. Einhorn Center for Community Engagement, Cornell University. n.d. 'What is community-engaged learning?' https://einhorn.cornell.edu/about/what-is-community-engaged-learning/

Faulkner, R. R. 1983. *Music on Demand: Composers and Careers in the Hollywood Film Industry*. New Brunswick, NJ: Transaction Books.

Florida, R., and S. Jackson. 2010. 'Sonic city: The evolving economic geography of the music industry'. *Journal of Planning Education and Research* 29, no. 3: 310–321. https://doi.org/10.1177/0739456X09354453

Frenette, A. 2013. 'Making the intern economy: Role and career challenges of the music industry intern'. *Work and Occupations* 40, no. 4: 364–97. https://doi.org/10.1177/0730888413504098

Frenette, A., and T. J. Dowd. 2019. *Who Stays and Who Leaves? Arts Education and the Career Trajectories of Arts Alumni in the United States*. Washington DC: National Endowment for the Arts.

Frenette, A., with A. Dumford, A. Miller, and S. Tepper. 2015. *The Internship Divide: The Promise and Challenges of Internships in the Arts*. Special report for the Strategic National Arts Alumni Project. Bloomington, IN: Indiana University Center for Postsecondary Research, School of Education.

Gallini, S., and B. Moely. 2003. 'Service-learning and engagement, academic challenge, and retention'. *Michigan Journal of Community Service Learning* 10, no. 1: 5–14.

Gaston-Bird, L., R. Mason and E. De Sena. 2021. 'Inclusivity in immersive audio: Current participation and barriers to entry'. Paper presented at Audio Engineering Society International Audio Education Conference, Nashville, TN, July 2021.

Henson, D., and S. Zagorski-Thomas. 2019. 'Setting the agenda: Theorizing popular music education practice'. In *The Bloomsbury Handbook of Popular Music Education: Perspectives and Practices*, 11–27. New York: Bloomsbury.

Horning, S. S. 2004. 'Engineering the performance: Recording engineers, tacit knowledge and the art of controlling sound'. *Social Studies of Science* 34, no. 5: 703–31. https://doi.org/10.1177/0306312704047536

Jacobson, J., and L. R. Shade. 2018. '*Stringtern*: Springboarding or stringing along young interns' careers?' *Journal of Education and Work* 31, no. 3: 320–37. https://doi.org/10.1080/13639080.2018.1473559

Kerrigan, S. 2013. 'Accommodating creative documentary practice within a revised systems model of creativity'. *Journal of Media Practice* 14, no. 2: 111–27. https://doi.org/10.1386/jmpr.14.2.111_1

Lave, J., and E. Wenger. 1991. *Situated Learning: Legitimate Peripheral Participation*. Cambridge: Cambridge University Press.

Meintjes, L. 2005. 'Reaching "overseas": South African sound engineers, technology, and tradition'. In *Wired for Sound: Engineering and Technologies in Sonic Cultures*, edited by Paul D. Greene and Thomas Porcello, 23–46. Middletown, CT: Wesleyan University Press.

Miège, B. 1989. *The Capitalization of Cultural Production*. New York: International General.

Pratt, D. 1998. *Five Perspectives on Teaching in Adult and Higher Education*. Malabar, FL: Krieger Publishing.

Preston, S., C. Chiappetta-Swanson, S. Beaudette, R. Talbot, and C. Collver. n.d. *Incorporating Community-Engaged Education into Courses: A Guidebook*. Faculty of Social Sciences, McMaster University. https://community.mcmaster.ca/app/uploads/2019/01/faculty-manual-guidebook-updated-version.pdf

Reddington, H. 2021. *She's at the Controls: Sound Engineering, Production and Gender Ventriloquism in the 21st Century*. Sheffield, UK: Equinox Publishing.

Rolston, C. P., and D. Herrera. 2000. 'The critical role of university-sponsored internships for entry into the professional music business: A report of a national survey'. *Journal of Arts Management, Law, and Society* 30, no. 2: 102–12. https://doi.org/10.1080/10632920009601289

Sawyer, R. K. 2006. *Explaining Creativity: The Science of Human Innovation*. New York: Oxford University Press.

Smith, S., K. Pieper, M. Choueiti, K. Hernandez, and K. Yao. 2019. *Inclusion in the Recording Studio? Gender and Race/Ethnicity of Artists, Songwriters and Producers across 600 Popular Songs from 2012–2017*. Los Angeles: University of Southern California Annenberg.

Sound Diplomacy, Secret Study Projects, Music BC Industry Association, and Vancouver Music Steering Committee. 2018. *Vancouver Music Ecosystem Study*. London: Sound Diplomacy.

Théberge, P. 2004. 'The network studio: Historical and technological paths to a new ideal in music making'. *Social Studies of Science* 34, no. 5: 759–81. https://doi.org/10.1177/0306312704047173

Thompson, D. 2012. 'Unpaid internships: Bad for students, bad for workers, bad for society'. *The Atlantic*, 10 May. https://www.theatlantic.com/business/archive/2012/05/unpaid-internships-bad-for-students-bad-for-workers-bad-for-society/256958/

Thompson, P. 2019. *Creativity in the Recording Studio: Alternative Takes*. New York: Palgrave Macmillan.

Thompson, P., and P. McIntyre. 2013. 'Rethinking creative practice in record production and studio recording education: Addressing the field'. *Journal on the Art of Record Production* 8.

Tough, D. 2010. 'Shaping audio engineering curriculum: An expert panel's view of the future'. Paper presented at Audio Engineering Society Convention 129, San Francisco, 4–7 November.
Vogelgesang, L., and A. Astin. 2000. 'Comparing the effects of community service and service-learning'. *Michigan Journal of Community Service Learning* 7, no. 1: 5–13.
Wolfe, P. 2019. *Women in the Studio: Creativity, Control and Gender in Popular Music Sound Production*. London: Routledge.
Yin, R. K. 2014. *Case Study Research: Design and Methods*. Thousand Oaks, CA: Sage Publications.

Author biography

Kirk McNally is a sound engineer specializing in the recording of popular and classical music, as well as in the performances of new musical works using electronics. Kirk is the associate professor of Music Technology at the University of Victoria, Canada. In this role, he serves as the program administrator for an undergraduate combined program in music and computer science, as well as the graduate program in music technology. His research and creative work have received support from the Canada Council for the Arts and the Social Sciences and Humanities Research Council of Canada (SSHRC).

10 Putting Down Roots: Making Music and Embracing Messiness in Graduate School

Taylor Ackley with Joe Sferra

Introduction

The sound of the Deep Roots Ensemble is equal parts classical chamber music, American folk music, and jazz improvisation, consisting of mandolin or banjo, cello, violin, flute, French horn, clarinet, and string bass, with four of the instrumentalists doubling as singers. We find joy in exploring approaches to music-making beyond what we encountered during our education – blending, blurring, and bringing together our musical backgrounds and aspirations. From our beginnings as an informal gathering of graduate music students, to our current work as a professional ensemble with two studio albums and a growing national profile, we have navigated the complex histories of the music we play and the intricate politics of the institutions we relate to. In this chapter I will present an autoethnography of my work with the Deep Roots Ensemble, examining the mess revealed by engaging with under-represented musical practices in American academic music.

The graduate study of music presents both a remarkable opportunity and a complicated enigma as students transition from the generalist approach of undergraduate instruction to a specific specialization. This process is intertwined with a shift from student to professional and includes an expectation of engaging with dense bodies of scholarship and demands for theory and precise language, which describes relationships with music that are subjective and often deeply personal. For students from underrepresented cultural or musical backgrounds, especially those who learned music outside an academic environment, several fraught circumstances arise. These include the expectation that one student speaks for a whole group of people, the necessity to disclose personal experiences which inform art or scholarship, or a general difficulty connecting personal experiences or cultural values onto contemporary educational and scholarly trends (see Leon 1999; Ramsey 2003).

As a person from a background of rural poverty and with a long family tradition of music-making, my experience in graduate school was characterized by access to life-changing opportunities intertwined with expectations of me and my art that were quite different from those of my peers. This began with the very first performance by what would eventually become the Deep Roots Ensemble. In a piece called 'Sonata for Horn, Cello and Banjo', I drew upon music I learned from my grandfather and conveyed all the musical materials to performers aurally, without the use of notation. In a composers' forum after the premiere, I was asked by a faculty member the ontologically loaded question of what constitutes 'the work' in music like this, with minimal discussion of the actual music I created.[1] This was in stark contrast to the sort of discussions that generally grew out of the premiere of more classically oriented, fully notated works by my peers.

The professor asked this question with the best intentions and had no idea that my piece responded to my father falling deathly ill, my family's loss of our home, and our return to poverty. Nor did he know that his question would make me doubt the value of my art and its place in an academic institution, reinforcing that the music of my background was fundamentally different from what other composers were doing. Ultimately, I benefitted greatly from considering the profound differences between different ways of making music, developing a scholarly practice and a body of creative work that engages with questions about art, value, and representation in American music. Looking back, this moment and my reactions to it are a fair representation of the complex intersection of privilege and marginalization which I experienced as a graduate student.

Methodology

This chapter will present an autoethnography describing the process of bringing my musical heritage into the centre of my academic and professional life throughout my graduate studies at Stony Brook University. I will discuss the Deep Roots Ensemble and our growth from a graduate student-led workshop into a professional performing group. By embracing the messiness of this process, I attempt to show how different ways of engaging with music can simultaneously contradict and support each other. Moreover, I will show

---

1. Lydia Goehr (1992) outlines many of the ideas and assumptions surrounding classical music, which clashed with elements of my work.

how studying and creating music is an ongoing process in which one rarely gets the opportunity to sort everything out before stepping onto the stage or in the front of a classroom. This chapter will primarily be from my perspective as the founder and director of the Deep Roots Ensemble, all sections are by me in the first person, except where otherwise noted. Because of the profoundly collaborative nature of the project, it was also important to include contributions from my long-time colleague and close friend Joe Sferra. One passage in the 'Performance Practice' section is entirely from his perspective and the 'Class, Equity and Inclusion' and 'Conclusion' sections of this chapter were written collaboratively.

My approach to autoethnography is grounded in two bodies of scholarship. First, I draw heavily on the tradition of writing by Black scholars which work to centre personal experience and family and community histories in the academic discussion of Black music-making in the United States (see Baraka 1963; Lewis 1996; Ramsey 2003; Crawley 2017). A particularly relevant example is *Race Music*, in which Ramsey (2003) draws upon historical research and his unique experiences as equally valuable sources. He proposes the term 'race music' as a scholarly lens which 'intentionally seeks to recapture some of the historical ethnocentric energy' of historically Black musical practices to draw upon traditional scholarly models as well as ethnographic perspectives, cultural memory, and self-reflexivity in his 'analysis, interpretation, and criticism' of this music (3). While his musical subject and personal identity differ substantially from my own, his insistence on intellectual honesty and openness has directly inspired how I talk about my cultural background and its connection to my music.

The second branch of scholarship which informs this chapter's approach is feminist ethnography, especially within the field of ethnomusicology. In the late 1990s and early 2000s, Michelle Kisliuk, Ellen Koskoff, and Kay Kaufman Shelemay produced scholarship which rejected ill-fated attempts at objectivity in favour of ethnographic work that openly situated the scholar as a person, reconsidering the relationship between ethnographers and their subjects/informants/research-collaborators (Kisliuk 2000; Koskoff 2005; Shelemay 1999). This writing is characterized by a remarkable openness about the research process, including presenting the authors' misconceptions and mistakes as valuable sites of learning for both them and their readers. In one striking example, Kisliuk (2000) describes how she completely misunderstood a gendered dance practice while learning from the BaAka people. After admitting her mistake, she examines how she projected her own Western, gender biases onto a cultural practice that was far more egalitarian than she assumed. This sort of openness has reshaped expectations in the humanities, opening the door for radically personal writing like Donna Haraway's (2016), blurring the lines between autobiography, science, philosophy, and poetry.[2] A more recent example of feminist ethnography, which is directly applicable to the goals of this chapter, is Emily Billo and Nancy Hiemstra's 'Mediating messiness: Expanding ideas of flexibility, reflexivity, and embodiment in fieldwork'. Billo and Hiemstra (2013) present an admirably open account of their entry into ethnographic fieldwork, describing how their educations did not adequately prepare them for the harsh realities of the field and showing the messy ways in which lived experience conflicted with their theoretical ideas and personal ideologies. Reading this work helped me permit myself to engage with big ideas before I had all the answers and encouraged me to embrace the messiness of my own story, my family history, and the rapidly evolving field of American folk and roots music studies.

With these approaches in mind, this chapter will present my experiences forming and directing a roots music ensemble, a project that became the primary activity of my graduate work in two master's degrees and a PhD. It will explore how leading and composing for this ensemble transitioned from a student activity to a professional practice. I will discuss how the demands of academia interact with the life of a professional musician in messy ways and will engage with questions about inclusion, diversity, and privilege. This chapter addresses these issues by presenting how the musical practice of the Deep Roots Ensemble participates in large, messy discussions surrounding contemporary music making.[3]

Forming the Deep Roots Ensemble

I come from a background of multigenerational poverty. My family's roots are in rural communities in the Southern and Western United States, where we have scrapped out livings through farming, ranching, mining, and various other forms of manual labour.[4] We are also musicians as far back as I can trace on my mother and father's sides. While the resources needed to study music in the traditional classical-oriented sense were far outside of our means, we

---

2. Haraway's ideas about the many sites of knowledge in *Staying with the Trouble* deeply informed my thoughts about the relationship between art and scholarship.
3. The Deep Roots Ensemble has two commercially released albums, *Song from the Bitterroot* (2018) and *Hard Tellin'* (2020). Should the reader wish to watch us performing I recommend the following videos: https://www.youtube.com/watch?v=tUtwZhdIRr0 and https://www.youtube.com/watch?v=dKmCx_Oo22E
4. The Deep Roots Ensemble's second album *Hard Tellin'* presents some of my family history in the songs 'Tools of the Trade', 'Exodus', and 'Fences'.

had our own traditions of playing and singing folk and roots music which have long been a source of great pride and a considerable reputation in our communities (see Bates 2012).

From my maternal grandfather, Gene Smith, I learned hundreds of songs and tunes as well as how to accompany and improvise. His repertoire and style form the foundation of the Deep Roots Ensemble's practice. He also taught me how to play mandolin, guitar, bass, banjo, and dobro. His mandolin was built in the late 1800s and came with his father's family to Oklahoma in a covered wagon in about 1900. I picked out my first solos on this instrument long before I realized how much the musical heritage it represents would mean to me and my career. My father Dennis Ackley is an outstanding guitarist who specializes in bluegrass, gospel, and western swing styles. When I was young, he was one of Northwestern Montana's most sought-after singing cowboys and collaborated with many well-known folk and roots musicians including the Fairfield Four, Rob Quist, and Vassar Clemmons. Among the numerous things I learned from him was a specific approach to singing harmony by ear, which I draw heavily on when working with the Deep Roots. My father and grandfather often performed together, and many of my most formative musical experiences were playing and singing with them.

The musical skills I learned from my family facilitated my education and a path out of the body-breaking manual labour and the economic precarity that had characterized much of my family's and many in our community's experiences. That said, my undergraduate musical education from 2008–2012 only encouraged me to use these skills as a basis for studying and making Western classical music (and to a certain extent, jazz). The instances where my education valued the musical heritage from which I developed these skills were few and far between (see Shevock 2016). My graduate studies in composition began in 2014 with basically the same premise, this time as much self-imposed as anything.

In the Spring semester of 2015, my father became very ill. After months in and out of the hospital, he lost his job, my parents spent the little savings they had on his medical bills, and our family lost our home. I turned in my last assignments for the semester (including my first writing on country music) and flew home to help. Over the course of a few weeks, we sold or gave away everything that didn't fit in a small horse trailer, feeling our last hopes of middle-class stability dissolve. After long days we would sit on our porch and play music just like we always had. I seriously considered dropping out of school after that summer but decided instead to create art based not on the music I had learned to value in school, but on the folk and country music which my family turned to when we had almost nothing else.[5]

Returning to school was hard. There were almost no resources available at my institution to help graduate students navigate issues of poverty. The expenses of beginning a career in academic music (from instruments and equipment to festival and travel costs) felt completely unobtainable. My saving grace was a remarkably supportive department and a shift in the cultural tides of academic music, which seemed to be growing increasingly receptive to artists from backgrounds outside of classical music. In the fall of 2015, I started holding workshops where I taught other graduate music students how to play and sing American folk and roots music. Our sessions explored learning by ear, improvising accompaniments, and harmonizing in a folk style.[6] Over two years, these workshops coalesced into an ensemble of seven to nine players with a sizable repertoire and an increasingly sophisticated approach to playing both traditional and original repertoire. In the spring of 2017, we held our first public recital as the Stony Brook Roots Ensemble. By the summer of 2018, we had an active performance schedule of around thirty public performances a year and released our first album as the Deep Roots Ensemble.

From 2015 to 2017, teaching, performing, and composing American folk and roots music became the central focus of my graduate work. This coincided with an effort to be much more open about my cultural background and my experiences of poverty.[7] The growing reputation of the Deep Roots Ensemble and my situation as the only person from a background like mine within Stony Brook's large music department offered incredible opportunities to share my ideas and observations. Along with public performance, I began lecturing about my music as a guest speaker in classrooms, public events, and conferences. This development pushed me to address big questions about music, class, and culture, before I had the scholarly training to do so with the rigor expected in academia. As Rosenberg (1993) has observed, folk practitioners are often prompted to develop and articulate ideologies about their music through contact with well-meaning outsiders (197). This prompted me to take on a second master's degree in ethnomusicology. This new branch of study was equally inspiring and frustrating as I was learning a great deal, but often felt that what I was reading conflicted with my personal experiences,

5. In the chapter 'Daddy's Second Line' Ramsey (2003) describes how loss and family music making inspired his academic work.
6. Hood's concept of 'bi-musicality' was an important theory in the early stages of this work (Hood 1960).
7. Yates is the first scholar I read from a background like mine who openly described his experiences (Yates 2009).

and that the field of ethnomusicology was built upon a different set of values than were held by the people I originally learned music from.[8]

The remainder of this chapter is devoted to unpacking some of the complexities of creating art and scholarship grounded in a personal connection with a musical practice outside of what is typically studied in American higher education. These sites of intellectual and artistic messiness provide valuable opportunities to discuss important issues in the study of folk and popular music and may offer insights into how music institutions can better serve students from marginalized communities and traditions. I hope this inspires educators to think creatively about the ways they can support and mentor musicians as they transition from students to professionals and that students reading this chapter are encouraged to explore big ideas that matter to them through making music.

Performance Practice

The most obvious departure of the Deep Roots Ensemble from norms in music education has been the development of a performance practice in which elements of musical traditions that are widely regarded as high art, specifically classical chamber music, are integrated into a folk-based style of playing and singing. While classical music has long drawn upon folk and popular music, attempting to bring performance of these kinds of music into spaces typically reserved for classical music is a much more recent development. Several institutions have bluegrass, folk, and old-time ensembles, including Berklee, East Tennessee State University, Warren Wilson College, Troy University, and Berea College, but for all of its roughly two dozen members across five years, the Deep Roots Ensemble was their first opportunity to study this music within an academic context. I have asked my long-time collaborator and founding member of the Deep Roots Ensemble, Joe Sferra, to write about his experience with the ensemble, learning to perform American folk and roots music. The remainder of this section is from his perspective.

Joe Sferra

While my formal study of music was devoted to classical music, I had two experiences as a child that helped me develop skills that I would eventually refine as a clarinettist and vocalist in the Deep Roots Ensemble. While studying piano, I played extensively from lead sheets, which cultivated my facility

---

8. Billo and Hiemstra (2013) explore the conflict between scholarship and personal experience, while Leon (1999) explores these conflicting values in scholarship on Peruvian music.

in improvising and accompanying. I also played clarinet in church, which prompted me to explore harmonizing melodies by ear. As a church musician, I also had to be prepared to modify arrangements in real-time, adding or skipping verses to accommodate timing in a service. While these skills were formative in my music making, I drew on them less and less as I studied music in school. When I began to play in Taylor's workshops, I felt that I was stretching muscles that I had long neglected. As the Deep Roots performed more regularly, the group featured flexibility and spontaneity that hearkened back to the experiences that first made me love music. Our performance practice facilitated a personal synthesis of my academic training and formative musical experiences through the folk-based approach that Taylor taught the group.

When we learn new music, Taylor teaches us the song or tune by ear, and we work out arrangements by playing and singing (Frisch 1987 outlines a similar method). We don't transcribe these rhythms or melodies, but sometimes we use lyric sheets in rehearsal and pencil in reminders about what to play. When performing, we use no notation, playing entirely from memory.[9] While this can be laborious, the payoff is incredible. By relying on memory, the repetition through performance continues the learning process. We play spontaneously and flexibly, so our understanding of our repertoire and connections with the other group members develops and deepens over time. In many performances, we select tunes and take requests from a call list of about fifty songs, shaping the programme in the moment. This flexibility plays out within individual pieces as well. If I'm soloing and gaining momentum, Taylor can call out 'Keep it going now!' and the group knows that I will keep playing and they should continue supporting me.[10] We can modify arrangements live based on our assessment of the audience, adding choruses, or playing the second half of a tune again. John Covach outlines that these practices are quite common in popular music, where modular song forms are assembled during a performance (Covach 2005: 76). Still, I hadn't experienced music-making like this in public performance since childhood.

While this flexibility in repertoire and form is our ideal, we sometimes must compromise as our profile has risen. When performing in formal recitals or large festival stages, we work out specific arrangements and play from a strict set list. Musical details are still improvised in these circumstances, but larger formal structures are more stringent. Working with guest artists also

9. For further discussion of the changing historical roles of transcription see Nettl (2015).
10. This sort of calling is common in roots performance and exemplified by Bob Wills; see his 1936 recording of 'Steel Guitar Rag' and Halberstadt (2001).

limits elements of our approach. Artists who haven't participated in our years-long aural learning process use lead sheets or need to be featured in more structured parts of our performances. While some of our most exciting concerts have included guest musicians, they generally require compromises of our performance practice.

As our audience sizes have grown, the need for amplification has produced a particularly challenging compromise of our ideals. Most of our members come from classical chamber music backgrounds and chafe against playing into microphones. We much prefer controlling our dynamics and instrument placement, 'mixing' ourselves in whatever space we are performing. We try to maintain that chamber music-based approach, even with amplification. Our microphone levels are set before the performance: we adjust our dynamics as we would in an acoustic setting and try not to rely on the mixing of an engineer. Sometimes we only perform with one or two microphones, which we each step up to when featured. By developing a response to amplification consistent with our performance practice, we have serendipitously recovered a technique from roots musicians of the mid-twentieth century. Our movements and playing around microphones resemble the choreography of groups like Bill Monroe and The Blue Grass Boys, where the instrumentalists would both approach and back away from a single microphone during performances and recording sessions.[11] By synthesizing our academic musical training and Taylor's folk methods, we have approached new musical situations with openness, even though amplified performances always feel like a departure from our ideals.

While reflecting on the Deep Roots Ensemble in preparation for writing this chapter, I was struck by how many integral aspects of our performance practice never came up during my formal education. As a college music student, I was primarily taught how to perform a fixed program of notated music with a specific ensemble. I rarely learned how to handle last-minute changes in repertoire, arrangement, or amplification with any consistency. I certainly wasn't pushed to learn music by ear. While there are college programs where this training is more common, particularly in jazz, old-time and bluegrass, this is not yet the norm in higher education. For me, the Deep Roots' performance practice combines the best of what I learned in academic music with the folk practices we have learned from Taylor, providing a way to play music that embraces the spontaneity and flexibility that I missed in so much of my other performance in academic settings.

11. Their performance of 'Uncle Pen' (1965) exemplifies this approach: https://www.youtube.com/watch?v=MeZPAQRl7TA.

Class, Equity, and Inclusion

Along with developing a performance practice, the Deep Roots Ensemble has fostered diversity, equity, and inclusion as performers and educators. This section presents both Taylor and Joe's thoughts and reflections on this process as well as their ethical and intellectual motivations for these efforts.

Academic and non-academic classical music institutions have increasingly prioritized diverse programming, particularly music by women and people of colour. Works by these composers, long excluded from the concert music canon, have become required repertoire for young performers (see Kutting 2020; Roberts 2020; Ross 2020; Sloan and Harding 2020). One of the strengths of American folk and roots music is that these same groups have been central contributors to its repertoire.[12] The programming challenges facing classical music are quite navigable for the Deep Roots Ensemble. Some of our most performed selections include works by Elizabeth Cotten and Dolly Parton and traditional repertoire made famous by Huddie Ledbetter, Jean Ritchie, and R. L. Burnside. Furthermore, when class is included in discussions of diversity, our programming's diversity is even more apparent.

We consider class an important facet of diversity in music education and performance. Classical music has been historically intertwined with wealth and continues to draw upon classist values and expectations (Bates 2012; Wood 2020). Musical institutions rightly make considerable efforts to diversify their people and repertoire, prioritizing equal representation of women and people of colour. Inclusion of the music of people from backgrounds of poverty and working-class communities presents different complications. One challenge is that poverty and working-class identity are often invisible or purposefully hidden. Thus, developing class-based diversity relies upon people from poor backgrounds being open about their experiences, but this openness is not yet widely encouraged within classical music. Perhaps this is because acknowledging the way class helps determine success in classical music challenges cherished beliefs in the meritocracy of American music education (Littler 2018).

The complications of exploring class in music extend to scholarship as well. The dominant theories of class within twentieth-century sociology, anthropology, musicology, and ethnomusicology grew out of Marxism. While influential, Marxist ideology has notoriously failed to connect with the poor and working-class in the United States, rendering the academic discussion of class

---

12. It should be noted that this does not mean that these artists did not experience discrimination in the commercial music industry and in their communities: see Pecknold (2013), Hughes (2015), Mather (2017), and McCusker (2017).

severely lacking in contributions from those most impacted by economic inequality (Robinson 1983; Yates 2009). Academic music institutions include discussions of class in their discourse without the equitable participation of those from poor and working-class backgrounds. Important strides towards addressing this have been made recently (with Anna Bull's class-based studies of classical music education in the United Kingdom being an important example), but the overall inclusion of those whose lives have been most shaped by class-based marginalization and discrimination is still remarkably small, especially considering what a large group of people they represent (Bull 2019).

Higher education's increasing inclusion of popular music is also addressing this somewhat (Allsup 2011; Larson 2019). Textbooks by Schloss, Starr, and Waterman include class discussions in their histories of popular music, describing artists whose work was shaped by poverty (Schloss, Starr, and Waterman 2012). Scholarship on country music by authors like Lloyd and Edwards, and blues music by Davis and Titon, centres conversations on class in the United States (Davis 1998; Titon 2013; Edwards 2017; Lloyd 2017). The recently published *Bloomsbury Handbook of Popular Music and Social Class* offers the most comprehensive discussion of class in popular music to date with effective integration of recent developments in the sociological study of class by scholars like Beverly Skeggs and Michael Savage (Peddie 2020). As academia discusses these musical styles further, the need for theoretical models for examining class and poverty grows more critical. Vincent C. Bates's work in developing critical social class theory in music education provides an excellent potential foundation for this discussion (Bates 2017). Daniel Shevock has drawn upon Bates to produce excellent autoethnography discussing complex intersections of whiteness and class in music education (Shevock 2016). The disciplines of musicology and ethnomusicology would do well to draw upon music education's grasp of the impact of class on music. Additionally, the radical centring of perspectives of scholars from backgrounds of poverty and the practice of scholars situating themselves clearly regarding their class backgrounds in the discourse on class – as advocated for by Vivyan C. Adair and Janet Zandy respectively – could have a transformative impact on this discussion (Zandy 1996; Adair 2005).

Perhaps the most profound critique of the academic discourse on class and music is found in the writing of country music scholar Nadine Hubbs. Hubb's (2014) work on gender, sexuality, and class establishes the idea of a 'narrator class', journalists and academics whose values align with upper-class tastes and the middle-class sense of propriety (37). She argues that writers, artists, and public figures from economically privileged backgrounds tend to misunderstand and misrepresent the values of the poor and working class.

This facilitates both the dismissal and appropriation of the musical practices of poor and working-class artists and communities. In the worst of circumstances, these appropriations can be presented as inclusive but instead perpetuate inequality. The following sections return to Taylor's perspective and describe his personal experiences.

Experiencing Class

In hopes of furthering the discussion of how classism can operate in American musical institutions, I offer the following observation as an example of the misrepresentation of the cultural values of American folk and roots music.[13] When I first entered college, I encountered a version of folk music very different from what I learned from my family. Musicians and professors I met praised artists like Joan Baez, the Kingston Trio, and Pete Seeger and seemed shocked that, as a folk musician, I was not familiar with them. Listening to their recommendations, I heard what sounded like a watered-down version of the music I grew up with: songs I knew sung by voices very different from my family's with almost none of the instrumental virtuosity we valued. I eventually learned that these artists (none of whom came from poor backgrounds) were part of a so-called folk revival (see Cantwell 1993). As Rosenberg (1993) has observed, the cultural values of this folk revival grew almost entirely from the white, educated middle- and upper-middle-class (members of Hubbs's narrator class). Its practitioners interacted and continue to interact with the working-class practices the revival drew upon in messy and inequitable ways. This was most obviously manifested in a preference for music that facilitated participation, but with little of the specialized performance techniques that grow from aural learning: folk music scrubbed clean of micro-tonality, crooked phrasing, and interactive improvisation. In effect, the musical nuance and proficiency gained from growing up in a working-class musical community was removed, allowing people with little connection to the music to join as 'equals'.

Turino establishes a useful framework for examining how values are manifested in music making. He describes some music as participatory, using the middle-class, revivalist old-time music events as an example, which he contrasts with 'presentational' practices like bluegrass, a participatory folk style adapted into virtuosic concert music (Turino 2008). This distinction does not always map cleanly onto actual music practices. Much of the music of my

---

13. Examples of examining classism feature in ethnomusicology: see Tsioulakis (2020), and in popular music studies, particularly in the UK, see Fuhg (2022), Raine (2020), and Wilkinson (2016).

youth was participatory and inclusive, welcoming anyone who wanted to play informally, but also celebrating contextually appropriate creativity and even virtuosity. From a young age I also performed with my father and grandfather in presentational contexts. These generally featured the same repertoire, flexible interaction, and improvisation of participatory contexts, but with a much higher expectation of proficiency. Even as a child it was clear to me: anyone could perform this way, but the opportunity to do so was earned.[14] When I encountered performance of the music which I had worked so hard to learn to sing and play being presented as so simple that anyone could participate in it without much effort, it felt like my music (and, by extension, myself) was not as valuable. This was in sharp contrast to how classical music was presented to me and taught in the institutions I attended. The Deep Roots Ensemble works to correct this perception by offering American folk and roots music as a practice in which anyone can participate, but which also rewards dedicated study and celebrates originality, creativity, and virtuosity.

Categories and Labels

One of the sites of profound messiness encountered by the Deep Roots Ensemble is in the terminology we use to describe our music. George Lewis points out that musical labels have values and ideologies embedded within them, some of which are exclusionary or even racist (Lewis 1996). Because the Deep Roots Ensemble self-define our practice, the words we use are essential. Our primarily well-educated, upper-middle-class audiences, our academic colleagues, and the working-class musicians I learned from each respond to our terminology differently. In educational settings, both as performers and scholars, we try to use precise language, reflecting an understanding of contemporary writing on American folk and roots music, which should be noted is in a period of rapid expansion and revision. As we learn more about how different groups of people identify, reject, and develop sensitivities to labels, the words we use have changed. We have used a range of terms, including traditional, folk, traditional American music, roots, American vernacular, and most recently American folk and roots music, with various capitalizations, shifting definitions, and varying degrees of confidence in our decisions. While appropriate in academic settings, regularly revising language is not a practical marketing approach for a professional performing ensemble hoping to build a following.

---

14. This nuanced connection between participation and presentation has been noted by scholars including Turino (2008) and Rosenberg (1993: 199).

Labels in American music have long been a site of messiness, with incompatible values inherited from both scholars and practitioners in commercial music. The earliest studies of American folk music were conducted by song collectors seeking a lost oral literary tradition from the British Isles, preserved in isolated white communities in Appalachia (Miller 2010). This approach defined American folk music as a practice that specifically excluded Black musicians and their influence on rural white musicians and dominated late nineteenth- and early twentieth-century scholarship. 1920s researchers like John Tasker Howard and John Lomax began to look at Black and white music, though they maintained false racial boundaries within musical practices (see Howard 1929; Lomax 2003; Miller 2010: 261).

With the rise of commercial recordings marketed to working-class audiences, record companies falsely assumed that musical performance and listening practices reflected racial segregation, creating the market categories of 'race records' and 'hillbilly'. This 'musical colour line' was so carefully enforced that the interracial collaborations which gave Southern music so much of its character were all but eliminated from the story of American music (Miller 2010). For example, the old-time string band Taylor's Kentucky Boys, who recorded a half-dozen tunes in 1927, were a racially integrated ensemble, featuring the black fiddler Jim Booker. Booker's driving fiddle style is perhaps the most outstanding aspect of their recordings, but when it came time to take a publicity photo, the group's white manager Dennis Taylor held a fiddle and posed with the two white members of the band, effectively eliminating Booker from the band's public image (Huber 2013: 28–29, 50–51). As hillbilly music and race records developed into old-time, country, R&B, and soul, this colour line remained a defining element of American music in the music industry and academic scholarship. As Hughes (2015) has demonstrated, it is only when both the shared legacy of American music and the profound inequity faced by Black musicians are considered that these racially divided genres can be understood.

In the twenty-first century, scholars like Miller, Hughes, and Mather have worked to demonstrate the contributions of Black artists to country music (Miller 2010; Huber 2013; Hughes 2015). Performers including Rhiannon Giddens, Dom Flemons, and organizations like the Black Banjo Reclamation Project and the International Bluegrass Music Association, are reshaping the public image of American folk and roots music by drawing connections across musical colour lines. The Deep Roots Ensemble aims to contribute to this development through our performances, workshops, and lectures. For this reason, we use 'Roots music' as opposed to terms with more racialized histories. It is an imperfect solution, but 'Roots' seems to be widely accepted and understood by our audiences. That said, on stage and in promotional materials we still rely on messy terms like country, blues, folk, and bluegrass.

In the years since forming our ensemble, the label 'Roots' has become increasingly widespread in popular press and academic contexts, but this has been relatively recent.[15] At our first performance as the Stony Brook Roots Ensemble, one professor showed up expecting me to be performing with Questlove and the Roots! While I would love the opportunity to play with this fabulous group, I was shocked that the term 'roots music', which I had heard for most of my performing life, was so illegible in this new setting. As the representation of folk and popular music grows in academic settings, I am hopeful that terminology will be better understood and require less revision. Still, the history of this music and the labels used to describe it remain a mess for the time being.

Conclusion

This chapter has purposefully presented big questions without offering any real answers. As Hughes has demonstrated, sometimes music can embrace messiness with nuance rarely achievable in writing (2015: 12). Perhaps this is because America's poor and working-class musicians have been contending with mess decades before scholars abandoned tidy labels and theories. Maybe American folk and roots music's creativity and flexibility facilitate cultural dexterity while the fixed nature of written scholarship and notated composition take longer to respond? Or perhaps we just want these things to be true? Either way, by positioning ourselves as an alternative to the classical-based practices which dominate the study of music higher education, the Deep Roots Ensemble willingly engages with issues that feel too big for any of us to address as individuals. Collaboration is inherently messy. Even in writing this chapter, the depth of the partnership between Joe and I extend far beyond what the structure of this text reveals. Joe's willingness to centre my experiences and perspectives in this piece of writing is a profoundly supportive act which reflects the remarkable comradery and advocacy that members of our ensemble have provided me as I have worked to tell these stories. So here, even in the last lines of our conclusion, my (Taylor's) personal voice has reentered this shared conclusion. While this could have been avoided, its inclusion is honest and reflective of the messiness of collaboration in creating something new for both of us. The lines between our written voices blur as

15. Informal searches for 'roots music' on NPR's website show results beginning in the early 2000s, but increasingly common in the last ten years, while JSTOR results also began around the new millennium but were largely from the last five years.

much as they do when we make music with each other; blending to tell a story which began as one person's but has grown into something we tell together. This spirit is woven into the history of the music the Deep Roots Ensemble plays as we work not to avoid mess but to make something beautiful within it.

References

Adair, Vivyan C. 2005. 'US working-class/poverty-class divides'. *Sociology* 39, no. 5 (December): 817–34.

Allsup, Randall E. 2011. 'Popular music and classical musicians: Strategies and perspectives'. *Music Educators Journal* 97, no. 3: 30–34. https://www.jstor.org/stable/23012588

Baraka, Amiri. 1963. *Blues People: The Negro Experience in White America and the Music that Developed from It*. New York: Marrow Quill Paperbacks.

Bates, Vincent C. 2012. 'Social class and school music'. *Music Educators Journal* 98, no. 4: 33–37. https://journals.sagepub.com/doi/abs/10.1177/0027432112442944?journalCode=mejc

Bates, Vincent C. 2017. 'Critical social class theory for music education'. *International Journal of Education & the Arts* 18, no. 7: 1–24. http://www.ijea.org/v18n7

'Bill Monroe & The Blue Grass Boys – Uncle Pen (1965)'. YouTube. https://www.youtube.com/watch?v=MeZPAQRl7TA (accessed 11 January 2021).

Billo, Emily, and Nancy Hiemstra. 2013. 'Mediating messiness: Expanding ideas of flexibility, reflexivity, and embodiment in fieldwork'. *Gender, Place, and Culture: A Journal of Feminist Geography* 20, no. 3: 313–28. https://doi.org/10.1080/0966369X.2012.674929

Bull, Anna. 2019. *Class, Control, and Classical Music*. London: Oxford University Press.

Cantwell, Robert. 1993. 'When we were good: Class and culture in the folk revival'. In *Transforming Tradition: Folk Music Revivals Examined*, edited by Neil V. Rosenberg, 35–60. Urbana and Chicago: University of Illinois Press.

Covach, John. 2005. 'Form in rock music: A primer'. In *Engaging Music: Essays in Music Analysis*, edited by Deborah Stein, 65–76. Oxford: Oxford University Press.

Crawley, Ashon T. 2017. *Blackpentecostal Breath: The Aesthetics of Possibility*. New York: Fordham University Press.

Davis, Angela Y. 1998. *Blues Legacies and Black Feminism: Gertrude 'Ma' Rainey, Bessie Smith, and Billie Holiday*. New York: Vintage Books.

Edwards, Leigh H. 2017. 'Country music and class'. In *The Oxford Handbook of Country Music*, edited by Travis D. Stimeling, 307–26. New York: Oxford University Press.

Frisch, Michael. 1987. 'Notes on the teaching and learning of old-time fiddle'. *Ethnomusicology* 31, no. 1 (Winter): 87–102. http://www.jstor.com/stable/852292

Fuhg, Felix. 2022. *London's Working-Class Youth and the Making of Post-Victorian Britain, 1958–1971*. Palgrave Studies in the History of Subcultures and Popular Music. Cham: Palgrave Macmillan.

Goehr, Lydia. 1992. *The Imaginary Museum of Musical Works*. Oxford: Oxford University Press.

Halberstadt. 2001. 'Bob Wills's unique call'. *Washington Post*, 8 April. https://www.washingtonpost.com/archive/lifestyle/style/2001/04/08/bob-willss-unique-call/bfd8c502-440c-49c4-9a57-6d0202fba570/

Haraway, Donna J. 2016. *Staying with the Trouble: Making Kin in the Chthulucene*. Durham, NC and London: Duke University Press.

Hood, Mantle. 1960. 'The challenge of "bi-musicality"'. *Ethnomusicology* 4, no. 2: 55–59. https://doi.org/10.2307/924263

Howard, John Tasker. 1929. *Our American Music: A Comprehensive History from 1620 to the Present*. New York: Thomas Y. Crowell Company.

Hubbs, Nadine. 2014. *Rednecks, Queers, and Country Music*. Berkeley and Los Angeles: University of California Press.

Huber, Patrick. 2013. 'Black hillbillies: African American musicians on old-time records, 1924–1932'. In *Hidden in the Mix: The African American Presence in County Music*, edited by Diane Pecknold, 19–81. Durham, NC and London: Duke University Press.

Hughes, Charles L. 2015. *Country Soul: Making Music and Making Race in the American South*. Chapel Hill: University of North Carolina Press.

Kisliuk, Michelle. 2000. 'Performance and modernity among BaAka pygmies: A closer look at the mystique of egalitarian foragers in the rain forest'. In *Music and Gender*, edited by Pirkko Moisala and Beverly Diamond, 25–50. Urbana: University of Illinois Press.

Koskoff, Ellen. 2005. '(Left *Out in*) *Left* (the *Field*): The effects of post-postmodern scholarship on feminist and gender studies in musicology and ethnomusicology, 1990–2000'. *Women & Music – A Journal of Gender and Culture* 9: 90–98. https://muse.jhu.edu/article/190641

Kutting, Linda Katherine. 2020. 'Classical music had a race problem 20 years ago. It still does'. *WBUR*, 22 July. https://www.wbur.org/cognoscenti/2020/07/22/classical-music-racism-linda-katherine-cutting

Larson, Robert. 2019. 'Popular music in higher education: Finding the balance'. *College Music Symposium* 59, no. 2: 1–14. https://www.jstor.org/stable/26902589

Leon, Javier F. 1999. 'Peruvian musical scholarship and the construction of an academic other'. *Latin American Music Review* 20, no. 2: 168–83. https://www.jstor.org/stable/780019

Lewis, George E. 1996. 'Improvised music after 1950: Afrological and Eurological perspectives'. *Black Music Research Journal* 16, no. 1: 91–122. https://www.jstor.org/stable/779379

Littler, Jo. 2018. *Against Meritocracy: Culture, Power and Myths of Mobility*. New York: Routledge.

Lloyd, Richard. 2017. 'The sociology of country music'. In *The Oxford Handbook of Country Music*, edited by Travis D. Stimeling, 283–306. New York: Oxford University Press.

Lomax, Alan. 2003. *Alan Lomax: Selected Writings 1934–1997*. Edited by Ronald D. Cohen. New York: Routledge.

Mather, Olivia Carter. 2017. 'Race in country music scholarship'. In *The Oxford Handbook of Country Music*, edited by Travis D. Stimeling, 327–54. New York: Oxford University Press.

McCusker, Kristine M. 2017. 'Gendered stages: Country music, authenticity, and the performance of gender'. In *The Oxford Handbook of Country Music*, edited by Travis D. Stimeling, 355–74. New York: Oxford University Press.

Miller, Karl Hagstrom. 2010. *Segregating Sound: Inventing Folk and Pop Music in the Age of Jim Crow*. Durham, NC and London: Duke University Press.

Nettl, Bruno. 2015. 'The fundamental skill: Notation and transcription'. In Bruno Nettl, *The Study of Ethnomusicology: Thirty-Three Discussions*, 72–88. Urbana: University of Illinois Press.

Pecknold, Diane. 2013. 'Introduction: Country music and racial formation'. In *Hidden in the Mix: The African American Presence in County Music*, edited by Diane Pecknold, 1–18. Durham, NC and London: Duke University Press.

Peddie, Ian, ed. 2020. *The Bloomsbury Handbook of Popular Music and Social Class*. New York: Bloomsbury Academic.

Raine, Sarah. 2020. *Authenticity and Belonging in the Northern Soul Scene*. Palgrave Studies in the History of Subcultures and Popular Music. Cham: Palgrave Macmillan.

Ramsey, Guthrie P. 2003. *Race Music, Black Cultures from Bebop to Hip-Hop*. Berkeley and Los Angeles: University of California Press.

Roberts, Maddy Shaw. 2020. 'Beethoven "cancelled"? Why people are debating whether the Fifth Symphony is elitist'. *Classicfm*, 21 September. https://www.classicfm.com/composers/beethoven/composer-cancelled-fifth-symphony-elitist-vox-debate/

Robinson, Cedric J. 1983. *Black Marxism*. Chapel Hill: University of North Carolina Press.

Rosenberg, Neil V. 1993. 'Starvation, serendipity, and the ambivalence of bluegrass revivalism'. In *Transforming Tradition: Folk Music Revivals Examined*, edited by Neil V. Rosenberg, 194–202. Urbana and Chicago: University of Illinois Press.

Ross, Alex. 2020. 'Black scholars confront white supremacy in classical music'. *The New Yorker*, 14 September. https://www.newyorker.com/magazine/2020/09/21/black-scholars-confront-white-supremacy-in-classical-music

Schloss, Joseph, Larry Starr, and Christopher Waterman. 2012. *Rock: Music, Culture, and Business*. Oxford: Oxford University Press.

Shelemay, Kay Kaufman. 1999. 'The impact and ethics of musical scholarship'. In *Rethinking Music*, edited by N. Cook and M. Everest, 531–44. Oxford: Oxford University Press.

Shevock, Daniel. 2016. 'Music educated and uprooted: My story of rurality, whiteness, musicing, and teaching'. *Action, Criticism, and Theory for Music Education* 15: 30–55.

Sloan, Nate, and Charlie Harding. 2020. 'How Beethoven's 5th Symphony put the classism in classical music'. *Vox*, 16 September. https://www.vox.com/switched-on-pop/21437085/beethoven-5th-symphony-elitist-classism-switched-on-pop

Titon, Jeff Todd. 2013. 'Music and the US war on poverty: Some reflections'. *Yearbook for Traditional Music* 45: 74–82. https://www.jstor.org/stable/10.5921/yeartradmusi.45.2013.0074

Tsioulakis, Ioannis. 2020. *Musicians in Crisis: Working and Playing in the Greek Popular Music Industry*. London: Routledge.

Turino, Thomas. 2008. *Music as Social Life: The Politics of Participation*. Chicago: University of Chicago Press.

Wilkinson, David. 2016. *Post-Punk, Politics and Pleasure in Britain*. Palgrave Studies in the History of Subcultures and Popular Music. Cham: Palgrave Macmillan.

Wood, Robert. 2020. 'The stubborn classism of classical music'. *The New Republic*, 10 December. https://newrepublic.com/article/160469/insidious-classism-classical-music

Yates, Michael D. 2009. *In and Out of the Working Class*. Winnipeg: Arbeiter Ring Publishing.

Zandy, Janet. 1996. 'Decloaking class: Why class identity and consciousness count'. *Race, Gender & Class* 4, no. 1: 7–23. https://www.jstor.org/stable/41674809

Author biographies

Taylor Ackley is a scholar, composer, and performer of American Roots music. His work explores and understands American folk and popular music through historical research, composition, analysis, performance, and ethnography. His integrated intellectual and creative practice builds upon lived experiences of poverty among the rural working-class to provide a foundational knowledge for studying, creating, and teaching music. He holds a master's degree and a PhD in Composition as well as a master's degree in Ethnomusicology from Stony Brook University and is currently an Assistant Professor of Music at Brandeis University. He directs the Deep Roots Ensemble and has three commercially released albums.

Joe Sferra is a composer, performer, and theorist who advocates for a broad musical curiosity as an essential trait of a modern musician, and he embodies this in his teaching and creative work. As a clarinettist, he is featured on both abstract electronic improvisation with the ACCAD Sonic Arts Ensemble for Ravello Records and American Roots music with the Deep Roots Ensemble for 4Tay Records. His compositions entertain with popular gestures while revealing a love for the harmonic and formal ideas of modernist concert music, and have been featured in performances in the USA, Canada, and Spain. He has served on the faculties of Earlham, Vassar, SUNY-Potsdam, and the Cleveland Institute of Music.

11 Reconceptualizing Higher Education Programmes in Music for a Rapidly Changing Global Creative Industries Sector: An Australian Perspective

Ryan Daniel

Introduction

Modern life is full of uncertainty, change, and disruption. The global Covid-19 pandemic, which began in early 2020, has exacerbated this state of flux and the third decade of the twenty-first century will be tumultuous. Although a focus on uncertainty typically reveals numerous limitations and constraints, it can also unearth possibilities that may not have previously been considered and that may be dormant, ready to reframe thinking and practice. The global pandemic has sent shockwaves around the world and is enforcing change at a number of levels in society, resembling Schumpeterian creative destruction (Schumpeter 1942). One area that is experiencing major disruption is the broad sector known as the creative industries, an area of the economy which is focused on the commercialization of intellectual property in creative disciplines such as music, photography, design, architecture, visual arts, and the media. Creative industries infrastructure includes opera houses, concert halls, stadiums, galleries, museums, and film studios, as well as open-air spaces (such as parks and beaches) that are used for such activities as festivals, light shows, and visual art displays.

The creative industries sector was one of the hardest hit during the early stages of the pandemic, with millions of artists, creatives, and support workers losing paid employment as numerous parts of the industry went into shutdown and creative productions were put on hold (Caust 2020; Daniel 2021).

Venues for interaction with the arts were closed and income from ticket sales, commissions, sponsorship, investment, and other revenue streams (e.g., festivals, touring, and art fairs) was lost. The music industry has been one of the hardest-hit areas (Messick 2021), given its ecosystem is largely built around live performance and audience engagement. While the situation when the pandemic took hold was dire, artists and creative workers around the world quickly found new ways to engage with their peers and audiences, most notably through virtual means – in particular video – and the creation of new digital content. One such example from the many new collaborative music video performances was 'Phenom' by Thao & The Get Down Stay Down, which harnessed Zoom technology to realize a particularly creative implementation of choreography (Thao & The Get Down Stay Down 2020).

Music is one of the largest areas of the creative industries, with global recorded music market revenues in 2022 worth more than US$26 billion (IFPI 2023). While sales of physical albums such as compact discs remain in decline, revenue through streaming services continues to rise (IFPI 2023; Pitt 2021); in fact the global pandemic saw a significant uptake in streaming services for music on platforms such as YouTube and Spotify (Behr 2020). In recent decades, the music sector has also had significant profile-raising through a range of competitions and reality singing shows, such as *American Idol*, *Britain's Got Talent*, *The Voice*, and *The X Factor*. These talent shows have launched the careers of a number of major artists, including One Direction, Kelly Clarkson, and Adam Lambert. Music theatre is also a major part of the industry, employing hundreds of thousands of musicians and arts support workers worldwide, with an ongoing stream of hit musicals being mounted in previous years. Prior to Covid-19, the Broadway Theatre District in New York City generated approximately US$1.5 billion in gross revenue from musical theatre in the 2018/19 season (Statista Research Department 2022).

In addition to the popular music domain, there is a global market and demand for Western art or classical music; this area features traditional orchestras, ensembles, chamber music, and solo artists. Orchestras are perhaps the most well-known exponent of music performance in the classical tradition, with the majority of countries and major capital cities home to fully professional or semi-professional orchestras. Some of the world's most well-known classical music groups, including the Berlin, New York, and Vienna Philharmonic orchestras, have been in existence for well over 150 years. Orchestras also support ballet and opera, each major disciplines of their own. At the time when the pandemic shocked the world into isolation, orchestras around the world were essentially partially or fully closed; the Metropolitan Opera in New York City, for example, cancelled its entire 2020–21 season, leaving the orchestral musicians without salaries and facing significant uncertainty (VanBesien 2021).

While there have been frequent reports of classical music relying on an ageing audience population (Dobson 2010), there is evidence that younger generations are engaging more with this style of music. This includes streaming music, where playlists can be chosen by mood and to assist with study or concentration, for example (Daniels 2019). Classical music also has relevance when younger listeners are looking for alternatives to popular music (Lorenzon 2019), and has a place in the ears of video gamers, where classical music is often featured in both original and remixed forms to enhance the content or aesthetic of the game (Gibbons 2018). Notable examples include the games *Eternal Sonata* and *Frederic: Resurrection of Music*, both of which feature Chopin's music and the composer himself as the game's protagonist (Gibbons 2018).

The teaching and learning of music comprise a ubiquitous feature of education in colleges and universities. For centuries, musicians have been drawn to study at the highest level in what were initially referred to in Europe as conservatoires, where apprentices were taught by an expert or master in an intensive environment. Institutions offering music as a focused study grew significantly in number during the nineteenth century in the United Kingdom, Europe, and United States in particular. By the second half of the twentieth century, the tertiary music sector had expanded rapidly, with the majority of major Western nations offering multiple options for students to study music in publicly funded conservatoires, colleges, and universities, as well as in private institutions. While post-school music study was typically in traditional classical fields such as musicology, composition, and performance, in the late 1900s the sector embraced jazz and popular music in their various forms. In the twenty-first century, those with a passion for music have a multitude of options to study at the tertiary level, from entry-level degrees (i.e., diplomas and bachelor degrees) through to masters and doctoral programs. There is also an emerging understanding of the problematic nature of primarily focusing on Western art music in the Academy, given that music in society is far more diverse in styles and in practice, with individuals often listening to or engaging with popular musical styles and engaging in informal learning (Small 1998; Smart and Green 2017).

The Music Industry: Surviving and Emerging from the Global Pandemic

The music industry is currently at a critical point given the disruption caused by the pandemic, and the impact that it will continue to have on how consumers engage with music (Gee and Yeow 2021; Messick 2021; Morrow, Nordgård, and Tschmuck 2022; Tolmie 2020). The future for the music industry remains unclear, given the numerous unknowns about the longer-term effects the pandemic will have on what is a complex music ecosystem (Messick 2021). As Morrow, Nordgård, and Tschmuck (2022: 8) state, 'it may be years before we can understand the true impact of the COVID-19 pandemic on the music business'. In addition to job losses, further austerity measures in numerous countries have severely impacted the global music industry. For example, the UK government recently announced plans for major tax increases and spending cuts to attempt to address what is estimated to be the country's longest recession on record (Smith 2022). This austerity strategy has now directly impacted the performing arts sector in England, with the esteemed music conductor Simon Rattle expressing his considerable disquiet at sudden funding cuts to several of the major performing arts organizations (music, opera, and theatre), describing it as 'cultural vandalism' (Rattle quoted in Westwood 2023). Botstein (2020: 353) adds that in terms of America and its post-pandemic future, there will continue to be 'no meaningful government support for the arts'. These types of measures that directly affect creative industries appear likely to be ongoing and it is unknown what impacts they will have for the global music industry. Further exacerbating global economic challenges is the ongoing war in Ukraine, which in the first half of 2023 appears to show no signs of abating and with future rebuilding costs projected to be trillions of dollars (Blank 2023).

In many countries, thousands of venues for live music and the small businesses that support them have closed or have faced devastating financial losses (Messick 2021). While online and digital music services are more relevant than ever before (Pitt 2021), the extent to which the music industry balances live performance environments with online and digital platforms remains unknown. This is further complicated by recent research which suggests that the corporate rhetoric presented by online platforms such as Spotify, Apple, and Amazon – with their claims about musical democratization and boosting musicians' careers – do not match the creative interests of the musicians themselves, who must choose either to cater to complex user-recommendation algorithms or stay true to their individual creativity (Hodgson 2021). Additional emerging trends which impact the music industry include the growing influence of Artificial Intelligence (AI) technologies (Civit et al. 2022) and non-fungible tokens (NFTs) (Krasikov 2022), both of which remain relatively nascent but are likely to play an increasing role in the music industry.

There is no question that in the decade of the 2020s, the world is facing major challenges, including geopolitical instabililties, the climate crisis, aging, the east–west divide, and food security. All of these global challenges or wicked problems will continue to have a direct effect on the creative industries sector, including one of its largest areas, the music industry. While the various challenges are real, there are also significant opportunities. Given that music is a cornerstone of contemporary life, there is a chance to reconsider what the future holds for those involved in its production and consumption, and how this influences higher education music programmes. The music industry is in flux and open for revitalization, ripe for new modes of production and consumption, new ways of thinking about the place of music in society, and new ideas about how the learning and study of music works in practice. The higher education music sector, which arguably represents the final stage of preparing graduates for industry, is therefore a critical player.

Music: A Challenging Career

There is a significant oversupply of labour in the creative industries (Daniel, Fleischmann, and Welters 2017) and the building of a sustainable career can be a daunting proposition (Goodwin 2019). This is very much the case with music; workforce supply drastically exceeds demand and sustaining a career is very challenging (Gee and Yeow 2021). Given the music sector is highly fragmented, the unregulated and rapidly shifting nature of the industry can have a major impact on a person's confidence and self-esteem (Crabtree 2020; Daniel 2022). Crabtree (2020), for example, recently identified and drew attention to the very significant power structures, economic disparity, systemic gender inequity, and frequent incidents of sexual harassment in the music industry, particularly for women musicians and which is investigated in terms of the Australian and New Zealand context by de Boise, Edmond, and Strong (2022), and Fileborn, Wadds, and Tomsen (2020). Latukefu and Pollard (2022) also espouse the importance of a far greater focus on cultural diversity in music and the previous experiences that students bring with them to higher education, particularly in the intense setting of the music conservatoire.

For those successful in securing work in the music industry, it can be a fragile and ephemeral existence, given the freelance nature of the work and reputation being more influential than skills or training. A great performance, composition, or recording lays the foundation for future work opportunities; conversely, a poor one can be catastrophic to an artist's reputation and result in diminished work opportunities. In addition, gatekeepers such as agents, musical directors, teachers, funding bodies, and policy makers can have a significant influence on the lived experience of musicians, including their career prospects and personal wellbeing (Crabtree 2020; Foster, Borgatti, and Jones 2011; Weller 2013). These challenges likely contribute to the fact that aspiring and working musicians are more prone to substance abuse and to mental illness than the general population (O'Donnell 2020).

One of the criticisms of higher education music training is that it features stressors including intense competition amongst peers, demanding teachers and coaches, and very high expectations in relation to what is seen as success. Musicians at the higher education level are regularly exposed to highly critical evaluations and exams, and physical and mental pressures. In addition, many students and graduates are required to find work outside the music industry to survive financially. The Hollywood films *Shine* (1996) and *Whiplash* (2014) reflect some of the realities of the various pressures that are faced by musicians. While the gradual onset of mental illness in *Shine* and the intense, almost torturous, teaching in *Whiplash* are exaggerated, they are indicative of some of the possibilities relevant to the pursuit of a career in music. In terms of research literature, Miksza, Evans, and McPherson (2019a) highlight the levels of stress in higher education music institutions and note the prevalence of mental illness and physical injuries. In a second paper, and in order to combat these challenges, Miksza, Evans, and McPherson (2019b) refer to the need to focus on building social networks, the potential of peer mentoring, and the prospect of providing training in coping mechanisms to deal with various stressors. They argue that the 'challenges students encounter upon enrolling in a university-level music program are serious and multifaceted' (Miksza, Evans, and McPherson 2019b: 157). Similarly, O'Donnell (2020) identified social supports (family, friends, and peers) as key contributors to a musician's capacity for resilience, along with personality factors (e.g., emotional awareness) and external supports (e.g., spirituality and health agencies). These support structures are arguably critical in the current work environment and for the post-pandemic music industry, an industry which in many ways is fragile and prone to sudden changes, exacerbated by the ongoing ripple effects caused by the digital revolution (Crabtree 2020; Daniel 2019). In order to better understand the music industry, chaos theory offers a means of understanding its idiosyncrasies and processes.

Chaos Theory and the Music Industry

Chaos theory has traditionally been understood in relation to systems in mathematics, science, and nature. Its premise is that order and chaos are not always diametrically opposed and while some systems appear chaotic from the outside, the inner workings may be highly ordered. Saitis (2017: 156) describes chaos theory as 'systems of nonlinear dynamical equations when iterated', and claims that it moved science from having an objective to a more subjective nature. Saitis (2017: 161) also describes how chaos theory became an effective means for understanding nature and life, explaining that 'irregularity, chaos, abrupt changes, discontinuity, self-similarity, scaling: all rule both the inner and outer beauty and harmony of nature and life'. One of the common ways to illustrate chaos theory is the idea of the butterfly effect as applied to the weather, where one small flap of a butterfly's wings in one part of the world might lead to a severe event such as a hurricane in another part of the world; small or tiny differences can have large effects (Saitis 2017).

Pryor and Bright (2011: 2) applied chaos theory to career development, where it 'pointed to the complexity of reality and its essential interconnectedness'. In the case of a career in music, certainty is often privileged over uncertainty when students study and train at the higher education level. When engaging with their instrument or voice, students develop a sense of mastery following years of practice and study. Tertiary training allows students to spend countless hours striving to be an elite performer, composer, conductor, multimedia artist, educator, or audio engineer, for example. In this environment, students can be led to believe by the institution or their teacher(s) that they will succeed as a soloist or lead singer, and that there is certainty in a music career (Connell 2020). A composer, musicologist, performer, or teacher trains in their craft for a lengthy period – often 10 to 20 years – then seeks to secure a sustainable, viable, and rewarding career in their area of practice. For example, a violinist trains to an expert or professional level, after which they aim to secure a solo career, an orchestral position, or membership of a chamber music ensemble (e.g., a string quartet), and if successful this career position could last them many years, even decades.

However, the reality of the music industry is that it has the potential to be a chaotic career path. Uncertainty and change are very likely (Connell 2020), in the sense that what students envision for their career when they enter tertiary study may not necessarily take place in reality. A career in music can also be very diverse, including teaching in a private studio or in schools, performing in commercial settings including weddings, corporate events and other functions, or working at music performance venues in administrative or other roles. Musicians may also work outside the music field (Connell 2020; Gee and Yeow 2021), with many developing portfolio careers that involve a variety of work roles and forms of employment that suit their preferred goals and lifestyle choices. While it is yet to be known what longer-term impacts the global pandemic will have on the music industry, it has undoubtedly had a profound effect on the sector. Musicians across the globe are experiencing significant stressors as they face a future in an industry which will be severely disrupted for some time, as the world seeks to bring the pandemic under control and rebuild the music sector which is experiencing severe hardships and a degree of chaos.

Chaos systems are highly sensitive, meaning that if two versions of the same system differ by only a very small amount, they will soon become divergent and very different from each other (Lipa 2020). For instance, two contemporary singers who may study with the same or similar expert teachers and reach a comparable level of expertise will rarely replicate the path that each follows in their career. One tiny flap of the butterfly's wings – the point of chaos – for one of the singers and it could result in a radically different career path, where stability moves to instability and vice versa. As an example of the potential chaos that musicians face, Connell (2020) describes how an opera singer participating in a research project was performing to adulating audiences in a particular season, but in a subsequent audition for a role was told that she would not be receiving a new contract, resulting in feelings of betrayal, loss, and failure. Similarly, musicians fall in and out of favour with agents, band managers, directors, and audiences, and it can only take a small incident to damage a career, such as a mediocre performance, an album release that fails to capture or develop a wider market, or a change in artistic and musical style that does not achieve its intended success. Prior to the global pandemic, musicians had to find within themselves a degree of resilience and fortitude to manage the various stressors that the industry invokes, in addition to maintaining their specific craft and expertise. While music offers a vehicle for those who create it and those who engage with it to seek solace during tumultuous times (Daniel 2021; Hansen 2021), for those seeking a sustainable career in the sector, there are a multitude of unknowns and uncertainties at play: a degree of chaos.

Higher Education and Music

A number of authors have argued the need to revisit and reframe music curricula in higher education, as a response to the nature of the music industry, the realities of a career in the creative industries sector, and the disruption of the pandemic. Similarly to Daniel (2006), Bjøntegaard (2015) identifies the benefits of going beyond one-to-one teaching only and to incorporate small-group learning environments. Simones (2017) proposes that there is a significant need to develop sustained teaching excellence in music instrument and voice teaching for those who are undertaking studies at the tertiary or higher education level, given the important impact this would have for future generations of teachers and performers. Given many graduates from tertiary studies engage in vocal or music instrument teaching in the private studio, enhancing the focus on studio teaching is seen as critical (Simones 2017). Botstein (2020) argues that professional musicians should work more closely with higher education and increase the reach of music education within broader society, thereby becoming more actively embedded in schools and communities. Gee and Yeow (2021) note there is clear evidence that while tertiary institutions offer strong training in musical technique and knowledge, the typical realities of a life and career of a musician are not given sufficient attention in curricula, and they argue that a more holistic education is needed, including a far greater focus on employability skills.

Tolmie (2020) recently argued that given the pandemic and inevitable disruption to the music industry, tertiary education institutions need to adopt a future-thinking approach, where students are provided with opportunities to become adaptable and creative risk takers with both local and global foresight. She also argues that music institutions need to 'bravely acknowledge change, embrace post-normal times, and transform to deliver a relevant quality education that enables preparation for these possible futures' (Tolmie 2020: 607). Matei and Ginsborg (2020) refer to the importance of higher education and music teachers in particular in providing health education to students, including how to maintain physical health and manage anxiety, the latter of which they argue is a prevalent problem in the music field that has been amplified as a consequence of the pandemic. They also argue the need to prepare musicians with high levels of resilience, given the ongoing chaos that is likely to be a part of the industry and the heightened stressors that musicians will experience for some time as the industry redefines and repositions itself in societies.

In his position paper, Patkovic (2020) argues for the importance of networking amongst musicians, formal study of the concept of resilience, and the development of a mentoring system where students are paired with an experienced musician who they can look to for advice and support. It is also the case in the current post-pandemic world that the ubiquity, social acceptance, and adoption of virtual meeting systems such as Skype and Zoom technologies means that new opportunities may continue to open up to musicians. For example, an early-career musician in an isolated location may be able to dialogue and work with an established artist in a different part of the world – something they would not have been able to achieve prior to the pandemic. Recent developments in low-latency video-conferencing technology with high quality and authentic audio (e.g., JackTrip) have also opened up new opportunities to collaborate in music performance with peers around the world, which were previously unavailable if not undertaken in person (JackTrip Labs 2020).

While involving only a small sample of classical musicians based in Europe, López-Íñiguez and Bennett (2020) propose that essential professional capabilities receive more focus in higher education music programmes. They refer to some of the typical realities and issues for music students which may not have received sufficient attention in curricula:

- Career realities often fail to match what graduates had imagined.
- Few graduates are cognizant of the breadth of opportunities available.
- There is 'no longer any dispute that musicians need myriad capabilities beyond performance if they are to create and sustain a career' (López-Íñiguez and Bennett 2020: 1).
- Students should be exposed to networking, projects with industry, and learn multiple genres (e.g., traditional classical, improvisation, composition, and contemporary styles).

These views are also endorsed in relation to the American music sector by Botstein (2020: 359), who references the importance of professional capabilities for musicians, and the increasing need to work more closely in and with the wider community, in order to 'spark enthusiasm and support for music and help cross divides in our social fabric that we rarely cross'. Weston (2020), in reference to an undergraduate contemporary music performance degree, also argues for the need to focus further on soft skills, such as interpersonal, networking, communication, entrepreneurial, and collaboration skills. Weston (2020) proceeds to argue that a twenty-first-century musician will be required to adapt to an industry characterized by disruption and sudden changes, and hence higher education should achieve an appropriate balance of both hard and soft skills in order that graduates sustain a career in a rapidly changing field.

Reimagining Higher Education for Future Generations of Musicians: An Australian Perspective

The core proposition of this chapter is that the learning and teaching of music in higher education should consider a move towards a new conceptual model. This is seen as not only an important reframing for future generations of musicians, but an approach that is arguably urgently needed in response to what has become a very different global music industry. This model is one that places the student as a self-guided learner who is linked with a number of key domains.

Industry engagement
Networking, mentorships, collaborative projects

Health
Physical and mental health knowledge and strategies

Peer learning
Teachers, colleagues, family, friends

Student as self-guided learner

Agency
Independence, resilience, determination

Practice
Expertise, identity, diversity

Crticial thinking
Reflection, analysis, reflexivity, imagination

Figure 11.1 A new conceptual model for higher education music teaching: an Australian perspective (created by the author)

As indicated in Figure 11.1, the conceptual model places the student at the centre of the learning environment, with six inputs or areas of personal and professional development. Each is seen to have equal importance and status, with students encouraged to engage with each area in both deliberate and flexible ways. For example, a student may feel they need to prioritize practice and critical thinking for a period of time. At some point in their studies they may focus on industry engagement. Educators would encourage students to take control of their learning and to constantly assess and reassess what inputs and outputs they require in order to maximize their potential.

Industry engagement is seen as critical for students to gain an in-depth understanding of the nature of the sector. This is not only important in terms of students engaging directly with practitioners and organizations, but demonstrates a need for curriculum designers to look for ways in which to bring industry into the learning environment, be this as simple as an informal meet and greet event, or more formal mentorships or collaborative projects. Given the increasing references in the literature to student mental health and well-being, embedding a focus on the importance of students' developing strategies for self-care as well as knowledge of support services will potentially enable them to be more aware of how to manage the various personal challenges that a career in the music industry involves. Similarly, a focus on developing agency and agentic skills such as resilience will further support students' preparedness for the music industry, which is both ordered but also chaotic, depending on the dynamic changes and opportunities that become available at various points in time.

Institutions would potentially create greater equity for potential students if they removed high-stakes auditions or other entrance procedures, allowing students from all parts of society to enrol and pursue their passion. Portfolios, interviews, and reflective tasks would potentially enable students to chronicle their distinct learning journey, and enable educators to monitor how students are engaging with key areas of development across the course of their studies. In terms of the often-contested practice of aligning students to one studio teacher, students would be encouraged to work with different teachers, to gather a wide diversity of ideas and suggestions, and to also work with their peers in supportive and both structured and unstructured ways. Students would increasingly see their teachers as colleagues – like-minded musicians who themselves are constantly learning and developing their craft and their careers. In the Australian context, the music industry has suffered major disruption due to the pandemic. As the sector rebuilds, there is an opportunity for higher education institutions to revisit their curricula in order to potentially better prepare students for a career in music. This is particularly important given Australia's isolation from the major music centres in the northern hemisphere and the likely ongoing complexities associated with international travel.

Conclusion

The creative industries sector and the music industry in particular will continue to play a major part in the economic, social, and cultural fabric of our world. Music is a powerful artform, one that has fascinated philosophers, composers, performers, learners, teachers, academics, listeners, and health professionals for centuries. Further, music became an escape and a comfort for many around the world during lockdowns and restrictions caused by the Covid-19 pandemic. While it can be difficult to decipher what makes music have such impact and power, it can be as simple as a favourite symphony, song, advertising jingle, or film score that moves us and that often brings with it emotional and distinctive memories. The music industry has successfully moved through the chaos caused by the industrial revolution, post-war reconstructions, changes in technology, digitization, and is well placed to continue to provide the world with inspiration, healing, and joy. However, recent signs and arguments propose that significant change is needed yet again, and that the future of the industry requires rethinking and soul-searching by those who offer programmes at the higher education level. While the pandemic has devastated the industry in many ways, and global challenges such as climate change, security, and geopolitical conflict remain serious complex issues to address and which will affect many industries worldwide, the pandemic has accelerated the need for change, hence there is an opportunity for policy makers, institutional leaders, and educators to take brave steps and make bold, future-oriented decisions. This type of progress will be critical in order that higher education programmes continue to graduate musicians who become champions in their own right, but who also offer a distinct contribution to the creative industries during what is likely to be a chaotic period of time ahead as the world rebuilds and heals.

Acknowledgements

The author would like to thank Dr Eileen Larsen for designing the Figure, and Ms Lauren Moxey who provided valuable editing assistance.

References

Behr, A. 2020. 'Five ways musicians are responding to the coronavirus crisis'. *The Conversation*, 1 May. https://theconversation.com/five-ways-musicians-are-responding-to-the-coronavirus-crisis-137444

Bjøntegaard, B. 2015. 'A combination of one-to-one teaching and small group teaching in higher music education in Norway – a good model for teaching?'. *British Journal of Music Education* 32, no. 1: 23–36. https://doi.org/10.1017/S026505171400014X

Blank, S. 2023. 'Rebuilding Ukraine the right way'. *Atlantic Council*, 8 January. https://www.atlanticcouncil.org/blogs/ukrainealert/rebuilding-ukraine-the-right-way/

de Boise, S. Edmond, and C. Strong. 2022. 'Gender and popular music policy'. In *The Bloomsbury Handbook of Popular Music Policy*, ed. S. Homan, 271–88. New York: Bloomsbury Academic.

Botstein, L. 2020. 'The future of music in America: The challenge of the COVID-19 pandemic'. *The Musical Quarterly* 102, no. 4: 351–60. https://doi.org/10.1093/musqtl/gdaa007

Caust, J. 2020. 'The year everything got cancelled: How the arts in Australia suffered (but survived) in 2020'. *The Conversation*, 17 December. https://theconversation.com/the-year-everything-got-cancelled-how-the-arts-in-australia-suffered-but-survived-in-2020-152180

Civit, M., J. Civit-Masot, F. Cuadrado, and M. Escalona. 2022. 'A systematic review of artificial intelligence-based music generation: Scope, applications, and future trends'. *Expert Systems with Applications* 209: 118190. https://doi.org/10.1016/j.eswa.2022.118190

Connell, K. 2020. 'Navigating a performance livelihood: Career trajectories and transitions for the classical singer'. *Music Education Research* 22, no. 5: 569–80. https://doi.org/10.1080/14613808.2020.1840537

Crabtree, J. 2020. 'Tunesmiths and toxicity: Workplace harassment in the contemporary music industries of Australia and New Zealand'. PhD diss., University of Technology Sydney. https://opus.lib.uts.edu.au/handle/10453/148011

Daniel, R. 2006. 'Innovations in piano teaching: A small-group model for the tertiary level'. *Music Education Research* 6, no. 1: 23–43. https://doi.org/10.1080/1461380032000182911

Daniel, R. 2019. 'Digital disruption in the music industry: The case of the compact disc'. *Creative Industries Journal* 12, no. 2: 159–66. https://doi.org/10.1080/17510694.2019.1570775

Daniel, R. 2021. 'The arts as a form of comfort during the COVID-19 pandemic'. In *The Societal Impacts of COVID-19: A Transnational Perspective*, edited by V. Bozkurt, G. Dawes, H. Gulerce, and P. Westenbroek, 109–21. Istanbul: Istanbul University Press. https://doi.org/10.26650/B/SS49.2021.006.08

Daniel, R. 2022. 'Reimagining higher education curricula for creative and performing artists: Creating more resilient and industry-ready graduates'. In *Mental Health and Higher Education in Australia*, edited by A. Francis and M. Carter, 151–60. Singapore: Springer. https://doi.org/10.1007/978-981-16-8040-3

Daniel, R., K. Fleischmann, and R. Welters. 2017. 'Professional development in the creative industries: Methods and insights from regional practitioners'. *Australian Journal of Career Development* 26, no. 3: 113–23. https://doi.org/10.1177/1038416217720780

Daniels, M. 2019. 'How classical music is becoming the next emerging streaming market'. *Forbes*, 22 July. https://www.forbes.com/sites/melissamdaniels/2019/07/22/how-classical-music-is-becoming-the-next-emerging-streaming-market

Dobson, M. 2010. 'New audiences for classical music: The experiences of non-attenders at live orchestral concerts'. *Journal of New Music Research* 39, no. 2: 111–24. https://doi.org/10.1080/09298215.2010.489643

Fileborn, B., P. Wadds, and S. Tomsen. 2020. 'Sexual harassment and violence at Australian music festivals: Reporting practices and experiences of festival attendees'. *Australian & New Zealand Journal of Criminology* 53, no. 2: 194–212. https://doi.org/10.1177/0004865820903777

Foster, P., S. Borgatti, and C. Jones. 2011. 'Gatekeeper search and selection strategies: Relational and network governance in a cultural market'. *Poetics* 40, no. 4: 247–65. https://doi.org/10.1016/j.poetic.2011.05.004

Gee, K., and P. Yeow. 2021. 'A hard day's night: Building sustainable careers for musicians'. *Cultural Trends* 30, no. 4: 338–54. https://doi.org/10.1080/09548963.2021.1941776

Gibbons, W. 2018. *Unlimited Replays: Video Games and Classical Music*. Oxford: Oxford University Press.

Goodwin, K. 2019. 'Developing self-efficacy and career optimism through participation in communities of practice within Australian creative industries'. *Australian Journal of Career Development* 28, no. 2: 122–31. https://doi.org/10.1177/1038416219849644

Hansen, N. 2021. 'Music for hedonia and eudaimonia during pandemic isolation'. In *The Anthology: Arts and Mindfulness Education for Human Flourishing*, edited by T. Chemi, E. Brattico, L. Fjorback, and L. Harmat, 1–13. London: Routledge. https://psyarxiv.com/s9jf6

Hodgson, T. 2021. 'Spotify and the democratisation of music'. *Popular Music* 40, no. 1: 1–17. https://doi.org/10.1017/S0261143021000064

IFPI. 2023. 'Global Music Report 2023: State of the industry'. *IFPI*. https://www.ifpi.org/wp-content/uploads/2020/03/Global_Music_Report_2023_State_of_the_Industry.pdf

JackTrip Labs. 2020. 'Technology'. https://www.jacktrip.org/technology.html (accessed 10 December 2020).

Krasikov, H. 2022. 'The NFT boom and bust: Musicians as productive laborers in the post-streaming music industry'. *Journal of Popular Music Studies* 34, no. 4: 39–60. https://doi.org/10.1525/jpms.2022.34.4.39

Latukefu, L., and J. Pollard. 2022. 'How can we prepare music students for early career challenges?' *British Journal of Music Education* 39, no. 2: 218–31. https://doi.org/10.1017/S0265051722000122

Lipa, C. 2020. 'Chaos and fractals'. *Cornell Math Explorers' Club*. http://pi.math.cornell.edu/~lipa/mec/lesson1.html (accessed 10 December 2020).

López-Íñiguez, G., and D. Bennett. 2020. 'A lifespan perspective on multi-professional musicians: Does music education prepare classical musicians for their careers?' *Music Education Research* 22, no. 1: 1–14. https://doi.org/10.1080/14613808.2019.1703925

Lorenzon, M. 2019. 'Study finds a large and young audience for classical music'. *Australian Broadcasting Corporation*, 16 August. https://www.abc.net.au/classic/read-and-watch/news/young-large-audience-for-classical-music/11418000

Matei, R., and J. Ginsborg. 2020. 'Physical activity, sedentary behaviour, anxiety, and pain among musicians in the UK'. *Frontiers in Psychology* 11: 3354. https://doi.org/10.3389/fpsyg.2020.560026

Messick, K. 2021. 'Music industry in crisis: The impact of a novel coronavirus on touring metal bands, promoters, and venues'. In *The Societal Impacts of COVID-19: A Transnational Perspective*, edited by V. Bozkurt, G. Dawes, H. Gulerce, and P. Westenbroek, 83–98. Istanbul: Istanbul University Press. https://doi.org/10.26650/B/SS49.2021.006.07

Miksza, P., P. Evans, and G. McPherson. 2019a. 'Motivation to pursue a career in music: The role of social constraints in university music programs'. *Psychology of Music* 49, no. 1: 50–68. https://doi.org/10.1177/0305735619836269

Miksza, P., P. Evans, and G. McPherson. 2019b. 'Wellness among university-level music students: A study of the predictors of subjective vitality'. *Musicae Scientiae* 25, no. 2: 143–60. https://doi.org/10.1177/1029864919860554

Morrow, G., D. Nordgård, and P. Tschmuck. 2022. *Rethinking the Music Business: Music Contexts, Rights, Data, and COVID-19*. Cham: Springer Nature Switzerland AG.

O'Donnell, H. 2020. 'Investigating the contributing factors to resilience in coping with adversity: A qualitative exploratory study of professional musicians in the context of COVID-19'. Masters diss., SRH Fernhochschule. https://static1.squarespace.com/static/5dd4504fa12e347f1317f22a/t/5f79841510373d562dd6f194/1601799196612/ODonnell_Thesis.pdf

Patkovic, D. 2020. 'Resilience in music: Viewpoints of artists' abilities to deal with crises in life'. *Trio* 9, no. 1: 70–77. https://trio.journal.fi/article/view/95771

Pitt, I. 2021. 'Life cycle effects of technology on revenue in the music recording industry 1973–2017'. *SN Business & Economics* 1, no. 9: 1–29. https://doi.org/10.1007/s43546-020-00004-x

Pryor, R., and J. Bright. 2011. *The Chaos Theory of Careers: A New Perspective on Working in the Twenty-First Century*. London: Routledge.

Saitis, C. 2017. 'Fractal art: Closer to heaven? Modern mathematics, the art of nature, and the nature of art'. In *Aesthetics of Interdisciplinarity: Art and Mathematics*, edited by K. Fenyvesi and T. Lähdesmäki, 153–63. Cham: Birkhäuser. https://doi.org/10.1007/978-3-319-57259-8_8

Schumpeter, J. 1942. *Capitalism, Socialism, and Democracy*. New York: Harper & Bros.

Simones, L. 2017. 'Beyond expectations in music performance modules in higher education: Rethinking instrumental and vocal music pedagogy for the twenty-first century'. *Music Education Research* 19, no. 3: 252–62. https://doi.org/10.1080/14613808.2015.1122750

Small, C. 1998. *Musicking: The Meanings of Performing and Listening*. Middletown, CT: Wesleyan University Press.

Smart, T., and L. Green. 2017. 'Informal learning and musical performance'. In *Musicians in the Making: Pathways to Creative Performance*, edited by J. Rink, H. Gaunt, and A. Williamon, 108–25. New York: Oxford University Press.

Smith, E. 2022. 'British government to usher in new era of austerity in effort to restore market confidence'. *CNBC*, 15 November. https://www.cnbc.com/2022/11/15/british-government-to-usher-in-new-era-of-austerity-in-effort-to-restore-market-confidence.html

Statista Research Department. 2022. Statista.com. 2020. 'Gross revenue of Broadway shows in New York from 2006 to 2019'. *Statista*, 24 January. https://www.statista.com/statistics/193006/broadway-shows-gross-revenue-since-2006

Thao & The Get Down Stay Down. 2020. 'Phenom'. https://www.youtube.com/watch?v=DGwQZrDNLO8 (accessed 15 December 2020).

Tolmie, D. 2020. '2050 and beyond: A futurist perspective on musicians' livelihoods'. *Music Education Research* 22, no. 5: 596–610. https://doi.org/10.1080/14613808.2020.1841133

VanBesien, M. 2021. 'Are labor and management (finally) working together to save the day? The COVID-19 crisis in orchestras'. In *Classical Music: Contemporary Perspectives and Challenges*, edited by M. Beckerman and P. Boghossian, 75–86. Cambridge: Open Book Publishers. https://www.openbookpublishers.com/product/1299

Weller, J. 2013. 'How popular music artists form an artistic and professional identity and portfolio career in emerging adulthood'. Ed.D. diss., University of St Thomas. https://ir.stthomas.edu/caps_ed_lead_docdiss/43

Weston, D. 2020. 'The value of "soft skills" in popular music education in nurturing musical livelihoods'. *Music Education Research* 22, no. 5: 527–40. https://doi.org/10.1080/14613808.2020.1841132

Westwood, M. 2023. 'Politicians are worried about an elitist tag ... this is cultural vandalism'. *The Australian*, 14 April. https://bit.ly/41k1wRe

Author biography

Ryan Daniel is currently Chief Academic Officer at Excelsia College in Sydney, and Adjunct Professor in the College of Arts, Society and Education at James Cook University. His research is published in *Creativity Studies, Creative Industries, International Journal of Cultural Policy, Arts and Humanities in Higher Education, CoDesign, Music Education Research*, and the *British Journal of Music Education*.

Index

A

A&R (artist and repertoire) 3, 37, 39–41, 44, 67, 72, 181
AAC (Association of American Colleges and Universities) 177–178, 180, 185–186
academia 2, 5, 24, 66, 89, 194, 196, 201
accounting 53, 60, 71–73
accreditation 6, 18–19, 23
actors 3, 180
administration 16–17, 19, 22–23, 41
advertising 80, 98, 111, 222
advice 38, 93, 110, 163, 218
AES (Audio Engineering Society) 174 *see also* equity
agency 4, 9, 37, 57, 95, 116, 167, 187, 215, 221
Akai (music sampler) 139 *see also* MPC
album cover 34, 93, 99
algorithm 69, 117–118, 175, 213 *see also* playlist; recommendation
Amazon (streaming platform) 69, 213
ambient (musical style) 136, 138, 176
Annenberg Study, the USC 179, 189
application 39, 83, 94–95
apprenticeship 4, 15, 34, 172, 175, 177
arrangement 155, 163–164, 198–199
art school 8, 129–132, 135, 138–139, 141–143 *see also* cybernetic; musicianship
Artificial Intelligence 111, 213
Ascott, R. (artist) 130, 133, 137–138 *see also* cybernetic; Groundcourse
assets 14, 39, 120
assignment 40, 54–55, 58, 178, 184, 195
Atmosphere (musical recording) 139
Attali, J. 76–77
audiovisual 15, 92, 94
authenticity 37, 43, 97, 100
autoethnography 2, 191–193, 201 *see also* Deep Roots Ensemble; ethnography
autonomy 6, 8, 44–45, 49, 116, 119, 130
avant-garde 131, 134–136, 139, 142
AWAL (record label) 111 *see also* record label

B

Bandcamp (website) 180–181
banjo 191–192, 195, 204 *see also* Deep Roots Ensemble

bass (musical instrument) 120, 139–140, 151, 162–163, 191, 195
Bauhaus 131–133, 142 *see also* art school
BBC (British Broadcasting Corporation) 2, 135
Beatles, the (musical group) 59
Beethoven (composer) 140
behaviour 3, 30–31, 35, 118, 133, 135
Berlin 16, 19–22, 27
biases 68–69, 84, 193
BIMM Institute (German university) 19, 22–27, 173 *see also* Berlin
Blacking, J. (ethnomusicologist) 133 *see also* ethnomusicology
BLS (Bureau of Labor Statistics) 2
bluegrass 195, 197, 199, 202, 204–205 *see also* Deep Roots Ensemble
BMG (record label) 16 *see also* record label
Booker, J. (musician) 204 *see also* fiddle
Bovell, D. (music producer) 141 *see also* Slits, the; cybernetic
Branca, J. (entertainment lawyer) 59 *see also* lawyer
brand 40, 44, 58, 70, 80, 123
Brisbane 148–150, 152
Bryars, G. (composer) 130–131, 136, 139–140 *see also* Eno, B.; Minimalist; Portsmouth Sinfonia
Budde (music publisher) 15 *see also* publisher
Burnside, R. 200 *see also* Deep Roots Ensemble; guitar; songwriter
Buster, P. (musical artist) 131 *see also* RnB; Ska
butterfly effect 216–217 *see also* chaos theory
BVMI (Bundesverband Musikindustrie) 12, 15–16 *see also* record label

C

Cabaret Voltaire (music group) 130, 137 *see also* electronic
Cage, J. (composer) 131–132, 137, 142
Cale, J. (composer) 136
California, University of Southern 179 *see also* Annenberg Study
campus 29, 31, 43, 58, 149, 174, 180
Canada 1, 9, 175, 181 *see also* UVic; SOCAN
capstone 180, 185–186 *see also* FTM; UVic
catalogue 22, 24, 26, 119, 122

228 Index

CBR (Cordova Bay Records) 176, 178–179, 181–184 *see also* FTM; Flood Tide; UVic
CEL (community-engaged learning) 8, 172, 175–176, 185–187 *see also* CBR
cello 75, 139, 191–192 *see also* Deep Roots Ensemble; sax
chamber 8, 191, 197, 199, 211 *see also* autoethnography; Deep Roots Ensemble; student-run
chaos theory 8, 215–216 *see also* butterfly effect
characteristic 23, 33, 72, 74, 76, 80, 110
charts 117, 150–151, 155
childhood 141, 198
chord 95, 110, 139, 151, 160 *see also* bass; charts; guitar
chorus 117–118 *see also* determinism, technological; songwriting
classism 202 *see also* autoethnography; Deep Roots Ensemble; graduate school
clothing 98–101 *see also* costume; Semiology; semiotic; visuals; wardrobe
cognition 6, 8, 69, 148, 158, 162, 167 *see also* metacognition
cognitive 30, 35, 68–69, 84–85 *see also* decision-making, 5R; SRL
cohort 42–43, 71–72, 138–139, 151, 186 *see also* A&R; MBPP; record label; student-led; student-run
competency 95, 159
competition 58, 70, 174, 211, 215
concert 12, 15, 61, 93, 151, 200, 202 *see also* visual analysis; visuals
conservatoire 51, 61, 212, 214 *see also* effectuation
Conservatorium 148–149, 152, 160 *see also* Queensland; USYD; Griffith University
Conservatory 9, 17, 19, 21, 52, 147–148 *see also* Munich, College of Music
contextual 74, 91–92, 95–96 *see also* decision-making, 5R; musicianship; PMHE; visual analysis
Coronavirus 16
costume 68, 98, 100–102 *see also* gorilla (test and experiment); visual analysis; visuals; expression; fashion
coursework 7, 54, 60 *see also* curricula
Crabtree, J. v, 6, 30, 50, 214–215, 223
creation 91, 119–120, 131–132, 150, 162–163, 165, 211 *see also* art school; cognition; songwriting
credit 25, 80, 150–151, 171, 185 *see also* accreditation; CEL; JMC Academy; WAAPA

criteria 34, 80, 147, 186
critical thinking 3, 9, 59, 95, 220
criticism 96, 99, 122, 193, 215
critique 115–116, 135, 182–183, 186, 201 *see also* CEL; determinism, technological
Csikszentmihalyi, M. 177 *see also* flow
curricula 6, 8, 16, 25, 27, 51, 122, 148, 173, 218–219, 221 *see also* undergraduate courses
cybernetic 130, 134, 136–137, 141 *see also* art school; Ascott, R.; Bovell, D.; Slits, the; Eno, B.

D

Dada (visual genre) 132, 136, 141
Dalwood, D. (visual artist) 7, 130, 141
dance 52, 134, 142, 193
Daniel, R. vi, 9, 210–211, 213–215, 217, 219, 221, 223, 225–226
Davies, H. v, 7, 64, 91, 108
decision-making, 5R 4, 7, 59, 67–69, 78, 80, 84–85 *see also* engineer; gorilla (test and experiment); grounded theory
Deep Roots Ensemble 8, 191–197, 199–200, 203–206 *see also* autoethnography; ethnography
deficit 52, 56, 116
DEI (Diversity, Equity and Inclusion) 3 *see also* equity
designer 3, 46, 56, 120, 221
desire 35, 123, 172–173, 185
determinism, technological 7, 110, 116
Deutsche POP (German university) 19, 22–25
Devo (musical group) 136
dialogue 115, 168, 183
digitalization 15–16
discourse 4, 34, 93, 98, 105, 165, 201
disruption 5, 210, 212, 217, 219
diversity 3, 32, 38, 43, 76, 108, 111, 174–175, 194, 200, 214, 221
DIY (Do It Yourself) 8, 93, 124, 132, 139, 142
downside risk 56, 59–60
drama 121, 136 *see also* narrative
Drillminister (artist) 112–115 *see also* Nouveau; visuality
drum 99, 120, 139, 151, 162–163 *see also* Roland
drummer 102–103
Duchamp, M. 132, 140, 142
Dylan, B. (musical artist) 119–120, 122 *see also* Subterranean Homesick Blues

E

ecosystem 109, 151, 211, 213
Edith Cowan University, the 148–149, 151 *see also* Perth; WAAPA
effectuation 6, 56, 58 *see also* lemonade principle; negotiation; networking; pitch; Sarasvathy, S.
electronic 137–138, 142 *see also* Cabaret Voltaire; overdubbing
elite 151, 216
employability 5, 53, 96, 218
employee 12–13, 27, 53, 150
employer 13, 16, 46, 53, 173
engineer 3, 5, 40–41, 82, 150, 199, 216 *see also* decision-making, 5R; JMC Academy; MBPP
England 9, 213
Eno, B. (musical artist) 7, 129–131, 133–139, 142 *see also* cybernetic; expression; Roxy Music; simplicity
enterprise 31–34 *see also* MBPP; PjBL
entrepreneurial 51–52, 55, 57, 61, 115, 173, 219 *see also* leadership; Vulfpeck
equity 3, 22, 80–81, 174, 176, 193, 200, 221 *see also* AES; DEI
Erfurt, University of 20
essay 96–97 *see also* LIPA
ethnography 2, 98, 193–194 *see also* autoethnography; Deep Roots Ensemble; feminist
ethnomusicology 193, 196–197, 200–202 *see also* musicology
experiential learning 7, 32, 171, 176 *see also* CEL
experimental 130, 132–135, 139–140, 142 *see also* art school; Portsmouth Sinfonia
expert 212, 216–217
exploration 129–130, 133, 137, 151, 183
expression 74, 101–103, 112, 123, 131, 135, 165 *see also* costume; Eno, B.; gesture

F

fashion 14, 61, 100, 130, 171 *see also* costume; wardrobe
female 71, 99–103, 179
feminist 165, 193–194 *see also* ethnography
Ferrograph (tape machine) 138
festival 3, 12, 17, 196, 198, 210
FHAM (University of Applied Management-Germany) 19, 22–26 *see also* Köln
fiddle 204 *see also* Booker, J.
financial 7, 41–42, 56, 59, 71, 84, 135, 213
flexibility 31, 47, 103, 194, 198–199, 205

Flood Tide (record label) 176, 179, 184 *see also* CBR; FTM
flow 80 *see also* Csikszentmihalyi, M.
Flynn, M. 7, 67, 69, 71, 73, 75, 77, 79, 81, 83, 85, 87, 89–90 *see also* decision-making, 5R
Foran, S. v, 8, 147, 149, 151, 153, 155, 157, 159, 161, 163, 165, 167, 169 *see also* JMC Academy
Frankfurt, College of Music and Performing Arts (German university) 14, 17–18, 21
freelance 9, 43, 150, 214
friendship 149, 159–161
FTM (Flood Tide Music) 176, 179–180 *see also* CEL; Flood Tide; record label; student-run
funding 4, 14, 39, 43, 214
fungible 70, 213 *see also* NFT
Futurism 132

G

Gang of Four (musical group) 135, 138, 141 *see also* Minimalist
gatekeeper 142, 214
gendered 175, 193
gesture 98, 101–103 *see also* expression
Giddens, R. (musician) 204
Google 69, 181
gorilla (test and experiment) 68–69 *see also* costume; decision-making, 5R
graduate school 192, 194, 196 *see also* Stony Brook
graduation 47, 51–53, 55, 61, 160
graphic 93, 115, 120, 131 *see also* visual analysis; visuals
Griffith University 148, 160 *see also* Conservatorium; Queensland
Groundcourse 133 *see also* Ascott, R.; Ipswich (art school); personality
grounded theory 7, 67, 74, 152 *see also* decision-making, 5R
guidance 4, 30–31, 35, 39, 54, 93
guitar 75, 135–136, 139–140, 151, 160, 163, 195, 198

H

Hamburg 17, 19, 21
harmony 122–123, 155, 163–164, 182, 195, 216 *see also* melody
Haydar, M. (musical artist) 113–114 *see also* Hijabi (Wrap my Hijab)
HdpK (SRH University of the Popular Arts) 20, 22–26
hegemonic 8, 113

230 Index

heritage 26, 192, 195
heuristic 69, 84
Hijabi (Wrap my Hijab) 113–114 *see also* Haydar, M.
hillbilly 204, 207 *see also* race
hip hop 129, 139, 142–143, 171
hMtMh (College of Music and Theater Hannover) 21
Holiday, B. (musical artist) 61
HPME (Higher Popular Music Education) 129, 141–143 *see also* IASPM
Human League, the (musical group) 138
humanities 14, 22, 193
hybridity 6

I

IASPM (International Association for the Study of Popular Music 91, 104 *see also* HPME; PMHE; PMS
ideation 39, 58, 122
illustration 37, 104
imagery 7, 104 *see also* objects
improvisation 147, 151, 191, 202–203, 219
incentive 34, 45
inclusive 4, 8–9, 175, 202–203
indie 71, 75, 129, 138, 143
industrial 15, 54, 112, 124, 137, 222
inequality 3, 201–202
informal 69, 74, 115, 132, 180, 191, 205, 212, 221 *see also* learning design; musicking; skillset
instruction 134, 140, 148, 163, 191
instructor 2, 30, 32, 58, 60–61, 148, 152, 178, 183
instrumental 85, 110, 116, 151, 161–162, 182, 202
intellectual 55, 80, 193, 197, 200, 210
intelligence 34, 111, 213
intention 45, 83, 97, 99, 192
interconnections 131, 134, 143
interdisciplinary 1, 6
Internet 55, 94, 171
internship 2, 7–8, 16, 26, 46, 53, 59, 171–176, 185, 187 *see also* CEL; SNAAP
interpersonal 3, 57, 59, 155, 173, 175
intersection 35, 109, 122, 132, 192, 201
investment 51, 58, 70, 165, 211
Ipswich (art school) 130, 133 *see also* Groundcourse
isolation 1, 85, 211, 221

J

JackTrip (network music platform) 218–219

JMC Academy 148–152, 154 *see also* Brisbane; engineer; Foran, S.
Joy Division (musical group) 139
judgement 68–70, 73, 77, 79, 84, 119
jungle (musical style) 129, 143

K

keyboardist 5, 103
KLF, the (musical group) 130–131
Köln (German city) 19, 21 *see also* FHAM

L

landscape 141, 180
laptop 155, 162
lawyer 59, 72, 80, 93 *see also* Branca, J.
leadership 2, 25, 38, 40, 45, 173 *see also* entrepreneurial; RSFLG; skillset; soft skills
learning design 30–33, 43 *see also* informal; motivation
Leeds (UK city) 95, 130, 135–136, 141 *see also* art school; Gang of Four
legacy 3, 123, 204
lemonade principle 57, 59 *see also* effectuation
lesson 26, 45–46, 129, 164
Lester Square (artist) 138, 142
licensing 4, 55, 122
lifelong learning 8, 178, 180, 185
LIPA (Liverpool Institute for Performing Arts) 91, 95–97, 99–102, 105 *see also* essay; Liverpool
listener 96, 113, 118, 123, 136, 182, 212, 221
literature 1, 9, 77, 122, 215, 221
Liverpool 90–91, 95, 131 *see also* LIPA
lockdown 72, 222
logo 93, 99, 179 *see also* merchandise
Lücke, M. v, 6, 12–13, 15–17, 19, 21, 23, 25, 27–29
Ludwigsburg, the University of Education in 17, 21

M

Macromedia University of Applied Sciences 18–19, 21–26 *see also* Hamburg; Köln
mainstream 70, 114, 134, 137, 142
male 71, 85, 99, 101, 103, 112, 179
mandolin 191, 195
Mannheim (German city) 17–19, 21
marginalization 112, 192, 201
Marxism 200
MBPP (Music Business and Professional Practice) 30–31, 33, 35–36, 38–39, 41, 43 *see also* engineer; enterprise; negotiation

McNally, K. vi, 8, 171, 173, 175, 177, 179, 181, 183, 185, 187, 189–190
mechanism 113, 117–118, 148, 177–180, 215
melody 122–123, 155, 163, 198 see also harmony; songwriter
merchandise 4, 42, 93, 99 see also logo
metacognition 35, 46
MeToo 110, 121
milestone 87, 180, 185–186
Minimalist 131, 136, 138, 142 see also Bryars, G.; Gang of Four; Reich, S.; Velvet Underground
minority 174, 176, 182
misogyny 3, 111
mixing 82, 149, 186, 199
modern technology 7, 137
Modernism 129–130
motivation 31, 44, 46, 178, 185 see also CEL; learning design
Motown 66, 118
MPC 139 see also Akai; sampler
MTV 107, 111–113, 123
MUCS (Music and Computer Science) 175
München (German city) 19–21
Munich, College of Music (German university) 17–18, 21
Münster (German city) 20–21, 28
music consumption 55, 113
music production 6, 26, 37, 39, 171
musicianship 129, 131, 136, 140–141, 143, 148, 151, 175 see also art school
musicking 131 see also informal
musicology 22, 26, 60, 200–201, 207, 212 see also ethnomusicology
MyCelia (blockchain startup) 55

N

Napster (streaming platform) 15
narrative 2, 69, 74, 93, 104, 121 see also drama; personae
Nashville 174
negative 59, 82, 109–110, 116, 122
negotiation 38, 59, 80, 84, 151 see also effectuation; MBPP
networking 3, 7, 52–53, 57, 173, 219 see also effectuation
Newcastle 130, 134
NFT (Non-Fungible Token) 70, 213 see also fungible
niche 115
noise 139, 141
normative 116–117
notation 140, 192, 198

Nouveau 112 see also Drillminister; visuality

O

O'Halloran, T. vi, 8, 147, 170
O'Hara, B. 64–65
O'Regan, J. vi, 8, 147, 170
Obama, B. 118
objects 70, 77, 98–99, 101, 104, 177 see also imagery
offering 95, 98, 149, 203, 205, 212
Oliveros, P. (composer) 131, 138
openness 193, 199–200
opera 12, 17–18, 78, 121, 210–211, 213, 217
opposition 100, 110
orchestral 5, 70, 212, 216
overdubbing 138 see also electronic
ownership 13, 116, 121

P

packaging 7, 91, 93
Paderborn, University of 18, 21
passion 123, 212, 221
Passmore, V. (artist) 138
pathway 3, 17, 59, 173, 175
Perry, V. 8, 147, 170, 201, 206
personae 93, 96–98, 103 see also narrative; tension
personality 40, 113, 133, 215 see also Groundcourse
Perth (city) 148 see also Edith Cowan University
Philharmonic, the Vienna 211 see also Vienna
phonograph 110
piano 136, 140, 182, 197
PiL (Public Image Limited) 140
pitch 58, 139, 180–181 see also CEL; effectuation
PjBL (Project-based learning) 32–33 see also enterprise; scaffolding
playlist 78, 118, 179–180, 182, 212 see also algorithm
PMHE (Popular Music Higher Education) 7, 92, 95, 101, 104 see also IASPM
PMS (Popular Music Studies) 95 see also IASPM
podcasts 3, 84
Popakademie (German university) 17–19, 21
population 71, 174–175, 212, 215
Portsmouth Sinfonia 130, 138–140 see also Sinfonia
poster 93, 99
postmodern 130–132
praxis 5, 55
preference 40, 69, 123, 182, 202
preparation 52, 56, 199, 218

presence 94, 96, 112, 173, 183
president 176, 179, 181, 187
privilege 123, 192, 194
problem-solving 3, 7, 40, 57, 133, 151, 167
producing 3–4, 42, 84, 149, 154, 176
promoter 41, 72
promotion 3, 30, 55, 96
psychology 14, 25
publicity 3, 5, 93, 204
publisher 15, 54, 84, 181

Q

qualification 15, 23, 141
qualitative 2, 8, 22, 30, 117, 119
quantitative 2, 18, 71, 117, 119
Queensland 160, 173 *see also* Griffith University
queer 101, 207
Questlove (musician) 205

R

race 5, 204 *see also* hillbilly
Raincoats, the (musical group) 130–131, 139, 141
Raine, S. ii, 3, 10
realization 26, 44, 46, 139, 159, 161
Reclamation, Black Banjo (organization) 204
recommendation 118, 202, 213 *see also* algorithm
record label 4, 6, 8, 34, 44, 46, 51, 60, 111–112, 115, 172–173, 176 *see also* FTM; Sony; Universal Music
record production 67, 76–77, 180, 185, 187
recording studio 4, 142, 172, 174
Reeperbahn (German festival) 12
reflective practice 6, 8, 35, 41, 44, 46
reflexivity 193–194
Reich, S. (composer) 131, 136 *see also* Minimalist
rejection 116, 121, 177
relevance 44, 51, 91, 96
requirement 15, 33, 40, 118–119, 122, 137
researcher 1–2, 4–5, 24, 55, 59, 173, 204
resilience 31, 165, 215, 217–218, 221
resistance 112–113, 115, 123, 171
revolution 138, 215
Rhodes, B. (manager) 135–136
RnB 131 *see also* Ska
Roland (TR808 drum machine) 139 *see also* drum; sampler
Rouvellas, M. 6, 30, 50
Roxy Music (musical group) 129, 137, 140 *see also* Eno, B.
royalty 3, 45, 58, 80

RSFLG (Recovery Support Function Leadership Group) 2 *see also* leadership
rural 192, 194

S

SAE (School of Audio Engineering) 20, 22–26
sampler 139 *see also* MPC; Roland
Sarasvathy, S. 56–60 *see also* effectuation
scaffolding 31, 33, 35–36, 172 *see also* PjBL; SRL
scene 85, 121, 130, 138, 142
Schumann Conservatory, R. (German university) 19
Scritti Politti (musical group) 141
Seeger, P. (musical artist) 202
self-guided 9, 219
Semiology 98
sexuality 101, 201
Sferra, J. vi, 8, 191, 193, 195, 197, 199, 201, 203, 205, 207, 209
silence 131, 134, 138–139, 143
simplicity 136–138, 141–142 *see also* Eno, B.
Sinfonia 130, 138–140 *see also* Portsmouth Sinfonia
singing 147, 195, 197–198, 211 *see also* vocalist
Situationist International (art movement) 130, 134–135, 140, 142
Ska 131 *see also* Buster, P.; RnB
skillset 54, 164 *see also* informal; leadership; soft skills
Slits, the (musical group) 134, 140–141 *see also* cybernetic
SNAAP (Strategic National Arts Alumni Project) 6, 52–54, 56, 59 *see also* internship
SOCAN (Society of Composers, Authors and Music Publishers of Canada) 181, 186 *see also* Canada
soft skills 39, 148–149, 158–160, 167, 219 *see also* leadership; skillset
songwriter 50, 71, 75, 95, 100, 118, 152, 166–167, 179 *see also* melody
songwriting 7, 80, 109–110, 116–119, 122–123, 148, 150, 152–155, 158, 164, 167, 177 *see also* determinism, technological; melody; skillset; tension
Sony (record label) 15–16, 111 *see also* record label
spontaneity 135, 198–199
Squeeze (musical group) 141
SRH University of the Popular Arts (German university) 20, 22–26
SRL (self-regulated learning) 35–36 *see also* scaffolding

Index 233

stability 53, 58, 195, 217
stagecraft 148, 155, 158, 161
Stevenson, I. 6, 30–31, 33, 35, 37, 39, 41, 43, 45, 47, 49
Stony Brook (American university) 192, 196, 205 *see also* graduate school
Strange, S. v, 7, 125, 128–129, 143–146
student engagement 35, 176
student-led 31–32, 192
student-run 8, 58, 60, 173 *see also* FTM
Subterranean Homesick Blues (musical work) 119 *see also* Dylan, B.
Surrealism 132
Surrey, the University of 172
synthesizers 142

T

talent 58, 78–79, 177, 181, 211
tension 7, 97, 109, 113, 118, 123, 184–186 *see also* personae; songwriting
TikTok 69, 94, 104, 111, 122
timeline 38–39, 41, 79, 179
timing 3, 80, 138–139, 198
toolkit 7, 69, 85, 98–99, 103, 105, 167 *see also* visual analysis
tour 59, 75, 93
transformation 33, 37, 55
transgender 101
transition 2, 30, 61, 73, 77, 191, 197
Treuchtlingen (German city) 19
tune 76, 195, 198, 204
tutor 72, 96, 131, 136, 147, 151, 155

U

UCAS (Universities and Colleges Admissions Service) 95
Ukraine 213
uncertainty 3, 57, 73, 82, 210, 216
undergraduate courses 6, 95 *see also* curricula
underrepresentation 72
undertaking 7, 38–39, 41, 51, 217
UNESCO (United Nations Educational, Scientific and Cultural Organization) 2
United Kingdom 147, 149, 172, 201, 212
Universal Music (record label) 15–17, 181 *see also* record label
USYD (University of Sydney) 154–155
UVic (University of Victoria) 175–176 *see also* Canada

V

Velvet Underground, the (musical group) 129, 131, 138 *see also* Minimalist

venture 58, 60, 111
vernacular 166–167, 203
Vienna 17, 211 *see also* Philharmonic, the Vienna
viewpoint 4, 143
vinyl 75, 94, 110
virtual 175, 211, 218
vision 8, 104
visual analysis 7, 92, 95 *see also* graphic; toolkit
visuality 7, 111–113 *see also* Drillminister (artist); Nouveau
visuals 94, 96–98, 104 *see also* graphic
vocal 110, 132, 139, 150–151, 161, 164, 218 *see also* singing
vocation 2, 31, 35, 46
voice 122–123, 142, 202, 205, 211, 216–217
Vulfpeck (musical artist) 111, 115 *see also* entrepreneurial

W

WAAPA (Western Australian Academy of Performing Arts) 149, 151–152, 154–155 *see also* Edith Cowan University
wardrobe 102 *see also* fashion
Warhol, A. (artist) 132, 142 *see also* Cage, J.; Eno, B.
wealth 69, 90, 200
Wedel University of Applied Sciences (German university) 14
Westfälischen (College of Music of the Westphalian Wilhelm) 20–21
Westphalian (College of Music, University of University Münster) 20–21
WGNCP (women and non-gender conforming people) 174
Whack, T. (musical artist) 119, 121
Wissenschaftsrat (German Science Council) 18
workplace 30–33, 55 *see also* learning design
workshop 33, 36, 138, 196, 198, 204
writer 72, 82, 92, 171, 201
Württemberg, the Popakademie Baden (German university) 18–19, 21

X

XR (Extended Reality) 93

Y

youth 203

Z

Zoom (webconferencing platform) 152, 211, 218

www.ingramcontent.com/pod-product-compliance
Ingram Content Group UK Ltd.
Pitfield, Milton Keynes, MK11 3LW, UK
UKHW020246060225
4464UKWH00047B/129